# CAMBRIDGE LIBRARY COLLECTION

*Books of enduring scholarly value*

## Cambridge

The city of Cambridge received its royal charter in 1201, having already been home
to Britons, Romans and Anglo-Saxons for many centuries. Cambridge University
was founded soon afterwards and celebrated its octocentenary in 2009. This series
explores the history and influence of Cambridge as a centre of science, learning,
and discovery, its contributions to national and global politics and culture, and its
inevitable controversies and scandals.

## Trinity College Library. The First 150 Years

Philip Gaskell (1926–2001) acknowledges in his Preface that 'one period in the
history of one college library may not seem much of a subject for a book', but, as his
1980 study shows, Trinity College Library has a history well worth investigating.
Gaskell, a former Librarian and Fellow of Trinity College, details how this library
grew from small beginnings in the mid-sixteenth century into arguably the greatest
of all Oxford and Cambridge college libraries. He links the growth of the library
to the intellectual life of the college at that time, outlining the achievements of a
number of eminent Trinity men in advancing England's spiritual, intellectual and
scientific development: Cartwright, Whitgift, Coke, Bacon, Essex, George Herbert,
Ray, Barrow and Newton. This is a fascinating insight into the early history and
accumulation of a college library now outstandingly rich both in contents and in
setting.

T0381810

Cambridge University Press has long been a pioneer in the reissuing of out-of-print titles from its own backlist, producing digital reprints of books that are still sought after by scholars and students but could not be reprinted economically using traditional technology. The Cambridge Library Collection extends this activity to a wider range of books which are still of importance to researchers and professionals, either for the source material they contain, or as landmarks in the history of their academic discipline.

Drawing from the world-renowned collections in the Cambridge University Library, and guided by the advice of experts in each subject area, Cambridge University Press is using state-of-the-art scanning machines in its own Printing House to capture the content of each book selected for inclusion. The files are processed to give a consistently clear, crisp image, and the books finished to the high quality standard for which the Press is recognised around the world. The latest print-on-demand technology ensures that the books will remain available indefinitely, and that orders for single or multiple copies can quickly be supplied.

The Cambridge Library Collection will bring back to life books of enduring scholarly value (including out-of-copyright works originally issued by other publishers) across a wide range of disciplines in the humanities and social sciences and in science and technology.

# Trinity College Library.
# The First 150 Years

*The Sandars Lectures 1978-9*

PHILIP GASKELL

CAMBRIDGE
UNIVERSITY PRESS

CAMBRIDGE UNIVERSITY PRESS

Cambridge, New York, Melbourne, Madrid, Cape Town, Singapore,
São Paolo, Delhi, Dubai, Tokyo, Mexico City

Published in the United States of America by Cambridge University Press, New York

www.cambridge.org
Information on this title: www.cambridge.org/9781108015936

© in this compilation Cambridge University Press 2010

This edition first published 1980
This digitally printed version 2010

ISBN 978-1-108-01593-6 Paperback

# TRINITY COLLEGE LIBRARY

*The first 150 years*

# TRINITY COLLEGE LIBRARY
## The first 150 years

PHILIP GASKELL

THE SANDARS LECTURES
1978–9

CAMBRIDGE UNIVERSITY PRESS

CAMBRIDGE

LONDON    NEW YORK    NEW ROCHELLE
MELBOURNE    SYDNEY

Published by the Press Syndicate of the University of Cambridge
The Pitt Building, Trumpington Street, Cambridge CB2 1RP
32 East 57th Street, New York, NY 10022, USA
296 Beaconsfield Parade, Middle Park, Melbourne 3206, Australia

First published 1980

Phototypeset in V.I.P. Bembo by
Western Printing Services Ltd, Bristol
Printed in Great Britain at the
University Press, Cambridge

*British Library Cataloguing in Publication Data*
Gaskell, Philip
Trinity College Library. – (Sandars lectures
in bibliography; 1978–9).
1. Trinity College, *Cambridge*. Library – History
I. Title   II. Series
027.7426′59   Z792.C/   79–41415

ISBN 0 521 23100 0

To the memory of
H. S. Bennett
1889–1972
Librarian of Emmanuel
and
A. N. L. Munby
1913–1974
Librarian of King's

# CONTENTS

*Lists of illustrations and plans*     ix

*Preface*     xi

*Terms and conventions*     xv

*Abbreviations*     xvii

## 1546–1600

1  College libraries in the sixteenth century     3
2  The libraries of Michaelhouse and the King's Hall     11
3  The establishment of Trinity College Library     19
4  The need for books at Trinity in the sixteenth century     22
5  The College Library in the mid-sixteenth century     25
6  The College Library in 1600     34
7  The development of the collection up to 1600     46
8  Private libraries     51

## 1601–1695

9  The New Library     61
10  Stanhope's Librarianship     75
11  Collections of manuscripts     79
12  The growth of the working collections, 1601–40     86
13  The arrangement of the books, 1601–40     92
14  Administration and reorganisation, 1641–74     107
15  The book stock, 1667–95     126
16  The last years of the New Library     134

## APPENDIXES

A  A catalogue of the College Library in 1600     147

B  The seventeenth-century Library catalogues                    213
C  Robert Beaumont's books, 1567                                215
D  Sir Edward Stanhope's will, 1603                             219
E  College Librarians and Sub-Librarians, 1609-95              227
F  Donations of manuscripts, 1604–94                           233
G  Donations of printed books, 1601–40                         237
H  The science books in c.1645                                 241
 I  Library regulations, 1651                                   259

*Index*                                                        261

# ILLUSTRATIONS

1 Conjectural drawing of an early lectern 5
2 Conjectural drawing of a four-shelf book-case 9
3 Trinity College in the 1590s 13
4 Detail from Loggan's view of Trinity, 1688 15
5 Lectern end in Queens' College Library 16
6 The Old Library of Trinity Hall 17
7 Two Cambridge roll-stamped bindings, c.1580 30
8 Handwritten titles on Old Library books 31
9 The College's inscription in an Old Library book 33
10 Beginning of the Old Library list in the *Memoriale* 36
11 Inscriptions on the title-page of a Skeffington book 43
12 Plan made c.1555 for laying out the principal court of Trinity 62
13 Detail of the 1555 plan 64
14 Detail of the 1555 plan photographed by transmitted light 65
15 Detail from Loggan's view of Trinity, 1688 66
16 Detail from West's view of the Great Court, 1739 67
17 Lectern of c.1600–5 in Trinity Hall Library 72
18 Conjectural drawing of the New Library 73
19 Detail from conjectural drawing of the New Library 94
20 Calf binding, probably by Hamond, c.1605–6 100
21 Inside the front cover of a calf binding 101
22 Running numbers on the fore-edges of Library books 102
23 Running number on fore-edge supplemented by paper tab 103
24 Printed donation label on title-page 105
25 Extract from alphabetical finding list, c.1640 109
26 Extract from draft class catalogue, c.1645–8 110
27 Extract from indexed class catalogue, 1667–c.1675 116

28 Extract from indexed class catalogue, c.1675–95      117
29 Extract from shelf-list of manuscripts, 1667      118
30 Extract from shelf-list of manuscripts, c.1675–95      136
31 First appeal circular for the Wren Library, 1676      138

## PLANS OF THE NEW LIBRARY

1 Possible arrangement of the cases, c.1604      70
2 Possible arrangement of the cases, 1640      95
3 Possible classification by donors, c.1612–18      98
4 Classification by donors, 1640      99
5 Proposed classification by subjects, 1645–8      111
6 Classification by subjects, 1667–95      114

# PREFACE

One period in the history of one College Library may not seem much of a subject for a book, but there are two reasons why it is worth investigating the early history of Trinity College Library in some detail. One is that a number of Trinity men – more perhaps than of the members of any other college – contributed importantly to England's spiritual, intellectual, and scientific development from soon after the foundation of the college in 1546 until the end of the seventeenth century,[1] so that the state of its working library during this period is of unusual interest. The other reason is that the investigation helps to illuminate the process whereby Trinity Library grew from small beginnings into the greatest of all the Oxford and Cambridge college libraries, rich both in contents and in setting.

To summarise the story: it appears that in 1546 Trinity inherited the libraries of its two constituent colleges, Michaelhouse and the King's Hall, but that Trinity was amongst those colleges which parted with virtually the whole of their pre-Reformation libraries during the religious upsets of the mid-century, so that scarcely any trace of its founding collections survived into the seventeenth century. There is in fact very little that we know for certain about the contents of Trinity's Library in the sixteenth century, though we can infer a good deal from the small and uneven collection of books which the College owned in 1600. Then the Library contained only about 325 volumes of printed books altogether, including a recently acquired collection of law books. Of the rest, about 250 volumes, two-thirds were divinity books, and no other subject was even remotely well covered. Most of the 250 had probably been in the Library since the 1560s. Since Trinity could easily have afforded to

[1] The most eminent of the early Trinity men were Cartwright, Whitgift, Coke, Bacon, Essex, George Herbert, Ray, Barrow, and Newton; but there were many others of only relatively less distinction.

build up its Library into something more useful during the later sixteenth century, this situation appears to have been acceptable to the College. Meanwhile the Fellows met their need for academic books by assembling substantial private libraries. There was no College Librarian.

The seventeenth century saw great and rapid changes. A new library apartment was completed as part of the Great Court in about 1604, and a College Librarianship was established in 1608. From then until the 1640s the book stock was quickly and purposefully built up. First came the gifts of superb monastic manuscripts which are still the Library's most spectacular treasures, and they were followed by a steady flow of academic printed books, a majority of them given by members of the College and other well-wishers, but a substantial minority chosen and bought by the College with its own funds and with money given for the purchase of library books. There was still a preponderance of divinity books in the Library, but other subject groups were deliberately improved as well, including the science sections. The later part of the seventeenth century, finally, was a time of consolidation, when the College paid more attention to organising and cataloguing the collections than to refining their contents, though there were further gifts of books. By the 1670s the Library in the Great Court was considered to be inadequate, and the College took the opportunity to complete Nevile's Court with a splendid new Library. The period ends with the removal of the books from the Great Court Library to the Wren in 1695.

There is unfortunately no large-scale general history of Trinity College to which this account could be referred. Of the short histories of the College the best are Rouse Ball, W. W., *Notes on the History of Trinity College, Cambridge*, London 1899, and Trevelyan, G. M., *Trinity College, an historical sketch*, Cambridge 1943, reprinted with additions 1972; and see also Rouse Ball's *Cambridge notes*, 2nd ed., Cambridge 1921, and vol. iii of the *Victoria County History of Cambridgeshire*, London 1959. Willis, R., and Clark, J. W., *The architectural history of the University of Cambridge*, 4 vols, Cambridge 1886, is essential; and it is supplemented by the Royal Commission on Historical Monuments' *Inventory of historical monuments in the City of Cambridge*, 4 vols, London 1959. There is a sketchy history of the Library in Sinker, R., *The Library of Trinity College, Cambridge*, Cambridge 1891; much more valuable is Sinker's scholarly *Biographical notes on the Librarians of Trinity College*, Cambridge 1897. The immediate predecessor of the present work is Gaskell, P., and Robson, R., *The Library of Trinity*

*College, Cambridge: a short history*, Cambridge 1971, the first part of which is now superseded.[1]

I am left with the pleasant task of acknowledging the advice and encouragement I have received from friendly experts, and of thanking them all warmly and sincerely. I was able to benefit from Bruce Purvis's work on the contents of Trinity College Library in the seventeenth century; and Elizabeth Leedham-Green's immense knowledge of the sixteenth-century Vice-Chancellors' Court records was essential to the investigation of the Fellows' private libraries. I was most fortunate in being given advice on the contents of particular sections of the Library by Gale Christianson, Rupert Hall, P. M. Rattansi, and Charles Webster (the science sections); by Shirley and Oliver Letwin, and Mary Ann Radzinowicz (the divinity and philosophy sections); by E. J. Kenney (the classics section); by Brian Wormald (the history section); and by Walter Ullmann (the law section). I was also generously helped with a variety of particular problems by Helen Baron, Roger Dawe, John and Pat Easterling, Neil Ker, David McKitterick, J. G. Pollard, Harry Porter, John Oates, and Quentin Skinner. Rosemary Graham and Robert Robson were kind enough to read my manuscript and make detailed criticisms. I am grateful, finally, to the Master and Fellows of Trinity College, Cambridge, and to the Syndics of Cambridge University Library, for permission to use and quote from copyright documents.

Trinity College                                                    PHILIP GASKELL
Cambridge
1976–9

[1] The present investigation has suggested the following amendments to Gaskell and Robson:
Gaskell and Robson p. 6: it appears to have been Michaelhouse Library, not King's Hall Library, that served as Trinity College Library in the sixteenth century (pp. 20–1 below).
Gaskell and Robson p. 7: Trinity's library books were chained in the sixteenth century, and unchained in 1604 (pp. 29, 71, 101).
Gaskell and Robson p. 8: there were only about 325 volumes in the College Library in 1600 (p. 38).
Gaskell and Robson p. 8: the sixteenth-century 'Library Keeper' was the fore-runner not of Stanhope's Librarians, but of the seventeenth-century Sub-Librarians (pp. 26–7).
Gaskell and Robson p. 10: for a revised account of the book stock in 1667, see Chapter 15, below. There was a collection of law books in the Library, but it was not catalogued.
Gaskell and Robson p. 11: although there was no regular allocation from endowment income for the purchase of library books in the seventeenth century, allocations were at least occasionally made from room rents (pp. 123–4).
Gaskell and Robson p. 12: the finding list (Add. MS a.103) was made in about 1640, not in about 1675–6 (Appendix B).
Gaskell and Robson p. 28: the 'efficient new catalogues' (Add. MS a.109, 127–8) were begun not in 1739–40 but around 1700 (p. 142).

# TERMS AND CONVENTIONS

*libraries* (general term)

    *library*                  a library apartment or building and the collection of library books in it

    *the Old Library*      TCL 1546–c.1604, location unknown

    *the New Library*     TCL c.1604–1695, in the Great Court

    *the Wren Library*     TCL from 1695, in Nevile's Court

*books* (general term)

    *item*                    a book as a bibliographical unit; a single manuscript, a copy of a printed edition

    *volume*                a book as a physical unit; one volume may contain one item, or part of an item, or several items

    *title*                    a specific entry in a book list

*catalogues* (general term)

    *inventory*            a list of books, giving only the first or chief work in each volume

    *shelf-list*            a list of books in shelf order

    *finding list*         a list of books with locations

    *catalogue*          a list of books in class order (*class catalogue*) or in alphabetical order of headings (*author catalogue*), with locations

As far as possible, authors' names and other headings follow Adams.

# ABBREVIATIONS

The following abbreviations are used:

Adams
Adams, H.M., *Catalogue of books printed on the continent of Europe, 1501–1600, in Cambridge libraries*, 2 vols, Cambridge 1967

*Ben*
TCL *Benefactions book*, ff. 1–30 of TC Add. MS a.106 (references are to the early manuscript pagination)

BL
The British Library

BM
The British Museum

*CAS Com.*
*Cambridge Antiquarian Society Communications*

*CAS Proc.*
*Cambridge Antiquarian Society Proceedings*

CUA
Cambridge University Archives (in Cambridge University Library)

CUL
Cambridge University Library

*DNB*
*The dictionary of national biography*, 2nd ed., London 1908–12

*Don*
TCL 'catalogue of books given to Trinity College', TC Add. MS a.150

Gaskell and Robson
Gaskell, P., and Robson, R., *The Library of Trinity College, Cambridge: a short history*, Cambridge 1971

Goff
Goff, F.R., *Incunabula in American libraries*, New York 1964

Innes
Innes, H.M., *Fellows of Trinity College, Cambridge*, Cambridge 1941

James
James, M.R., *The western manuscripts in the Library of Trinity College, Cambridge*, 4 vols, Cambridge 1900–4

| | |
|---|---|
| JB | Junior Bursar |
| Loggan 1688 | Loggan, D., view of Trinity College, c.1688, in *Cantabrigia illustrata*, Cambridge [1690] |
| *Mem, Memoriale* | *Memoriale Collegio Sanctae et Individuae Trinitatis in Academia Cantabrigiensi dicatum*, 1614, TC MS R.17.8 (references are to the early manuscript pagination) |
| Mullinger | Mullinger, J.B., *The University of Cambridge*, 3 vols, Cambridge 1873–1911 |
| *OED* | *The Oxford English Dictionary* |
| *Old plans* | Clark, J.W., and Gray, A., *Old plans of Cambridge, 1574–1798*, 2 vols, Cambridge 1921 |
| PRO | The Public Record Office |
| SB | Senior Bursar |
| Sinker, *Librarians* | Sinker, R., *Biographical notes on the Librarians of Trinity College on Sir Edward Stanhope's foundation*, Cambridge 1897 |
| STC | Pollard, A.W., and Regrave, G.R., *A short-title catalogue of books printed in England* [etc.] *1475–1640*, London 1926 (2nd ed. in progress) |
| TC | Trinity College, Cambridge |
| *TC Admissions* | Rouse Ball, W.W., and Venn, J.A., *Admissions to Trinity College, Cambridge*, 5 vols, London 1913–16 |
| TCL | Trinity College Library |
| TC Mun. | Trinity College Muniments |
| *Trans. Camb. Bib. Soc.* | *Transactions of the Cambridge Bibliographical Society* |
| Venn | Venn, J. and J.A., *Alumni Cantabrigienses*, Part I to 1751, 4 vols, Cambridge 1922–7 |
| VCC | Vice-Chancellor's Court |
| VCH | The Victoria County History |
| Willis and Clark | Willis, R., and Clark, J.W., *The architectural history of the University of Cambridge*, 4 vols, Cambridge 1886 |
| Wing | Wing, D.G., *Short-title catalogue of books printed in England* [etc.] *1641–1700*, 3 vols, New York 1945 (2nd ed. in progress) |
| Wormald and Wright | Wormald, F., and Wright, C.E., *The English library before 1700*, London 1958 |

| | |
|---|---|
| *1640* | TCL finding list, TC Add. MS a.103 |
| *1645* | TCL draft class catalogue, c.1645–8, BL MS Sloane 78, ff. 139ª–154ª |
| *1667* | TCL indexed class catalogue, 1667–c.1675, TC Add. MS a.101 |
| *1675* | TCL indexed class catalogue, c.1675–1695, TC Add. MS a.104 |

1546–1600

# CHAPTER 1

# COLLEGE LIBRARIES IN THE SIXTEENTH CENTURY

The history of Trinity College Library from the foundation of the College in 1546 to the installation of the books in the newly finished Wren Library in 1695 falls into two distinct periods dividing in about 1600. Although the development of the Library from 1600 on can be followed in some detail from surviving documents, the first half-century of its history is scarcely documented at all. Nevertheless there is some light in the darkness, for it is possible to make a list of the books that were in the collection in 1600. From this it appears that more than two-thirds of the books that were in the Library then are still in it today, so that the actual books can be examined for evidence of how the collection developed in the early days. Even this evidence, however, is so scanty that it has to be interpreted in the light of what is known about the other college libraries of Oxford and Cambridge; and I begin with a brief account of these libraries in the sixteenth century.[1]

In 1500 there were at Oxford ten colleges with libraries: University College (founded 1249), Merton (1264), Balliol (1293), Exeter (1314), Oriel (1326), Queen's (1340), New College (1379), Lincoln (1427), All Souls (1438), and Magdalen (1458); while at Cambridge there were eleven: Peterhouse (1284), Michaelhouse (1324), Clare (1326), the King's Hall

---

[1] This section relies heavily on N. R. Ker's admirable Sandars lectures of 1955, published as 'Oxford college libraries in the sixteenth century', *Bodleian Library record*, vi, 1959, pp. 459–515; see also his Bodleian Library exhibition catalogue, *Oxford college libraries in 1556*, Oxford 1956, and his 'Oxford college libraries before 1500', *The universities in the late middle ages*, ed. Ijsewija, J., and Paquet, J., Leuven 1978, pp. 293–311. There is no comparable survey of the Cambridge college libraries in the sixteenth century, but a good deal of scattered evidence indicates that they were essentially similar to those at Oxford; see inter alia Willis and Clark; the introductions to M. R. James's catalogues of the western manuscripts in the Cambridge college libraries; Streeter, B. H., *The chained library*, London 1931; and McKitterick, D., 'Two sixteenth-century catalogues of St John's College library', *Trans. Camb. Bib. Soc.*, vii, 1978, pp. 135–55. References to the printed inventories of Cambridge college libraries prior to 1500 are given in the notes to pp. 246–58 of Cobban, A. B., *The King's Hall*, Cambridge 1969.

(1337), Pembroke (1347), Gonville Hall (1347), Trinity Hall (1350), Corpus (1352), King's (1441), Queens' (1448), and St Catharine's (1473).[1] Just as the colleges at both universities had generally similar constitutions, so their libraries contained the same sort of books organised in the same sort of way. The heart of the college library was already the reference collection of books chained for the use of the Fellows in the Library apartment, but in 1500 the colleges still loaned library books to the Fellows, the older colleges having special loan collections of books that were distributed at annual meetings called *electiones*, at which each Fellow might choose a book or books for the year.

Very few library books were bought by the colleges, nearly all of them being acquired as a result of gifts or bequests. By 1500 the library apartments were mostly full – their capacity was limited by the type of library furniture in use – so that new books displaced old ones, those that were displaced going to the loan collections along with any new books that were more suitable for loan than for reference. The reference collections then numbered from about 100 to about 500 folio volumes, mostly manuscripts still, but including an increasing minority of printed books. The loan collections were now smaller than the reference collections, but might include as many as 375 volumes (as at Merton in 1500), nearly all of them manuscripts.

Coverage was uneven. Not only had the older colleges had time to build up better libraries than the younger ones, but a college might not happen to be given the books it needed. Nevertheless most of the colleges had good basic reference collections in divinity and law by 1500, and often in philosophy and medicine as well. This really mattered to the Fellows, since the academic books that they needed were not yet available in cheap printed editions that they could afford to own in any numbers, and they were obliged to rely chiefly on their college libraries for access to the central texts of the late medieval curriculum.

The college library apartments of 1500, most of which had been built in the first half of the fifteenth century, were typically first-floor rooms measuring from about 35ft × 15ft to about 60ft × 20ft inside. Windows were set at regular intervals of from 5ft to 7ft 6in in the two long walls, with a two-sided lectern projecting into the room between each pair of windows, and four single-sided lecterns set at the ends of the rows against

---

[1] God's House (1439, refounded as Christ's, 1506) is not known to have had a library; and the library of Jesus (1496) was established after 1500.

the end walls.[1] The lecterns had benches fixed between each pair, and each row occupied one third of the width of the room, the other third being a central passage. The lecterns had sloping desks on each side, originally perhaps only one desk but by 1500 either two desks one above the other or one desk and a flat shelf on each side (figs. 1, 5). The books were laid flat on

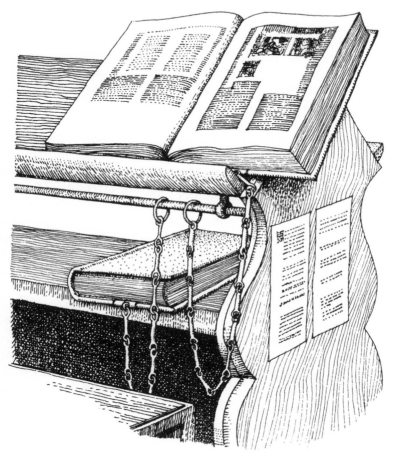

1 A conjectural drawing of a lectern of the sort that is likely to have been taken over by Trinity from Michaelhouse and the King's Hall, and used in the Old Library until c.1604. It can be seen why the chains were attached to the tail-edges of the covers, and why the titles were written on the bottom edges of the books. Shelf-lists were probably pasted on the lectern ends.

[1] Neil Ker has demonstrated that, contrary to the views of J. W. Clark and B. H. Streeter, no Oxford college library changed from lecterns to book-cases before 1589 (*Bodleian Library*

the desks or shelves, chained by their bottom (or less commonly their top) edges, and each folio volume occupied a space about one foot wide. The average number of volumes kept on a two-sided, two-decker lectern was therefore four times its length in feet. Since there was the equivalent of one such lectern to each of the windows in the long walls, and the length of each lectern was one third the width of the room, the approximate capacity of the whole apartment can be obtained by multiplying the width of the room in feet by $\frac{4}{3}$ (to get the average number of books per lectern), and then multiplying the result by the total number of windows. Thus a room measuring 35ft × 15ft, with a total of 10 windows, could accommodate about 200 volumes; and a room measuring 60ft × 20ft with 16 windows could take about 425 volumes.[1] In practice the limit for a large college library before the 1590s was about 500 volumes.

No college had yet appointed a Librarian, although the annual *electiones* were administered by Fellows who may also have cared for the reference collections. In any case the libraries were unsupervised, a library key being issued to each Fellow; hence the chains. Several shelf-inventories of college libraries have survived from around 1500, but no alphabetical catalogues. Users of these libraries appear to have made do with shelf-lists posted on the lectern ends, which were sufficient when the collections were such small ones, and were arranged in a traditional order.[2]

The older college libraries of Oxford and Cambridge remained in this general condition for the first three decades of the sixteenth century, there being if anything a reduction of activity as donations fell off, and as the organised distribution of the loan collections was given up in most colleges by about 1520.[3] Then, from the 1530s to the 1550s, the richer Oxford colleges began to buy library books in a conscious effort to catch up with the new learning, replacing their manuscripts with such things as the splendid new editions of the Greek and Latin Fathers from the scholar-printers of Basle. Similar purchases may have been made by the Cambridge colleges, but the evidence is lacking.

*record*, vi, 1959, pp. 470–2); and I know of no evidence that any Cambridge college library changed to book-cases before the end of the sixteenth century.

[1] It hardly needs to be said that these figures are the merest approximations. On the one hand a lectern desk might not be filled right up, while on the other the average space taken up by a volume might be reduced by piling the books up on a flat shelf; and there might be unsuspected variations in the library furniture.

[2] On classification, see pp. 109, 112 below.

[3] Though Neil Ker shows that *electiones* continued at Lincoln College, Oxford, until the 1590s. At Cambridge the last recorded *electio* appears to be one that took place at Corpus in 1517 (Fletcher, J. M., and McConica, J. K., 'A sixteenth century inventory of the Library of Corpus Christi College, Cambridge', *Trans. Camb. Bib. Soc.*, iii, 1959–63, p. 188).

There had always been some turnover of the stock of college libraries, but from the 1530s until about 1560 the pace of change rapidly increased. Its chief agents were, first, the replacement of old, outdated texts by new ones; secondly, wholesale disposal of the books belonging to the loan collections, which were not replaced; thirdly, the purging of library books on doctrinal grounds by the successive visitations of the Reformation and Counter-reformation; and fourthly, the loss of library books as a result of maladministration and neglect. The extent to which individual college libraries were affected by these factors varied enormously, being generally less at Oxford than it was at Cambridge. At Oxford the libraries of Merton, Balliol, Oriel, New College, Lincoln, All Souls, and Magdalen retained substantial numbers of their medieval manuscripts, whereas at Cambridge only Peterhouse, Pembroke, and Gonville and Caius kept many manuscripts, and then in smaller proportions than the Oxford colleges. At the other end of the scale University College and Queen's alone amongst the older Oxford colleges kept none (or very few) of their medieval manuscripts through the sixteenth century, while at Cambridge the libraries of Clare, Michaelhouse and the King's Hall (as Trinity), Trinity Hall, Corpus, King's, Queens', and St Catharine's had few or none of their old manuscripts in 1600.[1]

It appears that two of these Cambridge colleges, moreover, actually lost large numbers of their library books altogether. The Fellows of Clare, dismayed by the proposal of the Visitors of 1549 to unite their College with Trinity Hall, distributed all their worth-while library books amongst themselves. Less dramatically the Library of King's College was reduced by the combined effects of religious purges and of administrative neglect from perhaps 500 books in 1528 to 113 by 1557, and to a negligible rump by the late 1560s.[2] The two university libraries were also despoiled;[3] but in most colleges the old library books were exchanged rather than lost. In any case mid-century losses are unlikely to have undermined the intellectual

---

[1] See the sources referred to in p. 3 n. 1 and p. 6 n. 3; and Hunt, R. W., 'Medieval inventories of Clare College Library', *Trans. Camb. Bib. Soc.*, i, 1949–53, pp. 105–25; Cargill Thompson, W. D. J., 'Notes on King's College Library 1500–1570, in particular for the period of the Reformation', *Trans. Camb. Bib. Soc.*, ii, 1954–8, pp. 38–54; and James, T., *Ecloga Oxonio-Cantabrigiensis*, London 1600.

[2] For the distribution at Clare see Mullinger, ii, pp. 134–5; and on King's, Cargill Thompson, W. D. J., loc. cit.

[3] Oxford University Library lost *all* its books, and the library furniture was sold in 1556 (Wormald and Wright, pp. 168–9). At Cambridge the University Library survived the Reformation, but with its 1528 stock of 500–600 volumes reduced to 175 volumes by 1557 (Oates, J. C. T., and Pink, H. L., 'Three sixteenth-century catalogues of the University Library', *Trans. Camb. Bib. Soc.*, i, 1949–53, pp. 310–40).

life of the universities as much as similar losses would have done in 1500, since by this time many dons owned private libraries of academic books that were large enough to supply their prime needs.[1]

Five new college libraries were established in each of the universities during the sixteenth century: at Oxford those of Brasenose (founded 1509), Corpus (1517), Christ Church (1546), Trinity (1555), and St John's (1555); and at Cambridge those of Jesus (1496), Christ's (1506), St John's (1511), Magdalene (1542), and Emmanuel (1584).[2] These new collections, though dominated at first by their foundation gifts, came to resemble the older college libraries, and they were kept in the same sort of library apartments, chained to the same sort of desks.

The period from about 1560 to the mid-1580s saw a general improvement in the college libraries' holdings of Protestant theology, but otherwise there was little progress. Around 1580 a college's collection began typically with various Bibles, probably including a large one in several volumes with Lyra's glosses, and a concordance (few colleges yet owned the Complutensian polyglot). Next in the traditional order came the Greek Fathers – Josephus, Irenaeus, Eusebius, Epiphanius – commonly in the fine Basle editions of Froben and Episcopius; and after them the Latin Fathers, led by Augustine in nine or ten volumes, but also including Tertullian, Hilary, Jerome, and Gregory the Great; again it was the Basle editions that were most often chosen. The rest of the divinity books that were placed after the Fathers were strongest in biblical commentaries – especially the Protestant commentators such as Zwingli, Oecolampadius, Musculus, and Bucer – and in the history of the Church. Medieval theology was for the moment out of favour, and many scholastic texts had been thrown out; but few collections yet included much of Luther or of Calvin, or of the English controversialists. Altogether the divinity books were likely to make up about two-thirds of the whole library.

The classes which followed divinity varied more between the colleges. There would be dictionaries, but few classics, and those few probably in Greek rather than in Latin; they would not have included Virgil or Horace. Aristotle would be there, and probably Plato, both in Greek. Some of the libraries had small medical and scientific sections; and there might, finally, be a considerable section of law books, devoted equally to canon and to Roman civil law.

[1] See Chapter 8.
[2] The library of Trinity, Cambridge (1546), was not a new one; while Jesus, Oxford (1571), and Sidney Sussex, Cambridge (1596), did not have libraries in the sixteenth century.

Nearly all the printed books were folios imported from abroad and – apart from some Fathers, classics, and dictionaries in Greek – nearly all were in Latin. There were no recreational works, and none of the octavo text-books that were used by this time in both universities for teaching the junior courses.

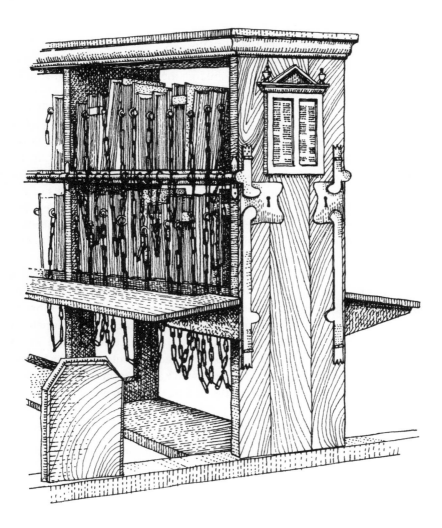

2 A conjectural drawing of a four-shelf book-case with chained books of the sort that was introduced at Oxford at the end of the sixteenth century. The chains were attached to the fore-edges of the covers.

The next period of change in the college libraries began in the 1580s with a widespread increase in the rate at which the collections grew. This resulted both from more and larger donations of books, and from an increasing reluctance to turn out old but still useful books to make way for new ones. There was also a revival of interest in the works of the medieval Schoolmen and in Catholic theology, but for the most part the existing sections of library books were simply expanded.

More library books meant that the colleges were obliged either to find more economical ways of keeping them – laying them out on lecterns was grossly extravagant of space – or to enlarge their library apartments, or to do both. Merton led the way in 1589 by replacing half its lecterns with book-cases[1] which had two flat shelves on each side on which the books stood upright, and were chained at their outward-facing fore-edges so that they could be pulled down and read on desks fixed below the shelves on each side of the case (fig. 2). This alteration increased the capacity of the library furniture by a factor of four or five, since the four shelves of such a book-case held 16–20 volumes to the foot, whereas the four desks of the lectern it replaced had accommodated only about 4 books to the foot; while more shelves could be added to the book-cases if they were needed. Most of the college libraries eventually changed over to book-cases in one form or another, Cambridge lagging behind Oxford.

More books also required more administration. A few colleges appointed Fellow-librarians – the first being the 'custos' of the library of Magdalen, Oxford, appointed in 1550 – but most of them did no more in the sixteenth century than employ a college servant, or occasionally a junior member of the college, to clean the library apartment and to set up the books. Records of benefactions became more detailed, and the inventories used for checking the books were well kept, but there were scarcely any full library catalogues before the end of the century.

---

[1] The term 'stall' was used by J. W. Clark and B. H. Streeter to distinguish this type of book-case from lecterns. The usage can be misleading, however, since the terms 'stall', 'desk', and 'seat' were all used in sixteenth- and seventeenth-century college libraries both for lecterns and for shelved book-cases.

# CHAPTER 2

# THE LIBRARIES OF
# MICHAELHOUSE
# AND THE KING'S HALL

The ancient colleges of Michaelhouse and the King's Hall each had a library at the time of their amalgamation and refoundation as Trinity College in 1546. All that we know about the Michaelhouse collection is that the College was given three divinity books and two law books by the Founder in 1327;[1] many books by William de Gotham, Master in 1387;[2] works of Augustine and Hugh of St Victor by John Ottringham, Master, by 1454;[3] 200 books by John Yotton, Master in 1492–3;[4] seven books by four donors in the early sixteenth century;[5] and six printed divinity books by William Filey DD, perhaps c.1525, of which three are still in Trinity College Library.[6] At the time of its dissolution, moreover, Michaelhouse commemorated about 150 other benefactors, some of whom, perhaps, had also given books to the College.[7] All this – and especially John Yotton's enormous donation – suggests that Michaelhouse had a large library by the 1520s; and it is likely, in view of the clerical character of the society, that it was a collection chiefly of divinity books.

Where Michaelhouse kept its books, however, we do not know. We have no Michaelhouse buildings records, and the buildings themselves were all pulled down long ago. All that is left are Trinity's sixteenth-century demolition and building accounts, and three perspective views of Cambridge made in the later sixteenth century when about half of the old Michaelhouse buildings were still standing, but none of these documents so much as hint at where the Library was located. Since, as we shall see,

---

[1] [Stamp, A. E.], *Michaelhouse*, privately printed 1924, p. 14.
[2] *Memoriale*, p. 21.
[3] [Stamp, A. E.], op. cit., p. 49.     [4] *Memoriale*, p. 22.
[5] The bequests of Thomas Colier, Fellow (3 law books; CUA, VCC Wills, c.1506); John Proctor BCL (2 divinity books; CUA, VCC Wills, 1510); Richard Nelson, Fellow (a Bible with chain c.1512; [Stamp, A. E.], op. cit., p. 55); and Henry Crossley, Fellow (a Hebrew bible; CUA, VCC Wills, 1526).
[6] See below, pp. 27–8.     [7] [Stamp, A. E.], op. cit., pp. 51–6.

there is reason to believe that the Michaelhouse library apartment remained in existence for some time after the foundation of Trinity, it was probably located in or near the central block of Michaelhouse that ran from what is now the south-west corner of the Great Court to the entrance porch of the Master of Trinity's Lodge; but this is a puzzle to which we shall have to return later[1] (fig. 3).

There is less mystery about the early history of the Library of the King's Hall, which can be followed in unusual detail in the great series of King's Hall account books that survives in the Muniment Room of Trinity College.[2] Even before the King's Hall was formally established as a College in 1337, the Society of the King's Scholars was given a collection of law books by Edward II that was valued at £10.[3] These books were later taken away again by Edward's widow, but by the 1360s the King's Hall – already specialising in legal studies – had at least 19 law books in its Library and half a dozen others.[4] A borrowers' list of 1385 names 75 law books and 5 others that were out on loan to the Warden and Fellows; and an apparently complete inventory of 1391 lists 101 volumes, 22 of them chained.[5] Of the 101 books of 1391, 48 were on civil law, the rest concerning canon law and medicine (16 each), grammar (11), and dialectic and divinity (5 each); it was undoubtedly the finest law library in Cambridge. In the fifteenth century there are records of various small gifts of books in the period 1410–28;[6] of many books given by Richard Holme, Warden, in 1424;[7] of 77 books given by Henry VI in 1435, one of which survives in the British Library;[8] of the possible purchase of 27 volumes from the executors of John Paston, Fellow and Steward, in 1443;[9] and of a manuscript (also now in the British Library) given by Roger Rotheram, Warden, in about 1477, but afterwards in the possession of E. Knevet, a member of the King's Hall in 1540–1.[10] There are also records of the binding and chaining of library books from 1399 to 1464.[11] There are no

[1] See below, pp. 20–1.
[2] Sayle, C. E., 'King's Hall Library', *CAS Proc.*, xxiii (NS xvii), 1920–1, pp. 54–76; Cobban, A. B., *The King's Hall*, Cambridge 1969, *passim*, and especially pp. 246–54.
[3] Sayle, C. E., loc. cit., p. 54.
[4] Sayle, C. E., loc. cit., pp. 55–6.     [5] Sayle. C. E., loc. cit., pp. 62–3, 64–70.
[6] Sayle, C. E., loc. cit., pp. 58–9.     [7] *Memoriale*, p. 18.
[8] Sayle, C. E., loc. cit., pp. 59–60, 71–2. The surviving manuscript is BL Cotton Claudius B.ix, ff. 2–263, Helinandus, 15th cent.; it was noted by Leland (Ker, N. R., *Medieval libraries of Great Britain*, 2nd ed., London 1964, p. 26).
[9] Sayle, C. E., loc. cit., p. 60, quoting Thorold Rogers. Sayle is inclined to doubt Rogers because he cannot locate his source, but it is hard to see how Rogers could have invented it.
[10] Sayle, C. E., loc, cit., p. 61; now BL Royal 12 C.xxi, Frontinus, 1458 (Ker, N. R., op. cit., p. 26).     [11] Sayle, C. E., loc. cit., pp. 58–61.

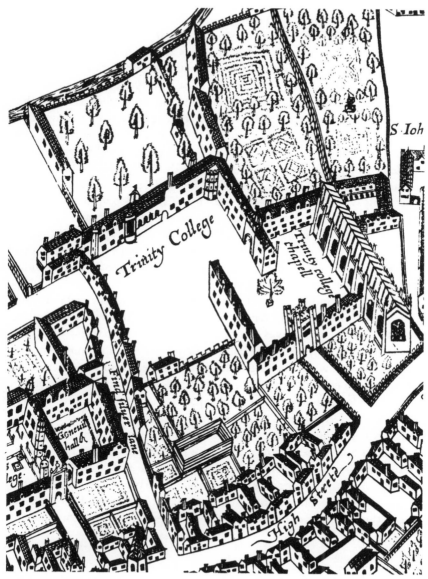

3 Trinity College in the 1590s, showing the range that had included the Lodge, Hall, Kitchen, and possibly Library of Michaelhouse immediately above the words 'Trinity College'. These buildings were replaced in the seventeenth century by the west range of the Great Court from R staircase to the porch of the Master's Lodge. (Detail from Hamond's plan of Cambridge, 1592; *Old plans*, 4; reduced.)

records of donations in the early sixteenth century, such as are found for Michaelhouse, and it may be that towards the end of its history the King's Hall had a less active and perhaps a smaller Library than did its neighbour.

The King's Hall library apartment seems always to have been situated on the northern boundary of the College with the Hospital of St John (later St John's College), north of the west end of Trinity College Chapel.[1] No details survive of its form or location in the fourteenth century, but between 1417 and 1421 a new Library was built, probably on the site of the old one, which served the College for the rest of its existence. The new Library was a first-floor room running eastwards from the north end of the King's Hall building that Trinity calls the King's Hostel[2] (fig. 4). It measured about 33 ft × 15 ft inside, and it had five windows in its south wall.[3] This would indicate a total capacity of about 200 volumes, a figure that agrees well enough with what we know about its contents. Trinity, as we shall see, appears to have put the King's Hall library apartment to other uses, and it was eventually pulled down in 1694, all but a small fragment of the north wall, which may still be seen (much restored) above a small courtyard beside the King's Hostel.[4]

There are still indications in Cambridge of what the Michaelhouse and King's Hall libraries may have looked like. The library apartment of Queens' College, which was completed in 1448, less than thirty years after the new library of the King's Hall, is a first-floor room running east and west with windows in the long walls. Before the east end was extended in the eighteenth century it measured 43 ft × 20 ft inside, and it had a total of twelve windows (with a theoretical capacity therefore of approximately 320 volumes).[5] At Queens', moreover, but at no other Oxford or Cambridge college, the old lecterns were not thrown out when the Library changed to book-cases in 1614, but were providently adapted and incorporated in the new furniture.[6] The lectern-ends are still there; the grooves that supported the lower desks are traceable inside (fig. 5). Queens' still has plenty of its sixteenth-century library books, the marks of their chains plain at the tail-edges of the boards, and the mind's eye can restore them to

[1] Caröe, W. D., King's Hostel, Cambridge 1909, p. 4.
[2] Caröe, W. D., op. cit., pp. 4–6.
[3] Dimensions from Caröe, W. D., op. cit., Plate M. The five windows in the south wall are shown in Lyne's map of 1574 (Old plans 1), and are implied in Loggan 1688; there were presumably similar features in the north wall.
[4] Caröe (op. cit., p. 12, fig. 8) reproduces a photograph of this fragment of the north wall taken during the restoration of 1905.
[5] Willis and Clark, ii, p. 50.
[6] Streeter, B. H., The chained library, London 1931, pp. 27–32.

4 A detail from Loggan's view of Trinity, 1688, showing three of the King's Hall Library windows, under the dormer windows to the right of the turret; the building was demolished soon afterwards, in 1694. (TCL X. 18.41; enlarged.)

5 A fifteenth-century lectern end in the Library of Queens' College, Cambridge, which was re-used at the beginning of the sixteenth century as the end of a book-case. Originally these lecterns had two sloping desks on each side, one above the other, and the diagonal groove on the inner face of the lectern end shown here supported the end of a lower desk.

6 The Old Library of Trinity Hall, Cambridge, showing the early seventeenth-century lecterns. (For the details of a Trinity Hall lectern, see fig. 17.)

their places side by side on the double desks of the ten two-sided and four single-sided lecterns.

Another Cambridge library of early appearance is that of Trinity Hall, the only college library at Oxford or Cambridge where lectern cases are still in use.[1] In fact this library apartment and its furniture – to which we shall be returning later – are of early-seventeenth-century origin, and differ in important ways from those of the fifteenth-century college libraries. Nevertheless the tall lectern cases at Trinity Hall, set in two rows in a library apartment of traditional form, do powerfully evoke what must have been the visual impact of a late-medieval college library (fig. 6).

## ADDENDUM (February 1980)

Neil Ker reports having seen a Michaelhouse book at Dulwich College: it is John, Damascene, St, *Theologia Damasceni* (? Paris 1519, not in Adams). In a contemporary binding, it is inscribed at the beginning 'Iste liber pertinet ad collegium diui Michaelis ex dono magistri hunkes'; and, at the end, 'Hunc librum contulit Ioannes hunkes collegio Diui Michaelis'. John Hunkes is not listed in Venn.

[1] See pp. 71–2.

# CHAPTER 3

# THE ESTABLISHMENT OF
# TRINITY COLLEGE LIBRARY

Trinity College was founded in 1546, and in 1560 it received the Statutes by which it was to be governed until the nineteenth century. These first fourteen years of the College's history, which spanned the reigns of Edward VI and Mary I, were troubled ones for Cambridge, and the times could hardly have been worse for the establishment of the College Library. Not that it was really a new Library, for it is certain that Trinity took over the library apartments of Michaelhouse and the King's Hall along with the rest of their buildings,[1] and no doubt it took over their books as well: Trinity continued to commemorate the donors of books to Michaelhouse and the King's Hall, and there were at least three Michaelhouse books in Trinity Library in the sixteenth century.[2] What is quite uncertain is how many books were left in the libraries of Michaelhouse and the King's Hall when these colleges were incorporated in Trinity in 1546.

In the 1520s the King's Hall may have owned some 200 library books, and Michaelhouse perhaps rather more. The two libraries could then have totalled 400–500 volumes altogether and, since Michaelhouse was primarily a clerical college and the King's Hall was primarily a legal one, there may not have been a great deal of duplication. In 1535, however, the Royal Injunctions imposed on the University when Thomas Cromwell became its Chancellor and Visitor forbade the study of scholastic theology and of canon law, either in the University or in any college;[3] and it is known that this resulted in the removal from many college libraries of large numbers of medieval text-books.[4] How far the libraries of Michaelhouse and the

---

[1] See pp. 20–1 below.
[2] The *Memoriale* commemorates books given by Richard Holme of the King's Hall (p. 18), and by William de Gotham and John Yotton of Michaelhouse (pp. 21–2). The three Michaelhouse books were those given by William Filey; see pp. 11 above, and 27–8 below.
[3] Mullinger, i, p. 630.
[4] Cargill Thompson, W. D. J., 'Notes on King's College Library 1500–1570', *Trans. Camb. Bib. Soc.*, ii, 1954–8, esp. pp. 42–3; Wright, C. E., 'The dispersal of the libraries in the sixteenth century', Wormald and Wright, esp. pp. 164–70.

King's Hall were depleted at this time is not known, but it is perhaps worth noting that Leland the antiquary saw only two manuscripts at the King's Hall in the 1530s which he thought worth mentioning, and at Michael-house none at all.[1] This does not prove that Michaelhouse and the King's Hall had already lost a lot of books – Leland may simply not have been interested in what he saw – but it does group their libraries with those of Trinity Hall, King's, and St Catharine's, the three other medieval Cam-bridge college libraries that were ignored by Leland, each of which lost all or almost all of its medieval library books during the sixteenth century.[2]

There is the further possibility that the Fellows of Michaelhouse and the King's Hall, realising in 1546 that their colleges were about to be dissolved, distributed some of their library books amongst themselves, as the Fel-lows of Clare were to do under the threat of dissolution in 1549.[3]

It may be, then, that the libraries of Michaelhouse and the King's Hall were considerably depleted by the time that they were taken over by Trinity, and that both collections of books could be fitted into one of the two library apartments. In fact only one was used, for the College building accounts for 1554–5 record that what is referred to as 'the old library' had by then been converted into rooms occupied by Mr Preston, one of the Chaplains, and by the Choir.[4] An entry in the accounts for 1556–7 then locates these rooms in the range of buildings, conveniently near the Chapel, in which the King's Hall Library had been situated[5] (fig. 4). This shows that by the mid-1550s the King's Hall library apartment was no longer used as a library; and the fact that it was referred to as 'the old

---

[1] Leland, J., *Collectanea*, iv, London 1770, p. 17. The two manuscripts that he saw at the King's Hall were 'Liber variarum Cassiodori', which is unidentified; and 'Historia Helinandi a creatione mundi ad tempora Henrici & Othonis imperatorum, complectens 44. libros', which had been given to the College by Henry VI in 1435 and which is now in the British Library (see p. 12 n. 8 above).

[2] Leland J., loc. cit., pp. 16–25. His largest haul was at Peterhouse, where he found over 100 books worth mentioning. He mentioned about 45 books at Queens' (which apparently replaced its old books with new ones later in the century), and about 30 at Clare (where the Fellows distributed the library books in 1549). He mentioned about 25 books at Gonville Hall, and 7–10 each at Pembroke, Corpus, and Jesus.

[3] Mullinger, ii, pp. 134–5.

[4] TC Mun., JB accounts, 1554–5:
f. 209ª: 'For makyn vpp 3 windoos in thold lybrarye where as mʳ preston ys'.
f.211ᵇ: 'For makyn ij large casementts for yᵉ singing booys in thold librarye'.
f.234ᵇ: 'For setting vpp of .44. Fooytt of old glasse wᵗʰ new Leade in mʳp'stons chamber, & in thold lybrarye for the synging booys'.
f.246ᵇ: 'for .4. barrs to mʳ p'stons casementts in thold lybrarye'.

[5] TC Mun., JB accounts, 1556–7:
f.291ª: 'for takyng downe yᵉ north wall of yᵉ Chambers from thold buttrye to tholde Chappell'. . .'for takyng downe yᵉ north wall of tholde buttrye & a pece of a wall Joyning to mʳ prestons Chamber'.

library' implies that there was another library apartment which was in use. This other library apartment was presumably that of Michaelhouse, for it is improbable that Trinity would have turned the King's Hall Library into rooms if it had not got Michaelhouse Library to use instead.

Since there is no indication in the surviving building accounts that Trinity built or otherwise contrived a new library apartment before one was included in the Great Court in about 1600, it would seem most likely that Michaelhouse Library continued to serve the College for the rest of the sixteenth century. There is unfortunately scarcely any clue to where it was situated. The Michaelhouse buildings which survived more or less intact until the end of the century were those in the range running from the south-west corner of the present Great Court to the porch of the Master's Lodge, of which the only clear view is that of John Hamond made in 1592[1] (fig. 3). Going from south to north, the range was preceded by two separate buildings in the area of Ovyng's Inn and Garret Hostel;[2] then came the main range with a stair turret, and a block with six windows and two dormers which may formerly have included the Lodge of the Master of Michaelhouse. Next came the Hall of Michaelhouse, which was still in use by Trinity, with its oriel, four windows and louvre, and with the entrance to the screens beyond it; then the buttery and kitchens (reconstructed, probably only internally, by Trinity in the mid-1550s[3]); and finally another block with four windows on the site of Gregory's Hostel. (The large stair turret at the north end of the range was put up in the 1550s as part of the new Master's Lodge which ran eastwards towards the King Edward Gate, which was still in its original position.) This was a considerable range of buildings, at least 250ft long and of unknown depth, in which there appears to have been plenty of room for a medieval library apartment that may have measured no more than 35ft × 20ft. Perhaps it was a first-floor room at the south end, in the area of Trinity's Old Combination Room; perhaps it was on the first floor at the other end, where the present Combination Room is. Alas we do not know.

[1] *Old plans*, 4. See also Willis and Clark, ii, pp. 465 ff., and Atkinson, T. D., 'On the Hall of Michael House', *CAS Proc.*, viii (NS ii), 1891–4, pp. 234–42. It should be noted that the scheme for a great court of Trinity College reproduced by Willis and Clark as ii, fig. 10 was made in about 1555, *not* (as misprinted in Willis and Clark, and copied by subsequent writers) in about 1595; see p. 61 n. 2 below.

[2] These buildings were possibly on the sites lettered 'L' and 'E' on Lyne's plan of 1574 (*Old plans*, 1). Lyne's western extension of the southern range of buildings had apparently gone by Hamond's time.

[3] Willis and Clark, ii, p. 471, imply that the old kitchen and buttery were rebuilt in 1555, but the building accounts could as well refer to internal reconstruction, with new ovens and the replacement of the kitchen chimney stack, which on the whole seems more likely.

# CHAPTER 4

# THE NEED FOR BOOKS AT TRINITY IN THE SIXTEENTH CENTURY

Trinity College was intended from the start to be large and rich. The scheme drawn up for Henry VIII in the spring of 1546, and the charters of foundation and dotation which followed in December of the same year, provided for a College of a Master and fifty Fellows with an annual income from endowments of about £1,640.[1] By contrast Michaelhouse and the King's Hall at the time of their dissolution had between them a total of thirty-three Fellows and a combined annual income from endowments of only £400.[2] The first, Edwardian, Statutes of Trinity which were confirmed in 1552 again provided for fifty Fellows, but in the Elizabethan Statutes of 1560, which were to remain in force for nearly three hundred years, the number was raised to sixty.[3]

Besides the sixty Fellows of the 1560 Statutes, some of whom were to act as College Lecturers, Tutors, etc., there were to be sixty-two junior Scholars; thirteen sizars (poor students); an unspecified number of pensioners (fee-paying students); four Chaplains and a Choir; and various other functionaries and servants.[4] All but two of the Fellows were required to study divinity, the two exceptions being allowed to study civil law and medicine respectively; and all but the two legal and medical Fellows were obliged to take holy orders within seven years of graduating MA.[5] The junior members of the College were supposed to follow a seven-year arts

---

[1] TC Mun., Box 29.C.II.a (*Distribucio Collegii*), and Box 34 (Charters of Foundation and Dotation). There is a convenient summary in Rouse Ball, W. W., *Cambridge notes*, 2nd ed., Cambridge 1921, pp. 3–21.

[2] Rouse Ball, W. W., op. cit., pp. 9–10.

[3] The sealed copy of the 1552 Statutes is missing, but there is a paper copy in TCL (O.6.7). The sealed copy of the 1560 Statutes is TC Mun., Box 34; the text was printed by the College in the eighteenth century: *Statuta Collegii sanctae et individuae Trinitatis in academia Cantabrigiensi*, Cambridge 1773. Marian Statutes were drawn up for the College in 1554, but they were never confirmed; they are now TCL O.6.7B.

[4] TC Statutes, 1560, cap. i.                              [5] TC Statutes, 1560, cap. xii, cap. xix.

course under the direction of the College Lecturers, similar to the course specified in the University Statutes of 1549 but differing from it in detail;[1] and each junior member was to be in the personal care of a Tutor, a Fellow who was held responsible for the industry, finances, and morals of a small group of pupils.[2]

The statutory requirement that nearly all the Fellows of Trinity should study divinity was complied with in the sixteenth century. Of the 134 (out of a total of 252) Fellows elected from 1561 to 1600 who took degrees higher than that of MA, 116 (87 per cent) became Bachelors of Divinity, of whom 44 went on to become Doctors of Divinity; whereas only 10 took higher degrees in law, and 8 took higher degrees in medicine.[3] Most of the new Fellows left the College within a few years, but nearly all of those who remained as teachers and administrators took holy orders and continued in the study of divinity. Like Michaelhouse, therefore, but unlike the King's Hall, Trinity in the sixteenth century was a college of divines.

Divinity meant primarily the study of holy writ, for which the Fellows needed Bibles in several tongues, and a variety of biblical commentaries. After this they required the works of the Greek and Latin Fathers of the Church, and studies of ecclesiastical history, general theology, and doctrinal controversy: subjects that could be of great practical as well as of intellectual and spiritual concern in the mid-sixteenth century. The medieval Schoolmen were, for the moment, out of fashion; but collections of sermons were useful in preparing for the preaching that was a requirement for the higher degrees in divinity.

Books were also needed for the junior arts courses that led to the degrees of BA and MA. Curricula were outlined and texts were prescribed in the University Statutes of 1549 and 1570, and in Trinity's own Statutes of 1560.[4] The texts proposed for Trinity's classes were, for dialectic, an unspecified introductory manual;[5] the 'Praedicabilia' of Porphyrius;[6] Aristotle's *Categoriae* and *De interpretatione*; the *De inventione* of Rudolphus Agricola; and Aristotle's *Sophistici elenchi*, *Analytica*, and *Topica*. There were then the 'philosophical' works of Aristotle (*Physica*, *De generatione et corruptione*, *Meteorologica*, and *De anima*); the *Rhetorica* of Cicero for Latin;

---

[1] TC Statutes, 1560, cap. ix. The University Statutes of 1549 are printed in Lamb, J., *A collection of documents illustrative of the history of the University of Cambridge*, London 1838, pp. 122–38.

[2] TC Statutes, 1560, cap. x.        [3] Innes; *TC Admissions*; Venn.

[4] University Statutes 1549, cap. iii–iv; 1570, cap. vi–vii. TC Statutes 1560, cap. ix.

[5] Perhaps John Seton's *Dialectica* (STC 22250 ff.); see Jardine, L., 'The place of dialectic teaching in sixteenth-century Cambridge', *Studies in the Renaissance*, xxi, 1974, at p. 45n.

[6] Presumably Adams P1917.

the Greek grammars of Clenardus, Ceporinus, and Theodorus of Gaza; and for Greek literature unspecified works of Isocrates, Demosthenes, Plato, Homer, and Hesiod.

How far these needs for academic books were met by the College Library and by the private ownership of books in the sixteenth century is discussed in what follows.

# CHAPTER 5

# THE COLLEGE LIBRARY IN THE MID-SIXTEENTH CENTURY

We know very little about what Trinity inherited from the libraries of Michaelhouse or the King's Hall, and there is no catalogue of Trinity Library that gives a clear idea of its contents before the end of the century. As we have seen, the Oxford and Cambridge colleges did little to improve their libraries in the mid-sixteenth century, even the richer colleges spending only trivial sums on books or library administration from the 1540s to the 1570s.[1] In common with most of the other Oxford and Cambridge colleges, Trinity did not appoint a Librarian in the sixteenth century,[2] and there is no record in the Bursars' accounts of money spent on books or binding or library administration before the 1580s.[3] Nevertheless the College did acquire library books during the sixteenth century, and some of them were probably bought; some of these books were certainly bound for the College; someone must have been responsible for them, and have seen to it that the library apartment was kept clean and tidy. There is evidence that in the seventeenth century, routine Library expenditure on books, binding, and administration was met from room rents which were

---

[1] See especially N. R. Ker on the Oxford college libraries in the sixteenth century (references in p. 3 n. 1).

[2] The *Distribucio Collegii* of 1546 (see p. 22 n. 1), and the Statutes of 1552 and 1560 (p. 22 n. 3), all specify College offices and posts from the Master down to the College servants and building tradesmen, so that the omission of the office of Librarian can hardly have been accidental.

[3] TC Mun., Senior and Junior Bursars' accounts (annual volumes to Michaelmas). For the period 1547–1600 the accounts to Michaelmas in the following years are now missing: *Senior Bursar*: 1549, 1556, 1557, 1558, 1559, 1562, 1563, 1568, 1573, 1575, 1581, 1584, 1598, 1599, 1600; *Junior Bursar*: 1547, 1548, 1549, 1556, 1558, 1559, 1562, 1572, 1573, 1574, 1575, 1576, 1579, 1585, 1590, 1592, 1593, 1594, 1595, 1596, 1597, 1598. (For the accounts missing for the period 1601–95, see p. 123 n. 4.) In spite of the gaps, enough of the Bursars' account books survive for us to be sure that (for instance) no binding expenditure was accounted for in them at times when books were certainly being bound for the Library (see pp. 29, 32).

not recorded in the Bursars' accounts,[1] and it may be that something of the sort occurred during the earlier period.

The arrangements for administering the College Library in the sixteenth century are hinted at in Library regulations that were incorporated in the Edwardian Statutes of 1552. The clauses referring to the Library come in the middle of Chapter 35, 'De custodia bonorum Collegii', and may be translated as follows:

Those who borrow books from the Library, or any other of the College's goods, shall write their names in the Vice-Master's day-books and shall promise a surety; he who does not make such a promise shall either pay double [the value of the item borrowed] or be removed from the College.

The Library shall be kept clean and swept with a broom every other day. For this, the Master and Seniors shall appoint one of the servants who shall see that it is well kept.

The College shall pay twenty shillings a year for buying books and placing them in the Library.

Whoever gives anything to the Library, not only shall his name be written at the beginning of the book, but also boards shall be posted at the finer end of the Library which shall include all the names of the donors, the gifts, and the time of the donation.[2]

To take the four regulations of 1552 in turn, it had always been the normal practice in college libraries to lend books against pledges, but this first regulation is the only evidence we have that such loans took place at Trinity; the Vice-Masters' day-books are lost, and we do not know how the system was used.

The servant who, by the second regulation, was to sweep out the library apartment every other day was probably a member of the regular College staff who was not paid extra for the work. No payments were recorded in the surviving accounts for cleaning the Library until 1582 when a man – later called the Library Keeper – was paid first 8s. and then 10s. a year for 'sweeping, setting up the bookes & keeping the liberary'.[5] This Library

[1] See pp. 123–4.

[2] Si qui libros è bibliotheca aut quid aliud bonorum Collegij mutuantur, ijdem in propraesidis commentarijs nomen suum subscribant, et de praestatione promittant, qui non praestiterit, uel duplum soluat uel Collegio excludatur.
  Bibliotheca munda seruetur, et alternis diebus scopis mundetur. Huic praeses et Senatus aliquem è ministris assignent qui eam bene asseruandam curet.
  Collegium Viginti solidos in libris emendis, et in bibliotheca collocandis quotannis pendat. Si quis, quid bibliothecae dederit, nomen eius non modo in principio libri inscribatur, sed etiam tabulae in pulchriore bibliothecae fine affigantur; quae, omnia donatorum nomina, dona et tempus donationis comlectantur.
  (TC MS O.6.7, pp. 48–9.)

[3] TC Mun., JB accounts, 1583–4, f.104ᵃ.

Keeper of the 1580s and 1590s, who made the books ready for use as well as cleaning the Library, presumably took the place of an earlier and humbler cleaner.

The third regulation of 1552, whereby the College was to spend 20s. a year on library books, implies senior management, no doubt a Fellow who had the unpaid job of overseeing the stock of the College Library. How much the College actually spent on books in the early days is not known, but it is unlikely to have been much; an average of 20s a year – the cost of two ordinary folio volumes[1] – is a possible figure for the second half of the sixteenth century.[2] No Library grant was made from endowment income, however, and any costs of books, of binding, and of library administration were met from another source – perhaps from room rents.[3]

The fourth regulation, which required donors' names to be written at the beginning of the books they gave and their donations to be recorded on boards posted up in the Library, was no doubt drafted in 1552 more in the hope of gifts to come than in gratitude for gifts already received. Books were indeed given to the Library during the mid-sixteenth century, but it appears that the practice of writing the donors' names in them did not become a regular one until the 1590s. It is not known whether records of donations were posted up in the Library.

Trinity's Edwardian Statutes of 1552 which included these earliest Library regulations were to have been superseded by new Statutes drafted in 1554;[4] but the Philip and Mary code was never confirmed, and it was the Elizabethan Statutes of 1560, which were based on the draft of 1554, which eventually superseded those of 1552. The new Statutes omitted all the 1552 Library regulations except the first, the one that concerned the loan of books and other things against pledges; and that one may have been retained only because it referred to College goods in general, not to books alone.[5] But although it was decided not to continue the regulation of the Library by Statute, the administration of the collection is likely to have gone on much as before.

---

[1] Books retailed in the mid-sixteenth century for about a halfpenny a sheet, so 20s. bought two folio volumes of about 480 pages each (Gaskell, P., *A new introduction to bibliography*, Oxford 1972, rev. 1974, pp. 178–9).

[2] See p. 49.  [3] See pp. 25–6.  [4] TC MS O.6.7B.

[5] In 1560 the wording, but not the sense, of the surviving Library regulation was changed, as follows:

Si quis libros è Bibliothecâ, aut aliud quicquam ex bonis Collegii mutuetur, in dictis Registris sua manu scribat, & de iisdem reddendis fidem det. Qui autem non reddiderit, aut duplum solvere, aut tantisper commeatu carere dum solverit, volumus.

(TC Statutes, 1560, cap. xxix; text from the printed version of 1773, p. 61.)

Our knowledge of the contents of the Library before the 1590s is sadly limited. Six printed books survive which were given to Michaelhouse by William Filey, perhaps in 1525. Three of them are still in Trinity Library: the *De proprietatibus rerum* of Bartholomaeus Anglicus; the histories of Petrus Comestor, Eusebius, and Bede; and the commentaries on the Epistles of the humanist Faber Stapulensis, who was condemned in 1521 by the Sorbonne for heresy.[1] The other three books given by Filey to Michaelhouse are now in other collections; they are two of the New Testament commentaries of Aquinas, and a liturgical compendium by the medieval canonist William Durandus, the *Rationale divinorum officiorum*.[2] This division suggests that Trinity (or possibly Michaelhouse) Library was well purged of Catholic books during the Reformation, but that the Library was not so thoroughly purged of reformist books during the Counter-reformation. Another early possession was a manuscript noted by Leland between 1546 and 1550, but gone by 1600.[3]

We know pretty well what books were in the Old Library in 1600, and we still have about two-thirds of them. It appears from inscriptions in some of the 170 surviving volumes, and from references in the *Memoriale* to sixteenth-century donors, that a good many of these books reached the Library well before the end of the century. This is a question to which we shall return when we have considered the stock of the Library as it was in 1600.[4]

We know even less about how the College Library was kept and

---

[1] The three books given to Michaelhouse by William Filey which are still in Trinity Library are:

Bartholomaeus Anglicus, *De proprietatibus rerum*, 2°, Nuremberg, A. Koberger, 1492; Goff B–141; OL94.

Petrus, Comestor, *Historia scholastica*, 2°, Strassburg, G. Husner, 1503; Adams P883. (Bound with) Eusebius, Pamphili, and Bede, the Venerable, *Ecclesiastici historia*, 2°, Hagenau, J. Rynman and H. Gran, 1506; Adams E1088; OL132[1-2].

Faber, Jacobus, *Epistola ad Rhomanos, ad Hebraeos* (comm. J. Faber), 2°, Paris, H. Stephanus, 1512; Adams B1837; OL79.

[2] The three other books given to Michaelhouse by Filey are:

Aquinas, Thomas, St, *Super quatuor evangelia*, 2°, Venice, B. Locatellus, 1493; Goff T–232; Ampleforth Abbey.

Durandus, Gulielmus, *Rationale divinorum officiorum*, 2°, Lyons, J. Huguetan, 1515; not in Adams; Lambeth Palace.

Aquinas, Thomas, St, *Super epistolas Pauli*, 2°, Paris, J. Petit, 1518; Adams A1485; St John's Coll., Cam.

[3] '*In bibliotheca colleg: S. Trinitatis. Sermones fratris Gulielmi Badonensis. Opus non omnino ineruditum*' (Leland, J., *Collectanea*, iv, London 1770, p. 17). This note must have been made between 1546, when Trinity was founded, and 1550, when Leland went mad. All that is known about brother William of Bath and his sermons derives from Leland, who says that he was a Somerset man (Leland, J., *Commentarii de scriptoribus Britannicis*, ii, Oxford 1709, p. 345). No copy of William's book is known to have survived anywhere.

[4] See pp. 49–50.

administered in the sixteenth century than about what it contained, though there is a hint in the condition of ten Old Library books which escaped rebinding in about 1605, following the move to the New Library[1] (fig. 7). Not surprisingly these survivors show that the books were chained to the Old Library lectern desks, the chain staples being attached to the tail-edge of one of the boards.[2] This was the ordinary way of chaining books to lecterns in sixteenth-century college libraries, it being less usual to attach the chains to the top edges of the boards.[3] (Chaining at the fore-edge came later – though not at Trinity – when the volumes stood upright in book-cases.)

Trinity's old library books had their titles written on their tail-edges (fig. 8). The position of these labels – which was unusual, although the University Library numbered some of its books on their tail-edges at this time[4] – may indicate that the lower decks of the Trinity lecterns were not sloping desks, as they were at Queens', but were shelves on which the books were laid on their sides, an alternative arrangement that was not uncommon.[5] (Labelling the fore-edge, again, came later when the books stood upright.)

The surviving Old Library bindings themselves fall into three groups. First are four early books (a folio and three small books dated 1519–44) which were bound in roll-stamped calf probably in the 1530s and early 1540s, before they came into the Library.[6] Next are three folios and a quarto, dated 1541–65, which are handsomely and uniformly bound in roll-stamped brown calf over oak boards. A cropped College inscription

[1] On the rebinding programme of c.1605, and the probable reason for it, see pp. 96, 101. Nearly all the folio volumes, which then comprised about seven-eights of the collection, were rebound, the few that escaped possibly being out on loan. The small books were not rebound in 1605, but most of them were rebound later.

[2] The smiths' bills in the sixteenth-century Junior Bursars' accounts do not refer to these chains. This may be just another omission in the accounts, but in any case there were probably plenty of chains left over from the libraries of Michaelhouse and the King's Hall.

[3] For the Oxford libraries see Ker, N. R., 'Oxford college libraries', *Bodleian Library record*, vi, 1959, pp. 470–1, 508; for the Cambridge libraries, Streeter, B. H., *The chained library*, London 1931, pp. 31–2. A check of the libraries referred to by Streeter suggests that chaining at the bottom edges of the boards was even more usual than he thought.

[4] It appears from surviving bindings that in the late sixteenth century some of the University Library books were chained at the top edge and some at the bottom; and that the running number of the volume was written on the top or bottom edge of the book near the chain staple (information from J. C. T. Oates).

[5] For libraries of the fifteenth to seventeenth century in which the lower decks of the lecterns were flat shelves on which the books lay on their sides, see Streeter, B. H., *The chained library*, London 1931, pp. 16–26, 291–2.

[6] OL92 (1519), roll unidentified; OL156 (1544), Oldham FC.*e*(1); OL161 (1536), Oldham DI.*h*(3); OL163 (1537), Oldham CH.*c*(10). (For the 'OL' references see Appendix A; for the 'Oldham' references see Oldham, J. B., *English blind-stamped bindings*, Cambridge 1952.)

7 Two Cambridge bindings of roll-stamped calf made for the College c.1580. The short title was written in ink across the bottom edge of the book, and a chain hasp was riveted to the tail edge of either cover. (TCL M.9.31, OL155; K.17.15, OL28.)

8 Handwritten titles on the bottom edges of a group of Old Library books. (TCL (top to bottom, left-hand pile) C.7.71, OL165; I.13.58, OL161; Z.8.139, OL167; C.7.74, OL168; (middle pile) C. 29.16, OL152; I.13.77, OL166; K.2.1, OL154; K.16.2, OL156; (right-hand pile) II.3.59, OL146; M.9.31, OL155; K.17.15, OL28; I.17.5, OL58.)

in one of them indicates that these books were bound after they had come into the Library; and the roll used was assigned by Oldham to a Cambridge binder of the 1570s and 1580s.[1] Lastly come two small books dated 1530–63 which are bound in plain dark brown calf over mill-boards, with a large oval blind stamp on the covers. These bindings have stylistic links with those executed for the College by William Hamond c.1605, and they seem unlikely to be earlier than the 1590s.[2]

As we noted in connection with the Library regulation of 1552, the College did not begin to record the donors' names in books given to the Library until very late in the sixteenth century. The earliest gift of books in which the donor's name is known to have been written was the Skeffington bequest of 1592.[3] There were two further instances in the 1590s, after which most gifts were marked with an inscription, a book-plate, or an initialled binding to indicate the name of the donor.[4]

Some of the Library books, however, were inscribed in the sixteenth century with the name of the College as a mark of ownership. Thirty-seven of the 170 surviving Old Library volumes were inscribed in this way, eighteen of them being written – perhaps around 1570 – in a single hand[5] (fig. 9). These inscriptions – twenty-six of them in Latin, eleven in English – are clear evidence that someone, most likely one of the Fellows, looked after the Library books in the mid-sixteenth century.[6] The purpose of inscribing these books with the name of the College is less clear, since some (perhaps all) of them were chained,[7] and there seems to be no obvious connection between the inscriptions and particular donations.[8] It may be that individual volumes were marked with the name of the College if they were unchained and lent out of the Library.

There is no direct evidence of how the College Library books were arranged and catalogued in the sixteenth century. The scheme of classifica-

---

[1] OL28, OL29, OL58, OL155: all Oldham HM.g (2).
[2] OL146, OL154.          [3] See p. 42.          [4] See p. 104.
[5] The 37 books with TC inscriptions are the following (those marked '+' being in the single hand of c.1570): OL2 (2 vols), OL4+, OL8+, OL14, OL16+, OL24+, OL28+, OL29+, OL32 (4 vols, 2+), OL38+, OL48+, OL58+, OL61, OL62 (2 vols), OL79+, OL82, OL92, OL100+, OL109+, OL118+, OL130, OL146, OL147, OL149, OL155+, OL156, OL161, OL166, OL178+, OL179+, OL181, OL196.
[6] The inscriptions are too short for the confident identification of these hands with those of Fellows who signed the Admissions book in the 1560s and 1570s.
[7] Eight of the ten books in Old Library bindings, all of which were chained, have Trinity College inscriptions.
[8] It appears that some (but not all) of the books marked in a single hand c.1570 were bequeathed by Robert Beaumont in 1567; and that some of the books inscribed in English were associated with the bequest of William Bill, who died in 1561 and whose books may have been received in 1562. See pp. 46–8.

9 The College's inscription on the title-page of an Old Library book, probably written c.1570. (TCL A.14.8, OL4; reduced.)

tion used is likely to have been the traditional one according to which the books were arranged when they were listed following their removal to the Old Library.[1] No doubt there was an inventory of the books in the Library, and shelf-lists were probably posted on the lecterns, but no such lists survive; and, as usual with chained books, class marks were not written in the volumes themselves. It is also noticeable that, although the marginalia of previous sixteenth-century owners are often found, once a book had come into the Library it was very rarely annotated thereafter (apart from occasional pen-trials on the end-papers).

One other article of library equipment came early to Trinity. John Dee, the mathematician and astrologer who was a Charter Fellow, gave his pair of great Mercator globes and his astronomer's staff and ring to the College when he left Cambridge for Louvain in 1548.[2] It is most probable that these objects were kept in the College Library, as were for instance the pair of astrological globes bought by New College, Oxford, in 1547, and the globe table bought by Magdalen College, Oxford, in 1549;[3] they may still have been in the Old Library when Sir Edward Stanhope drafted his will in 1603, but new globes were presented soon afterwards, and no more is heard of Dee's equipment.[4]

[1] See pp. 109, 112–13.
[2] Taylor, E. G. R., *Tudor geography*, London 1930, p. 256; French, P. J., *John Dee*, London 1972, p. 25.       [3] Ker, N. R., *Oxford college libraries in 1556*, Oxford 1956, p. 11.
[4] In bequeathing money for the public register book of the Library Stanhope referred to 'all the particular Bookes, Mapps, Globes ore other ornaments whatsoever belongenge . . . to the saide Colledge Librarie' (Edward Stanhope's will dated 28 February 1602/3, TC Mun., Box 31, no. 2, p. 10). On the new globes, see pp. 104, 106.

# CHAPTER 6

# THE COLLEGE LIBRARY IN 1600

The earliest surviving inventory of the books in the College Library is included in the manuscript register of benefactors to Trinity known as the *Memoriale*.[1] The initiative for this undertaking came from Sir Edward Stanhope, a Fellow of 1564–72, whose will, dated 28 February 1603, made very generous provision for the Library. Amongst other things Stanhope bequeathed £20 for making and placing in the Library a large vellum register book which was to contain the names and arms of all the benefactors to the College and of its Masters. 'This Booke', he went on, 'must further bee kepte for the publike Register Booke of all the particular Bookes, Mapps, Globes ore other ornaments whatsoever belongenge or hereafter to beelonge to the saide Colledge Librarie.'[2]

Stanhope died in 1608, and the register book was duly written out and illuminated, probably following notes and sketches left by Stanhope himself.[3] The scribe, it appears from the College accounts, was John Scott, who probably completed the first lists of benefactors, of Masters, and of donations to the Library between 1612 and 1614, at a cost, including a lavish binding, of about £40.[4] The *Memoriale*, as it was then named, continued in use until the 1670s, chiefly as a record of donations to the College Library, and it remains in the Library as MS R.17.8.

[1] *Memoriale Collegio Sanctae et Individuae Trinitatis in Academia Cantabrigiensi dicatum*, 1614; TC MS R.17.8.

[2] Transcript in TC Mun., Box 31, no. 2, p. 10.

[3] The entry which describes Stanhope's own bequest to the College suggests that he himself supplied descriptions and drawings for the *Memoriale* ('Librum registrarium ipsius sua opera descripsit ac delineauit', *Memoriale*, p. 63).

[4] Scott's name does not appear in the *Memoriale* but it is clear from entries in the Senior Bursars' accounts that he was its maker (1615: payments for binding the 'Ledger book' totalling £3.18s.6d.; and to John Scott in part payment for the Ledger book £1.7s.6d. 1616: 'to Scott for the Legier booke in full payment till the 2ᵈ March 1615 [= 1616] for all then done', £33.0s.6d. It is not clear whether Scott provided the vellum, or whether it was charged for in a missing account, for instance that of 1611). Scott was still employed to make entries in the *Memoriale* in 1621, when he was paid 5s. for '2 Cotes & inscriptions in the Library booke' (SB accounts, 1621).

The heading of the section of the *Memoriale* which concerns the Library may be translated as follows:

Catalogue of books placed in the Library of Trinity College, Cambridge, by the generosity of the College's benefactors.

We think, moreover, that amongst all these benefactors, those who have helped to fit out that old as well as this new Library, either by meeting expenses or by buying books, are especially worthy of being included here; and their names and arms, together with the books, are recorded in the following pages.[1]

This heading is followed by notes on seven sixteenth-century benefactors to the Library. Then comes the first of the lists of Library books, with this introduction:

The following books belonging to the Old Library were bought for the benefit of scholars partly by the venerable men whose names are given in the preceding pages [that is, the seven sixteenth-century benefactors just mentioned] and partly by the College at its own expense.[2] (See fig. 10.)

This first list of books belonging to the Old Library – which, as we shall see, was probably succeeded by the New Library in about 1604 – consists of 201 titles, which I have numbered OL1 to OL201.[3] In spite of its heading the list includes a few books that were acquired by the Library between 1604 and 1617, including the *Memoriale* itself.[4]

The OL list is followed by detailed records of fifty-four individual donations to the Library, and one other short list, all but one of which are found to refer to books, etc., which became part of the Library after 1600. The sole exception is a list of books bequeathed to the College by Thomas Skeffington in 1592, and which I have numbered TS1 to TS59.[5]

---

[1] Catalogus Librorum repositorum in Bibliotheca Collegij Sanctae et Individuae Trinitatis in Academia Cantabrigiensi munificentia Benefactorum eiusdem Collegij.

Inter Benefactores etiam illos omnes anumerandos et reponendos iure optimo existimauimus: qui quoquo modo, vel suis sumptibus, vel Librorum impensis, Bibliothecam tam veterem illam, quam nouam hanc exornandam curarunt; quorum nomina et insignia vna cum libris, sequentes paginæ referent. (*Memoriale*, p. 85.)

[2] Subsequentes hi libri ad veterem Bibliothecam pertinentes partim a viris Venerabilibus quorum nominum in praecedenti paginae fit mentio, partim ipsius Collegij proprijs sumptibus in studiosorum gratiam comparati Fuerunt. (*Memoriale*, p. 87.)

[3] *Memoriale*, pp. 87–9. See Appendix A.

[4] These were OL29⁶*, OL35*, OL41*, OL42*, OL46*, OL47*, OL71*, OL191*, OL197*, OL198*, OL199*, OL200*, OL201*. The last four entries were added, probably c.1617, after the completion of the rest of the list in 1612–14. (Only one book in the OL list (OL37*) appears to have been acquired after 1600 but before the move to the New Library in about 1604.)

[5] *Memoriale*, p. 98. See Appendix A.

Subsequentes hi libri ad veterem Bibli
othecam pertinentes partim à viris Venerabi
libus quorum nominum in præcedenti paginæ
sit mentio, partim ipsius Collegij proprijs sump
tibus in studiosorum gratiam comparati Fuerunt.

| | |
|---|---|
| Athanasij opera græcè | Henriquez summa theologiæ |
| Biblia hebræa Vatablj vol: 2 | Toletus in Lucam |
| Biblia Gallicè | Rich: de Media Villa — vol 2 |
| Biblia Munsterj | Henricus Agandauo |
| Biblia Hieronymi latinè | Alberti Magni — vol: 3 |
| Conciliorum. vol: 3 | Ocham — vol: 2 |
| Conciliorum Canones | Vasquez in Thomam |
| Theophilactus in Euang. græ | Caietani — vol: 3 |
| Oecumenius in Euang: lat: | Nicholai Lyræ — vol: 6 |
| Cyrilli opera | Durandus in Sententias |
| Augustini operum — vol: 9 | Pineda in Job — vol: 2 |
| Gregorij Magni — vol: 2 | Villalpandi in Ezechielem vol: 3 |
| Epiphanius latinè | Alfonsus de Castro |
| Gassij Collectanea — vol 2 | Dionisius a Rickell in psalmos |
| Historia sacra multorum patrum | Thomas Stapletonus |
| Antidotum contra hæreses | Hosij opera |
| Lactantij opera | Catonj opera theologica |
| Philo Judæus | Marloratus in nouum Testament |
| Irenæi opera | Gualtherj — vol: 2 |
| Basilius latinè | Zuinglij — vol: 4 |
| Tertullianus | Pellicanus in vetus testament |
| Nazianzenus græcè | Whitgistus contra Cartwright |
| Justinus Martyr græcè | M: Hanelthoms loci comunes |
| Hilarius | Aretius selinus in psalmos |
| Dionisius Areopagita | Clauis Scripturæ |
| | |

10 The beginning of the list of Old Library books in the *Memoriale*, probably
copied out by John Scott in 1612–14. Entries give authors and short titles only, but
the list is arranged here in shelf order, the first shelf of 24 volumes ending with
Gregory (OL12) and the second beginning with Epiphanius (OL13). (TCL MS
R.17.8, f. 87; reduced; see Appendix B.)

It therefore appears that a catalogue of the books that were in the College Library in 1600 can be based on the combined OL and TS lists, adjusted to take account of alterations made after that date. Although the titles in these two lists are severely abbreviated in the *Memoriale*, they can be traced through their successive appearances in later catalogues of the Library, which in most cases provide enough detail to identify the books themselves, if they are still in the Library, or to identify the edition referred to if they are not.[1] Identifications can often be confirmed by running numbers written on the fore-edges of some of the volumes referred to which show that the OL and TS lists are shelf-lists, that is that they record the titles in the order in which the books were shelved in the New Library when the lists were written out in 1612–14. The shelf order of the lists also makes it possible in some cases to guess at the formats of absent or doubtful volumes.[2]

A catalogue made in this way of the College Library as it was in 1600 is given in Appendix A. It turns out that the 260 titles of the OL and TS lists referred to 331 items in 348 volumes.[3] Of the 331 items of the catalogue, 237 (72 per cent) are still in the Library. Of the 94 items which are now absent from the Library, it has proved possible to discover the author, title, and edition of 51; the author and title of 30; and the author alone of 10. Only 3 items are completely unidentified.[4] These figures have to be adjusted, however, since at least 21 of the OL items (marked with asterisks in the catalogue[5]) were added to the collection after 1600. There are, moreover, some evident uncertainties: there may have been books in the Library in 1600 which had gone by the time the lists were made in 1612–14;[6] a few items other than those marked with asterisks may have been acquired after 1600;[7] and some of the books entered in the lists which are not now in the Library may have included additional, unlisted items.

---

[1] For an account of the later TCL catalogues, see Appendix B.

[2] For the order of these books in the New Library, see pp. 112–13. It is uncertain that the order in which they had been kept on the Old Library lecterns was more than approximately repeated in the more capacious New Library.

[3] For the meaning of 'title', 'item', and 'volume', see p. xv.

[4] OL15, OL75, OL174.        [5] See p. 35 n. 4.

[6] For instance 'A great new Concordance' was bought for the Library for 22s. in 1591 (TC Mun., JB accounts, 1591, f. 184ᵃ). This book is not recorded in the OL list and it is not now in the Library. It may have been in the Library in 1600, however, and was possibly exchanged for a later gift (perhaps the Concordance given by Shaw in 1601, *Memoriale*, p. 99, or that given by Nevile in 1612–13, *Memoriale*, p. 93).

[7] The starred items are those which definitely came into the Library after 1600. We cannot be sure that a few other items on the OL list did not also come into the Library after 1600, even though there is no evidence that they did.

Bearing all this in mind, the numbers of listed titles, volumes, and items in the Old Library in 1600 are likely to have been approximately as follows:

### The College Library in 1600

|                 | OL list      | TS list    | OL + TS      |
| --------------- | ------------ | ---------- | ------------ |
| titles          | 188          | 59         | 247          |
| volumes         | 256          | 69         | 325          |
| volumes present | 170 (66%)    | 40 (58%)   | 210 (65%)    |
| items           | 233          | 77         | 310          |
| items present   | 165 (71%)    | 52 (68%)   | 217 (70%)    |

A general view of the College Library at the end of the sixteenth century – apart from the Skeffington bequest of 1592, which was a special collection of law books and will be considered separately – is given by a classification of the 233 OL items according to their arrangement in the New Library in the mid-seventeenth century, when they were allotted to twenty main classes.[1]

Two-thirds of the books on the OL list concerned religious studies in one way or another, reasonably enough since this was a Fellows' Library, and all but two of the Fellows were required to study divinity. This divinity section of the Library was strongest in the sixteenth-century Protestant writers of the second rank, chiefly in their capacity as biblical commentators: Brenz, Bucer, Bullinger, Martyr, Melancthon, Musculus, Oecolampadius, Pellican, Zwingli. Then there were the Fathers of the Church in the great Basle editions, and a fairly full section of ecclesiastical history, including the Lutheran history of the Magdeburg Centuriators and the reply of Baronius. Sermons and practical theology were also well covered, candidates for the higher degrees in divinity being required to preach in order to qualify.

On the other hand there were some notable omissions. There was not yet any major polyglot edition of the Bible in the Library; there was no Greek Testament, and no Erasmus. There were a few Anglican works in English (Barthlet, Latimer, Nowell, Whitgift), but no Luther and scarcely any Genevan Puritanism. There was, indeed, a copy of Knox on predesti-

[1] This was done by noting the positions of the OL books in the 'class catalogues' of c.1645, 1667, and c.1675 (see Appendix B).

|        |                                                              | items |       |
|--------|--------------------------------------------------------------|-------|-------|
| I      | Manuscripts                                                  | 1     |       |
| II     | Bibles                                                       | 4     |       |
| III    | Greek Fathers                                               | 12    |       |
| IV     | Latin Fathers                                               | 10    |       |
| V      | Councils                                                    | 3     |       |
| VI     | Liturgy                                                     | 2     |       |
| VII    | Commentaries, systematics                                  | 39    |       |
| VIII   | Sermons, practical and general theology                    | 24    |       |
| IX     | Controversy, casuistry                                     | 21    |       |
| X      | Scholastics (in Sententias 7; others 3)                    | 10    |       |
| XI     | Ecclesiastical history                                     | 24    |       |
| XII    | History (ancient 14; modern 5)                             | 19    |       |
| XIII   | Orators (Greek 3; Latin 3)                                 | 6     |       |
| XIV    | Poets (Greek 8; Latin 1)                                   | 9     |       |
| XV     | Philology, lexicography                                    | 21    |       |
| XVI    | Philosophy (Platonic 4; Peripatetic 12; modern 1)         | 17    |       |
| XVII   | Medicine                                                  | 1     |       |
| XVIII  | Mathematics, astronomy, geography, natural philosophy     | 3     |       |
| XIX    | Law (civil 2; canon 2)                                    | 4     |       |
| XX     | Oriental (Biblical 2; Talmudic 1)                         | 3     |       |
|        | *Summary*                                                 |       |       |
|        | Divinity (inc. MS and Oriental)                           | 153   | (66%) |
|        | Philology, lexicography                                   | 21    | (9%)  |
|        | History                                                   | 19    | (8%)  |
|        | Philosophy                                                | 17    | (7%)  |
|        | Greek and Latin orators and poets                        | 15    | (6%)  |
|        | Medicine, mathematics                                    | 4     | (2%)  |
|        | Law                                                      | 4     | (2%)  |

nation, but not one of Calvin's *Institutes*; and, apart from Whitgift *contra* Cartwright, scant reference to the Puritan controversies that shook the College in the later sixteenth century.

The generally Anglican tendency of the collection was certainly deliberate. The Puritan Master Robert Beaumont had bequeathed nine works by Calvin to the College in 1567,[1] but none of them were in the Library in

[1] Calvin's *Institutes; De scandalis; De vitandis superstitionibus; Harmonia ex tribus evangelistis composita*; and commentaries on Genesis, Prophets, Isaiah, Psalms, and Epistles. For Beaumont's bequest, see pp. 47–8.

1600. These may simply have been refused by Beaumont's Anglican successor Whitgift; or there may have been a general purge of the collection after Beaumont's time, for the College Library was noticeably more Anglican and conformist in 1600 than had been the Fellows' private libraries in the 1560s.[1]

Despite the obvious gaps, the divinity books on the OL list provided the Fellows with a reasonably comprehensive background for their studies, but the rest of the books – a mere 80 items – were a very scrappy lot. There were a few dictionaries, and small collections of ancient history and Greek literature; but there was virtually no Latin literature, mathematics, medicine, or law. There was of course no English literature, and only one manuscript, the Athanasius in Greek bequeathed by the Marian Master John Christopherson in 1558.[2] There were none of the little text-books used for teaching the junior courses; while of the ten texts prescribed by the College Statutes for the BA and MA courses,[3] the Library contained editions of only four.[4]

The majority of the OL books – 146 items, 71 per cent – were in Latin but a substantial fraction – 45 items, 22 per cent – were in Greek, or in Greek and Latin. Other languages were meagrely represented: there were 6 items in English, 3 each in Hebrew and in French, and 1 each in Italian and in Spanish.[5] An even larger majority of the 257 OL volumes – 226, 88 per cent – were folios, only 31 being quartos and octavos.

The dates and places of printing of the 206 OL items for which we have these details make a clear pattern. In date they are grouped emphatically around the middle of the sixteenth century, no fewer than 98 – nearly half – of them having been printed in the 1540s and 1550s, and very few having been printed before the 1530s or after the 1560s. Many of these 206 items, moreover, were printed in Switzerland: 79 (38 per cent) of them were printed in Basle, Geneva, and Zurich; while an even larger proportion – 42 per cent – of the items printed in the 1540s and 1550s came from the Swiss printing centres, chiefly Basle. (See the chart opposite.) We will return to this pattern when we try to identify the donors of the books on the OL list.

---

[1] See pp. 49–50, 52, 54.
[2] OL1. Thomas James noted this manuscript in his *Ecloga Oxonio-Cantabrigiensis*, London 1600, p. 138; and also a manuscript of Trivet's *Annales*, which was not listed anywhere in the *Memoriale* and which is not now in the Library.
[3] Apart from Aristotle, and counting the three Greek grammars as one; see pp. 23–4.
[4] OL73 (Demosthenes), OL86 (Plato), OL110 (Hesiod), OL175 (Homer).
[5] English: OL57, OL129, OL157, OL165, OL168[1], OL168[2]. Hebrew: OL172, OL173, OL190 (and there is a little Hebrew in OL4). French: OL3, OL69, OL139 (French and Latin). Italian: OL115. Spanish: OL195.

*Dates of printing of 206 OL items*

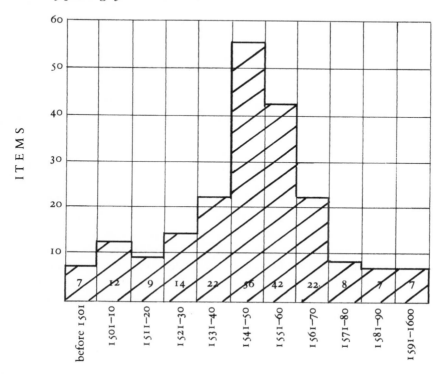

*Places of printing of 206 OL items*

| | |
|---|---|
| Switzerland | 79 |
| Germany | 42 |
| Italy | 38 |
| France | 31 |
| Low countries | 10 |
| England | 6 |

But to return first to the TS list of law books bequeathed by Thomas Skeffington, a past Fellow: in his will, dated 16 June 1591, Skeffington directed that his books should be offered to Trinity for its Library, provided that his executors were given first choice of any particular books that they wanted for themselves.[1] The will was proved on 25 October 1592; Thomas Fortho, a Fellow, went up to London to select books for the College; and the books were in Cambridge, inscribed and listed by the middle of 1593[2] (fig. 11). The TS list in the *Memoriale*, which is probably a complete record of the collection received in 1593, consists of 59 titles, and it refers to 69 volumes, 77 items; of which 40 volumes, 52 items, are still in the Library.

Of the 77 TS items, 55 (71 per cent) are law books: 29 of them concerning civil law, 17 canon law, and 9 law generally. It is an interesting though uneven collection, suggesting an unusual range of legal interests. Skeffington was undoubtedly well read in both civil and canon law, and also in French law; and he was up to date in owning works by Alciatus, Bodin, Budaeus, Maranta, Rebuffus, etc. As a working lawyer he had a particular interest in procedural and practical questions. But there are some surprising gaps: in Roman law the Digest and Codex of Justinian, and in canon law the Clementines, and the Extravagantes of Boniface VIII. Here the explanation may be that Skeffington had in fact owned some of these books, but that they were removed from the collection by his executors

---

[1] Skeffington (or Skevington, as he spelled his name at Trinity) came up as a pensioner in 1565, and graduated BA in 1568–9, MA in 1572, and LLD in 1579; he was a Fellow from 1571 to 1578. He was admitted Advocate in London in 1582, and became a member of Doctors' Commons. He died in 1592.

Skeffington wrote his name and one of three mottoes in Greek on the title-pages of his books: 'γηράσκω δ'ἀεὶ πολλὰ διδασκόμενος' [sic] ('I learn much all the time as I grow old' [Solon], on 29 title-pages); 'οὐδὲν γλυκύτερον ἢ πάντα εἰδέναι' ('nothing is sweeter than knowing all things', on 5 title-pages); 'πολλὰ μανθανόμενος πλείο .λανθανόμενος' ('learning a lot, forgetting more', on 2 title-pages).

In his will of 1591 (PRO Prob. II/80, ff. 218–20), Skeffington directed that, in each of his books placed in the College Library, 'by some of that colleage to my name be vnderwritten this *Additum* [:] *quondam socius huius Collegij*: and after this sentence *Ante Pelarge iam seruo*' (f.219ᵃ). The last phrase is the attempt of the copyist of the will to latinise Skeffington's 'ἀντιπελαργίαν servo', which is apparently intended to mean 'I maintain this act of cherishing for others'.

[2] TC Mun., SB accounts 1592–3: 'to Mʳ Furtho se for his charges at London about Dʳ Skevington his bookes, vijˢ viᵈ. Item cariarge of them from London, xxiiijˢ ixᵈ. Writing his name in them and a Catalogue iijˢ iiijᵈ.' Elaborate inscriptions, as specified in Skeffington's will, were beautifully written on the title-pages, probably by John Palmer, Fellow 1582–97, whose italic hand was one of the finest in late Tudor Cambridge (Fairbank, A., and Dickins, B., *The italic hand in Tudor Cambridge*, London 1962, pp. 27, 31, and Plate 24; *DNB*; TC Mun., *Admissions and admonitions*, pp. 11, 24). The 'Catalogue' may have been a list or lists posted on the lectern-ends.

RICHARDI

## Stanihurſti Dublinienſis

DE REBVS

# IN HIBERNIA

GESTIS, LIBRI

QVATTVOR,

Ad cariſſimum ſuum fratrem, clariſſimumque virum,
P. PLVNKETVM, Dominum Baronem Dunſaniæ.

*Acceſſit his libris Hibernicarum rerum Appendix, ex*
SILVESTRO GIRALDO CAMBRENSI
*peruetuſto ſcriptore collecta;*

Cum eiuſdem STANIHVRSTI adnotationibus.

*Omnia nunc primùm in lucem edita.*

LVGDVNI BATAVORVM.

## Ex officina Chriſtophori Plantini.

M. D. LXXXIIII.

---

11 Inscriptions on the title-page of a Skeffington book. The Greek tag ('nothing is sweeter than knowing all things') and the signature in the middle were written by Skeffington himself; the College's inscription at the foot of the page was probably written by John Palmer in 1592–3. (TCL X.10.106; TS54; reduced.)

before it was offered to the College; otherwise it is hard to see, for instance, why he should have owned the Code of Theodosius, but not that of Justinian.

The other 22 TS items were mere odds and ends (divinity, 2 items; history, 6; orators, 4; philology and lexicography, 4; philosophy, 2; and sciences, 4); but they did include a three-volume octavo Hermogenes of 1570–1 (TS55) which Skeffington may have acquired for teaching rhetoric.[1]

Taking the College Library in 1600 as a whole, exactly 50 per cent of the 310 OL and TS items concerned divinity, and 19 per cent were law books; the rest being lexicography and philology, 8 per cent; history, 8 per cent; philosophy, 6 per cent; Greek and Latin orators and poets, 6 per cent; and sciences, 3 per cent. In character the collection resembled an eccentric private library, rather than a deliberately assembled institutional one, and this reflected its haphazard development by means of a series of individual donations.

Other Oxford and Cambridge college libraries – especially those which had been built up during the later sixteenth century – showed similar eccentricities. Their shelf-lists commonly underwent continuous revision at this time, and there are apparently no exact parallels; but a useful comparison can be made between Trinity Library and that of King's College, Cambridge, at the beginning of the seventeenth century. At King's, where the Library was 'utterly spoiled' by 1569, restocking began with the purchase of some divinity books in the early 1570s, and then continued with a variety of donations, resulting in the collection of 457 volumes that was described in a surviving shelf-list which is dated 1612.[2] This shelf-list is incomplete, but the total number of volumes is given, and enough of it survives for the main subject groups to be enumerated with fair confidence. At King's in 1612, as at Trinity in 1600,[3] the emphasis was on divinity and law:

---

[1] Skeffington, who resided as a Fellow from 1571 to 1578, was a Regent Master from 1572 to 1577; he was probably not a College Lecturer.

[2] King's MS Lib. 1, ff. 134–52. For the Library in the sixteenth century, see Heywood, J., and Wright, T., *The ancient laws . . . for King's College . . .*, London 1850, pp. 229, 233; Cargill Thompson, W. D. J., 'Notes on King's College Library, 1500–1570', *Trans. Camb. Bib. Soc.*, 1954–8, pp. 38–54.

[3] The 457 volumes at King's in 1612 are compared with the contents of Trinity Library in 1600, rather than in 1612, because (as a result of a series of donations that were not paralleled at King's) Trinity Library grew from 326 volumes in 1600 to over 1,100 volumes in 1612, and changed character in the process.

| | Trinity, 1600 | | King's, 1612 | |
| | vols | % | vols | % |
|---|---|---|---|---|
| Divinity | 171 | 53 | 291 | 64 |
| Law | 60 | 18 | 73 | 16 |
| other subjects | 94 | 29 | 93 | 20 |

The lists for five of the thirteen occupied lecterns[1] of the divinity section at King's in 1612 are now missing, but those which remain show that it was essentially similar to the divinity section at Trinity in 1600; it was probably rather more comprehensive, possibly as a result of the deliberate purchase of divinity books at King's in the 1570s. The law books at King's were a notably fine collection of legal classics given by John Cowell the civilian.[2] Cowell, who died in 1611, was a former Fellow of King's who became Regius Professor of Civil Law and Master of Trinity Hall. His law books, which were equally strong in canon and civil law, were not so up to date as Skeffington's, but they were more juristic and scholarly: the collection of an academic rather than a practising lawyer. The other subjects, finally, were covered at King's (as at Trinity) sparsely and unevenly. The medical and mathematical sections were stronger, with about 20 and 10 volumes respectively; and King's with Horace (two commentaries), Juvenal, and Plautus, did better in Latin literature than Trinity with Prudentius; neither Library had any Virgil. But in Greek literature King's had only a single volume of Homer, whereas Trinity had Homer plus three commentaries, and also Aristophanes, Euripides, and two collections of Greek poets. King's, again, had an edition of Aristotle's works, but no Plato.

King's College Library in 1612 was thus very like Trinity Library in 1600 in what it included and omitted. Where the two libraries differed it was not generally as a result of policy on the part of one or other of the colleges, but of what the sky happened to drop in the way of gifts. It all depended on who your benefactors were.

[1] Called 'columnae' in the 1612 shelf-list. (For 'columna' Latham, *Revised medieval Latin word-list*, gives 'a book stand'; and J. W. Clark, *The care of books*, gives 'a set of shelves'.) At King's twenty-four of them held an average of 19–20 volumes each, and were probably two-sided, two-decker lecterns about five feet long.
[2] King's MS Lib. 1, ff. 4–5; for Cowell see *DNB*.

# CHAPTER 7

# THE DEVELOPMENT OF THE COLLECTION UP TO 1600

There are no lists which tell us plainly how or when the individual books on the OL list came into the Library, or what they replaced. Most of them were printed after 1546, and cannot therefore have been inherited from Michaelhouse and the King's Hall, but that is about all that can be said for certain. In order to get some idea of how the collection developed during the second half of the sixteenth century, and of its value to the College, we now consider the seven benefactors who are named as donors of books at the head of the OL list – Filey, Bill, Beaumont, Dodington, Meade, Sledd, and Wroth – and also Christopherson, the Marian Master, who is named elsewhere in the *Memoriale* as a donor of Library books.

*William Filey*, a senior member of Michaelhouse who never belonged to Trinity, 'gave many valuable books to this College in 1549'.[1] Filey, who graduated BA in 1505–6 and DD in 1522, became rector of Somersham, Huntingdonshire, in 1525 and died there in 1551. His will, which was both signed and proved in May 1551, does not specify any bequests to Trinity,[2] but the Junior Bursar's accounts for 1551 recorded payments of 1s.4d. to Thomas Helperbye, a Fellow, 'for his costs in bringing of Doctor phylowes books', and of 5s.4d. 'to hym that caryed the books'.[3] Only one book, OL127, is identified as having been given by Filey to Trinity, but three of his gifts to Michaelhouse are included in the OL list (OL79, OL94, and OL132).[4]

*William Bill*, twice Master of Trinity, died in 1561 leaving 'a quarter of his divinity books to the College'.[5] Amongst them may have been an odd

---

[1] 'multos magni pretij Libros huic Collegio contulit Anno Do: 1549' (*Memoriale*, p. 85).
[2] Huntingdon County Record Office, Archdeaconry will register 9, ff. 21–2; there is no surviving inventory.
[3] TC Mun., JB accounts, 1551, f.44ᵇ. The evidence of the will and the accounts throws some doubt on the *Memoriale* date of 1549.    [4] See also pp. 27–8 and notes.
[5] 'quartam partem Librorum suorum Theologicorum Collegio reliquit' (*Memoriale*, p. 85).

volume of Musculus (OL32[1]) which has the initials 'W.B.' on the title-page. Bill's will was proved on 17 December 1561.[1]

*John Christopherson*, Master of the College from 1553 to 1558, between Bill's two terms of office, made elaborate provision for the College Library in his will dated 6 October 1556:

> Firste I gyve unto the College all my Books, as well those that be w'in the College, as those that be at London prynted and wryten, all of whiche I will that a true Inventory be made by the Vice-M[r], the Deanes and the Bursers, and the same Inventory to be wryten in parchement and kept in the Towre, and an other Copie to remayne w[t] y[e] Vice Ma[r] and an other w[t] the Deanes. And the same Books to be placed in the Library of the said College, as sone as it shal be Buylded, to the use of all the fellowes & Scholers of the said College and theyr Successors for ever.[2]

Christopherson died in prison in December 1558, and – according to the *Memoriale* – he 'adorned the Library with the most beautiful books in three languages in 1558'.[3] But in fact his will was not proved until February 1563, and it is unlikely that any books bequeathed by him reached the Library before then. No inventory of his books, if one was made, has survived; and the only book now in the Library that is known to have belonged to him is the manuscript Athanasius, OL1, which he had lent to the Basle printers Froben and Episcopius for the use of the editor of their Athanasius of 1556.[4]

*Robert Beaumont*, who became Master in 1561, died in 1567 leaving the College 'all those Dyvynitie bookes onlye which I have / and the College wanteth', together with £40 'for stallynge & glasynge of the new lybrarye', and 'my syxe pictures of our founder / his parents & chyldren to be set in the librarye as sone as it is buylded'.[5] Beaumont's probate inventory specified 111 titles in a total of about 320 books, of which at least 94 were

---

[1] His books may therefore have reached the Library in 1562; and four of the surviving OL books are dated '1562' on their title-pages: OL32[3], OL32[4] (two more volumes of the Musculus, also initialled 'J.B.'), OL181, OL196. It may be significant that two volumes of Driedo, OL62, were apparently inscribed 'Trinity colleg' in the same hand as was the 'W.B.' volume, OL32[1].

[2] TC Mun., *Wills and charters*, p. 180; proved February 1563 (Cooper, C. H. and T., *Athenae Cantabrigienses*, i, Cambridge 1858, p. 189).

[3] 'Bibliothecam pulcherrimis trium linguarum libris exornavit Anno Dom: 1558' (*Memoriale*, p. 73).

[4] OL1 is inscribed 'Est D. Joannis Christofersoni, Angli, Frobenio et Episcopio ab ipso crediti' ('the property of Dr John Christopherson the Englishman, lent by him to Froben and Episcopius'). The editor of the 1556 Athanasius (Adams A2083, not in TCL) was Petrus Nannius, who acknowledged Christopherson's loan in his prefatory dedication (sig. α3[b]).

[5] CUA, Beaumont's will, 1567. The *Memoriale*, p. 86, repeats the phrases referring to the books and the £40, but does not say that the pictures were intended for the Library.

the titles of divinity books.[1] Only about 30 of these 94 titles, however, are found in the OL list, so that it follows either that the rest of them were not acceptable to (or not required by) the College at the time of Beaumont's death, or that they were put into the Library in 1567 but were later taken out again. Amongst the titles listed in Beaumont's inventory but not included in the OL list were his holdings of Luther (2 titles), Erasmus (3 titles), and Calvin (9 titles), and it may be that the missing books of this Puritan Master were refused or purged by his Anglican successor Whitgift. None of the surviving OL books have inscriptions which identify them as Beaumont's, though a few very tentative identifications may be made.[2] As to the rest of Beaumont's bequest, nothing was done about building a new library until the end of the century; and the royal portraits stayed in the Master's Lodge, where he directed that they should be kept until the new library was built.[3]

The other four gifts of books and money for the Old Library which are mentioned in the *Memoriale* were made some thirty years after Beaumont's bequest, around the end of the century. Their order in the *Memoriale* is probably the order in which they were received.

*Bartholomew Dodington*, calligrapher, Regius Professor of Greek from 1563, and Fellow of Trinity 1580–3, left £10 to the College when he died in 1595 'for the increase of the Library'.[4] No books bought with this money have been identified.

*Michael Meade*, College tenant of the rectory of Ware, gave 20 marks (£13.6s.8d.) 'to be spent on books that would be most suitable for the Library'.[5] Meade, who had been tenant of Ware since 1548, was dead by 1598,[6] and the most probable date for his gift is 1595–7. Two of the books on the OL list (OL60, OL129) are inscribed as the gift of Michael Meade.

*John Sledd*, who came to Trinity as a pensioner in 1568 and who was a Fellow from 1576 to 1597, 'gave some books to this Library, tokens of his heartfelt gratitude';[7] this was probably in 1597, when Sledd resigned his Fellowship. None of the books on the OL list are identified as having been

---

[1] CUA; the part of the inventory which lists Beaumont's books is given in Appendix C.
[2] See Appendix C.
[3] They were the large portrait of Henry VIII (College portraits catalogue, i, no. 81a), moved from the Lodge to the Hall c.1894; the smaller portraits of Henry VII (80), Elizabeth of York (55), Edward VI (54), and Mary Tudor (107), all in the Lodge; and the portrait of Elizabeth I, also apparently a small one, which was formerly in the Lodge but is now missing. There is no evidence that any of them were hung in the New Library.
[4] 'in incrementum Bibliothecae' (*Memoriale*, p. 86).
[5] 'in libris Bibliothecae maxime idoneis impendendas' (*Memoriale*, p. 86).
[6] TC Mun., Box 44.
[7] 'Libros aliquot grati animi sui indicia huic Bibliothecae contulit' (*Memoriale*, p. 86).

given by Sledd, but it appears that two of the books given by Skeffington (TS49, TS50) were replaced by similar books which are inscribed as Sledd's gift.[1]

*Sir Robert Wroth* MP, College tenant of Enfield, 'gave some especially notable books for the increase of the Library on account of his particular love of learning and the learned'.[2] Wroth died in 1616, but the date of his donation was probably between 1597 (the likely date of Sledd's gift) and 1603–4, when the Old Library was succeeded by the New. No books given by Wroth have been identified.

The pattern of these donations is clear. Apart from Filey, most of whose gifts of books were made to Michaelhouse rather than to Trinity, these donors of OL books fall into two distinct groups: there were first the three Masters, Bill, Christopherson, and Beaumont, who gave what were probably substantial collections of divinity books in the 1560s; and secondly there were the four miscellaneous donors (Dodington, Meade, Sledd, and Wroth) who made what appear to have been fairly small gifts around the end of the century. The only other recorded donation was that of Skeffington's law books, bequeathed in 1592.

It seems likely, moreover, that this pattern of donations was the chief influence on the actual development of the Library before 1600. It is possible that the College bought library books in the sixteenth century (as it was to do in the seventeenth) from funds such as room rents that were not accounted for, but it is not likely to have bought many; while we know from the mid-century probate inventories that it was not then customary for Fellows of Trinity to leave books to the College.[3] On the face of it, therefore, it seems likely that most of the books on the OL list were given by the donors named in the *Memoriale*, the greater part of them coming from Bill, Christopherson, and Beaumont in the 1560s. This hypothesis is supported by the dates of printing of the books in the OL collection, which are strongly concentrated in the 1540s and 1550s, rather than being spread out over the second half of the century.[4]

Thus it appears likely that half or more of the books on the OL list were already in the College Library by 1570; and that, apart from the possibility

---

[1] Now III.14.5 and S.6.39. The inscriptions in these Sledd books, like those in Skeffington's books, were probably written by John Palmer (see p. 42 n. 2).

[2] 'pro singulario suo in literas et literates amore, quosdam praecipuae notae libros ad augmentum Bibliothecae addidit' (*Memoriale*, p. 86).

[3] See Chapter 8.

[4] See p. 41. The dates of printing of Skeffington's books, given in 1592, were similarly concentrated in the 1560s and 1570s.

that a number of books offensive to strict Anglicans were removed from the collection in Whitgift's time, the stock of the Library did not change much from then until the arrival of Skeffington's law books and the other, smaller donations of the 1590s. For most of the later sixteenth century, therefore, this small and eccentric collection of divinity books in the Old Library was all that Trinity – always the richest of the Cambridge colleges – offered to its Fellows. Obviously it was not enough; and the Fellows, like the junior members of the College for whom no library facilities at all were provided, were obliged to shift for themselves.

# CHAPTER 8

# PRIVATE LIBRARIES

Since the early Fellows of Trinity could not rely solely on the College Library for access to the academic books that they needed for their work, they also bought books for themselves. University men had indeed owned academic books before the mid-sixteenth century, though not apparently in large numbers. Seventeen of the wills of senior members of Cambridge colleges that were registered in the Vice-Chancellor's Court from 1502 to 1526 referred specifically to books.[1] Sixteen of them mentioned from 2 to 16 titles, average 6; the seventeenth, that of Thomas Colier of Michaelhouse, mentioned 47.[2] These testators may have owned a few more books than they mentioned in their wills, but probably not many: books were not yet easy to come by, and the college libraries still met most of their needs.

But the college libraries then failed to keep up with the need for new books, and by the middle of the sixteenth century, when new books could more readily be bought, the private libraries of individual fellows were much larger than before. The wills of twenty Fellows of Trinity were proved in the Vice-Chancellor's Court from 1550 to 1589, and for thirteen of them detailed probate inventories survive.[3] All thirteen inventories

---

[1] In CUA. Books are mentioned in these wills as specific bequests; and it seems likely (though not certain) that as a rule these testators mentioned most of the titles in their collections. (Information from Dr Leedham-Green.)

[2] Brian Kyddall, Peterhouse, 1502, 16; Robert Mennall, Buckingham. 1503, 9; Robert Burgoyne, Peterhouse, 1504, 14; John Frysby, King's Hall, 1504, 3; John Fabbe, God's House, 1504, 15; John Brown, St Nicholas Hostel, 1506, 5; John Suttell, St Nicholas Hostel, 1506, 2; Thomas Colier, Michaelhouse, 1506, 47; Alan Stevynson, Pembroke, 1506, 3; Roger Wedyr, St Catharine's, 1506, 4; John Lownde, Peterhouse, 1506, 2; John Sycling, Christ's 1506, 5; Robert Clyfton, Michaelhouse, 1508, 5; John Proctor, Michaelhouse, 1510, 3; Henry Skinner, Peterhouse, 1514, 2; John Sentuary, Corpus, 1516, 2; Henry Crossley, Michaelhouse, 1526, 9.

[3] In CUA. Inventories were required for probate from 1534; they were made by appraisers appointed by the Vice-Chancellor, who were paid at the rate of 2d. in the pound value of the estate. The probate lists do not specify all the titles in the collections inventoried, but an

described substantial private libraries, ranging in size from about 45 to about 162 books, average 105.[1] The College Library itself may have had no more than 162 titles at the time; and, although these private libraries contained more small, cheap books than the College Library is likely to have done – mostly the little text-books used for teaching the junior courses – they also contained many substantial, expensive works of scholarship. Most of them, moreover, were valued at a third or more of their owners' estates, and many were impressively learned.

The collections of Martin Parkinson, William Liffe, and James Key, who all died in 1569, will serve as examples of the Fellows' private libraries. Parkinson began humbly as a sizar of Trinity in 1555, but his election to a Fellowship in 1560 was the first step in an unusually successful career. When he died in 1569 at the age of 31 Parkinson was both College and University Preacher, he had served as Lecturer, Dean, Bursar, and probably Tutor of Trinity, and he had recently been appointed Archdeacon of the East Riding. This made him a wealthy man, with board and lodging and perhaps £15 a year from the College, and a further £50–£60 a year from the Archdeaconry.[2] He seems to have spent his money chiefly on his library, which at the time of his death was a notable theological collection of about 159 books that was valued at £33.11s.9d., nearly three-quarters of the value of his whole estate. His most costly book was a ten-volume Augustine valued at £3.13s.4d., and he owned seven other multi-volume sets valued at a pound or more.[3] His collection was especially strong in Church Fathers and ecclesiastical history, but he also had a Greek and Latin Testament, a Greek Bible, and a seven-volume Hebrew Bible; the Protestant commentators Bucer, Gualter, Melancthon, and Musculus; some Luther and Erasmus, and Calvin's *Institutes*; and, amongst several small controversial works in English, 'An awnswer towchyng mynisters app[arell]', a Puritan tract printed at Rouen in 1566.[4] His library

attempt has been made here to turn collective entries (which are valued) into numbers of 'books'.

The book list from a sixteenth-century probate inventory (that of Robert Beaumont, not a Fellow but Master of Trinity, who died in 1567) is given in Appendix C.

[1] See the table opposite.

[2] Venn; *TC Admissions*; TC Mun., *Admissions and admonitions 1560–1759*, SB accounts. Parkinson's Tutorship is inferred from the fact that the inventory lists three bedsteads in his 'great Chamber'. The value of the Archdeaconry in 1535 was £56 net (*Valor ecclesiasticus*, v, p. 1).

[3] These were sets of Chrysostom, Cicero, Concilia, Dionysius Carthusianus, Jerome, the Magdeburg Centuriators, and Musculus.

[4] STC 10388. Parkinson also owned Coverdale's *Letters* of martyrs; *A defense of priestes mariages agaynst T. Martyn*; and Mainardi's *Anatomi of the Mass*.

*Fellows' private libraries, 1550–89*

| Name | Elected Fellow | Died | Prob. age at death | Prob. total of books | Average value per book | Value of books as % of Estate | Contents |
|---|---|---|---|---|---|---|---|
| GYLPYN, Godfrey | 1546 (Charter) | 1550 | 38 | 122 | 2s. 1d. | 35 | Protestant divinity; some Latin literature, text-books |
| CLERKE, Henry | 1546 (Charter) | 1552 | 29 | 45 | 7½d. | 3 | 10 titles listed; miscellaneous |
| HELPERBYE, Thomas | 1546 (Charter) | 1554 | 39 | 88 | 1s. 11d. | 15 | 52 titles listed; Catholic divinity, teaching books |
| MALHAM, John | 1548 | 1557 | 31 | 83 | 1s. 11d. | 42 | titles not listed |
| PEMBER, Robert | 1546 (Charter) | 1560 | 57 | 162 | 1s. 1d. | 47 | comprehensive, cultivated collection of Catholic divinity, literature, etc. |
| HAWES, Henry | 1555 | 1560 | 26 | 140 | 1s. 3d. | – | wide range of subjects other than divinity; teaching books |
| BEAUMONT, John | 1560 | 1565 | 35 | 150 | 1s. 6d. | 35 | 125 titles; divinity, teaching books |
| COCKCROFT, Henry | 1547 | 1567 | 42 | 79 | 1s. 5d. | 32 | 52 titles listed; divinity, teaching books |
| PARKINSON, Martin | 1560 | 1569 | 31 | 159 | 4s. 3d. | 70 | fine divinity collection; also strong in Greek (see text) |
| LIFFE, William | 1563 | 1569 | 26 | 122 | 3s. 11d. | 49 | wide range of subjects other than divinity (see text) |
| KEY, James | 1563 | 1569 | 25 | 59 | 4¾d. | 7 | small collection of cheap teaching books (see text) |
| SHARPE, Nicholas | 1573 | 1576 | 27 | 92 | 2s. 4d. | 29 | general collection of divinity and teaching books |
| ANGER, William | 1576 | 1589 | 38 | 64 | 2s. 3d. | 28 | 44 titles listed; modest divinity and teaching collection |

*Source*: Cambridge University Archives, Vice-Chancellor's Court inventories.
*Notes*: The probable ages at death are calculated from the dates of matriculation or graduation. The probable totals of books include estimated numbers in grouped entries.

also included, in Greek, Aeschylus, Aristotle, Demosthenes, Euripides, Herodotus, and Isocrates; but no Latin poets, and relatively few of the little teaching books in dialectic, etc., that most of the other Fellows owned in considerable numbers. Altogether Parkinson's library was a very well-considered collection, better in various ways than the College Library at the end of the century, which did not include all the authors mentioned here. Parkinson did not leave his books to Trinity, but he did direct that eighteen named BAs and undergraduates – his pupils, presumably – should have one book each 'as yow shall thynke mete for habilite and lernyng'.[1]

William Liffe came to Trinity as a pensioner in 1560, and was a Fellow from 1563 until his death in 1569 at the age of about 26. He was then College Lecturer in Greek Language, receiving board and lodging from the College and a stipend totalling £7.6s.8d. a year.[2] He probably had other resources, for his private library of 122 titles was valued at £23.17s.8d., and his whole estate at twice as much. His collection included a few valuable divinity books (an Augustine, some Protestant commentators, the Magdeburg Centuriators, and the complete works of Calvin), but its main emphasis lay elsewhere, especially in Greek and Latin literature and in dialectic. In Greek he owned texts of Anacreon, Euripides, Hesiod, Homer, and Sophocles; and in Latin, Cicero, Horace, Livy, Ovid, Sallust, Terence, and Virgil. There were Plato and Aristotle in Greek; the dialectic text-books of Agricola, Aristotle (in Latin), Clichtoveus, Ramus, and Seton; the rhetorical texts of Cicero, Hermogenes, and Isocrates; and the Greek grammar of Ceporinus. Again this was a balanced and learned library, containing several important works that were not added to the College Library until the seventeenth century. Like Parkinson, Liffe bequeathed no books to the College, but left one to each of his pupils.[3]

James Key was a sizar of 1561 who was a Fellow from 1563 until his death in 1569, when he was about 25. He was thus Liffe's contemporary, but he seems to have received only his keep and £4.6s.8d. a year from the College.[4] His private library was a very modest one, totalling only about 59 volumes valued at £1.1s.9d. altogether, or seven per cent of his estate. It consisted for the most part of small teaching books worth a few pence each. The only title valued at more than a shilling was an *Adagia* of Erasmus (3s.). There was a Greek Testament (but Homer was in Latin);

[1] Parkinson's inventory and will, CUA.
[2] Venn; TC Mun., *Admissions and admonitions 1560–1759*, SB accounts.
[3] Liffe's inventory and will, CUA.
[4] Venn; TC Mun., SB accounts. Key's name was also spelled Caius, Kaye, and Caye.

and then the usual text-books in dialectic, rhetoric, grammar, and arithmetic. It was a practical but limited collection, intended for teaching, not research. Key made no specific bequests of books in his will.[1]

The private libraries of the other ten Fellows for which we have probate inventories dating from 1550 to 1589 were essentially similar to these three. Some were more specialised than others, but none was strong in subjects other than divinity, ancient history and literature, philosophy, and teaching books; there were no good collections of legal or medical books. Similarly, too, not one of these libraries was given to the College.

It is true that there were Fellows of Trinity in the sixteenth century who had libraries of other sorts: Nicholas Simpson, for instance, Fellow from 1551 to 1554, who died in 1561 leaving a fine collection of medical books to various individuals; and of course Thomas Skeffington, Fellow 1564–72, who left his law books to the College in 1592.[2] It is also true, as we have seen, that the mid-sixteenth century Masters of Trinity (Bill, Christopherson, and Beaumont) left collections of books to the College in the period 1558–67.[3] Nevertheless, although it seems likely that at least some of the books in these expensive and essentially similar private libraries were bought because the College Library was inadequate, there is no indication that the Master and Fellows tried to help themselves either by spending College money on books or by encouraging gifts to the College Library.

The small text-books needed for the junior courses were not kept in the College Library, use of which was in any case restricted to the Fellows, so the junior members of Trinity also acquired books of their own. We have the probate inventory of John Wood, a Trinity BA who died intestate in 1558 owing a collection of 81 inexpensive text-books;[4] and, although no probate inventories of sixteenth-century Trinity undergraduates happen to survive, there are the inventories of the estates of eight undergraduates of other colleges who died in the period 1545 to 1566, all of whom owned small libraries averaging about 35 inexpensive books each.[5]

---

[1] Key's inventory and will, CUA.

[2] Simpson's inventory and will, 1561, CUA (misdated by Venn); for Skeffington see p. 42.

[3] See pp. 46–8.

[4] Wood's inventory, 1558, CUA (printed by Lisa Jardine in 'Humanism and the sixteenth-century Cambridge arts course', *History of education*, iv, 1975, p. 30).

[5] Inventories, CUA: Richard Kyrke, King's 1545, 14 books; Peter Nelson, Peterhouse, 1547, 16 books; Christopher Levins, Corpus, 1547, 24 books; Thomas Barker, Magdalene, 1549, about 75 books; Henry Spring, Trinity Hall, 1549, about 24 books; Thomas Stapley, Trinity Hall, 42 books; Rudolph Gonas (Ralph Jones?), Clare, 1551, 55 books; Henry Crosse, Peterhouse, 1566, about 35 books. (The lists for Kyrke, Gonas, and Crosse are printed by Lisa Jardine in 'The place of dialectic teaching in sixteenth-century Cambridge', *Studies in the Renaissance*, xxi, 1974, pp. 46–7n.)

There is also the evidence of the private account books of John Whitgift who, when he was Master of Trinity from 1567 to 1577, acted as Tutor to 46 pupils (8 Fellow-Commoners, 17 pensioners, 12 sizars, and 9 of unknown status), and kept a note of his expenditure on their behalf.[1] As Tutor, Whitgift settled his pupils' bills, paying amongst other things for books supplied to 24 of the 46. These were mostly the usual small text-books costing one or two shillings apiece, though some of the richer students bought more expensive books as well. Junior members of the College also obtained books from each other, those who were finishing their courses passing their text-books on to those who were about to begin.[2]

We have, finally, Lisa Jardine's list of the books that were named thirty times or more in the probate inventories of 150 senior and junior members of Cambridge University who died between 1535 and 1590.[3] It consists of thirty-seven works (of which the authors or titles are given); and only ten of them were available in Trinity College Library in 1600. It is also interesting to note that, of the twenty-odd works prescribed for junior courses in the University Statutes of 1549 and 1570, only seven occur in Jardine's list.

Plainly it was high time for the College to set about improving its Library. The long years of neglect may have been connected with the expectation – a confident one, apparently, as early as the 1550s – that there would soon be a new and worthier Library apartment which would be

---

[1] Lambeth Palace Library MS 807 part 1; printed by S. R. Maitland in *The British magazine*, xxxii, 1847, pp. 361–79, 508–28, 650–6; xxxiii, 1848, pp. 17–31, 444–63. (See also Robert Wright's tutorial account for the Earl of Essex, 1577, printed in Cooper, C. H., *Annals of Cambridge*, ii, Cambridge 1843, pp. 352–6.)

The entries for books in Whitgift's tutorial accounts are extracted and annotated in Gaskell, P., 'Books bought by Whitgift's pupils in the 1570s', *Trans. Camb. Bib. Soc.*, vii, 1979, pp. 284–93. Whitgift did not, as is sometimes said, take only rich men's sons as his tutorial pupils. The status of his 46 pupils may be compared with that of all the 538 men who matriculated at Trinity during his Tutorship, of whom 7 per cent were Fellow-Commoners, 39 per cent pensioners, 50 per cent sizars, and 4 per cent of unknown status (*TC Admissions*). It is also sometimes said that Whitgift actually sold books to his Tutorial pupils, but it is more likely that the Master settled their booksellers' accounts.

[2] There is evidence of this practice in many sixteenth-century text-books which were given to the College Library in the seventeenth and eighteenth centuries. For instance the TCL copy of Grimalius, *De optimo senatore*, 4°, Venice 1568 (Adams G1260, S.3.90) has three inscriptions of ownership: 'Bull of Queenes College, 1557'; 'Marcus Huttonus 1581'; and 'Timo: Hutton' (the Huttons matriculated as pensioners at Trinity in 1579 and 1588 respectively). On the fly-leaf are the names of two other Trinity men who may or may not have owned the book: 'Andrew Neuman' (pensioner 1578, Fellow 1585); and 'Bramfeld' (William Bramfyld, pensioner 1580–1). The book was given to TCL by John Laughton, Librarian 1679–83, d. 1712.

[3] See the table opposite.

## Books most commonly owned by Cambridge men in the later 16th century

| title | prescribed text | in TCL, 1600 |
|---|---|---|
| Aesop, *Fabulae* | | |
| Agricola, Rudolphus, *De inventione dialectica* | T | |
| Aristotle, *Ethica* | U | OL97 |
| —— *Politica* | U | OL97 |
| Bible, N.T., Greek | | |
| Caesar, *Commentaria* | | |
| Calepinus, Ambrosius, *Dictionarium* | | |
| Cicero, *De officiis* | | |
| —— *Epistolae* | | OL109 |
| —— *Orationes* | T | |
| Erasmus, Desiderius, *Adagia* | | |
| —— *Colloquia* | | |
| —— *De duplici copia* | | |
| —— *Enchiridion* | | |
| —— *Paraphrases* | | |
| Euripides (a work) | U | OL145 |
| Gellius, Aulus | | |
| Homer (a work) | U T | OL175 |
| Horace | | |
| Justinus | | |
| Livy | | * |
| Lucian, *Dialogi* | | OL120 |
| Ovid | | |
| Petrus, Lombardus, *Sententiae* | | OL40 |
| Plato (a work) | U T | OL86 |
| Plautus | | |
| Plutarch | | OL96 |
| Quintilian | U | |
| Sallust | | |
| Terence | | |
| Valerius Maximus | | OL95 |
| Valla, Laurentius, *Elegantiae de lingua latina* | | |
| Virgil | | |
| Vives, Johannes Ludovicus (a work) | | |
| (an arithmetic primer) | U | |
| (a Greek–Latin lexicon) | | † |

U: text prescribed in the University Statutes of 1549 and 1570
T: text prescribed in the Trinity College Statutes of 1560
*: in Italian and Spanish, but not in Latin
†: lexicons in Greek only
(Adapted from Jardine, L., 'Humanism and the sixteenth-century Cambridge arts course', *History of education*, iv, 1975, pp. 16–17.)

newly stocked with good books. In the event it was not until after the turn of the new century that the Fellows of Trinity were to get a Library that was worthy of their great College; while a century more was to pass before the junior members of the College were to be provided with any library facilities at all.

1601–1695

# CHAPTER 9

# THE NEW LIBRARY

In his will dated 6 October 1556 John Christopherson, Master of Trinity, left the College all his books 'to be placed in the Library of the said College, as sone as it shal be Buylded'.[1] The Library that the College was then intending to build is shown on an old plan for laying out the principal court of Trinity. This plan is undated, and it was later altered by means of patches pasted over parts of it, but the original draft can be assigned with some confidence to the year 1555 (fig. 12).[2] It shows a Library range running eastward from the King Edward Gate (in its original position), south of and parallel to the proposed new Chapel, and ending 20 feet short of the Great Gate.[3] Adjacent to the King Edward Gate was a block containing a squared spiral staircase leading up to the library apartment, which was raised on an arcade and measured about 80ft × 28ft inside; with windows at seven-foot intervals and ordinary lectern cases it would have accommodated about 800 volumes.

On 14 December 1560 the preamble to a commission issued on behalf of Trinity by Queen Elizabeth for the provision of building materials and workmen spoke of 'a Chappell and librarye lately begonne in the tyme of our late deere syster Quene Marye which remayneth at this presente

[1] TC Mun., *Wills and charters*, p. 180.
[2] This plan, mounted and framed, now hangs in TCL; Willis and Clark (ii, p. 465) speak of it as 'now preserved in the Library', but nothing is known of its earlier history. Its date is established by the inclusion of the buildings on either side of the King Edward Gate, which were built in 1554–5 (Willis and Clark, ii, p. 469); and by the dimensions shown for the Chapel, 182½ft × 40ft, which differ markedly from the dimensions established in the Chapel contract of 1556, 157ft × 33ft. (In 1556–64 the building of the Chapel proceeded according to the dimensions given in the contract, after which the east end was extended beyond the line of the Great Gate; see Willis and Clark, ii, p. 563.)
Willis and Clark (ii, pp. 465–72) knew that the plan dated from the mid-1550s, but their reproduction of it was wrongly dated 'about 1595', a misprint which has led others astray.
[3] Willis and Clark are wrong in saying that the scheme for this Library, as well as for the Library to the west of the Chapel, was 'drawn on separate paper, and pasted on to the plan' (ii, p. 467); this scheme was undoubtedly part of the original draft, which was later amended by means of a slip of paper pasted over its west end.

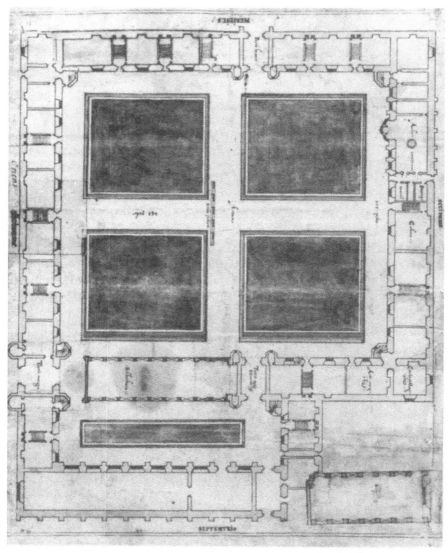

12 A plan made c.1555 for laying out the principal court of Trinity College, shown
here with north at the top. As it was first drawn the Library was placed just inside
the Great Gate, with a staircase next to the King Edward Gate (which was still
in its original position). Later emendations to the plan included patching over the
Library staircase with plain paper; and the addition on another paper patch of a
Library in an alternative position to the west of the Chapel, in the top left-hand
corner. (Plan in TCL; reduced.)

vnfynished'.[1] The building of the Chapel had started in 1556 and remained unfinished in 1560;[2] as to beginning the library, there are a number of references in the accounts for 1554–5 to work on new buildings next to the King Edward Gate.[3] Some of these references are certainly to the range containing part of the Master's Lodge to the west of the Gate, but some of them probably concern the building that is shown in Hamond's plan of 1592 adjacent to the east side of the Gate,[4] exactly where the block containing the Library staircase was placed in the plan of 1555 (fig. 3).

A large new Library, therefore, was planned and probably begun in the mid-1550s, but it was never completed. In 1567 Robert Beaumont bequeathed £40 'for stallynge & glasynge of the new lybrarye',[5] but no more is heard of it until the accounts record in 1589–90 that 'the place for the librarie' was considered, and that stone was provided for it.[6] This entry cannot refer to the New Library that was eventually built which was in a part of the Great Court which was not even planned until 1593–6; and it may be that in 1589–90 the College was considering two amendments that were made to the library scheme of 1555 by means of patches pasted on to the old plan. One of these amendments increased the length of the library apartment originally drawn from about 80ft to about 108ft by taking in the area of the staircase (figs. 13, 14); the other showed a free-standing library building to the west of the Chapel, raised on an arcade and measuring about 85ft × 32ft inside. These amendments would have increased the capacity of the proposed libraries, with ordinary furnishing, to about 1,000 and 1,200 volumes respectively, but again neither of them was built.

Having no pressing need for shelf-space, the College might have gone on planning but not actually building its new library for some years more, but the appointment of Thomas Nevile as Master in 1593 raised the College's building programme to a new level of activity.[7] The principal court planned in 1555 would have been spacious and interesting, but Nevile's scheme was greater still. The Great Gate range was continued southwards, the Hall and Chapel ranges were projected to meet at a new north-west corner, the clutter of buildings within the main ranges was cleared away, and – most revolutionary of all – the venerable King Edward Gate was taken down and re-erected further back against the west end of the Chapel. It was the top floor of the range that ran eastward from the

[1] Willis and Clark, ii, p. 472.
[2] Willis and Clark, ii, pp. 563 ff.
[3] *Old plans*, 4.
[4] Willis and Clark, ii, p. 481.
[5] Willis and Clark, ii, p. 469.
[6] CUA, Beaumont's will, 1567.
[7] Willis and Clark, ii, pp. 474–7.

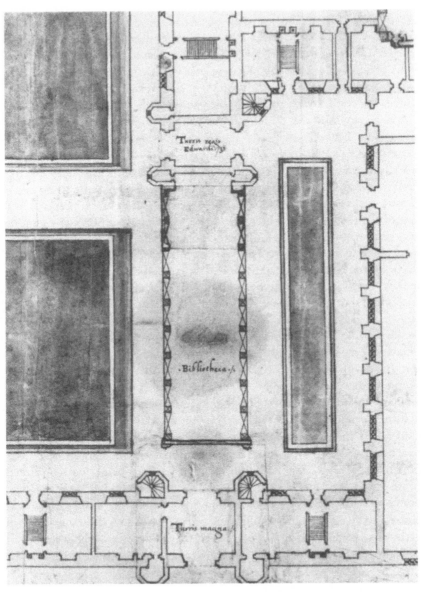

13  A detail of the 1555 plan (see fig. 12) to show the Library between the two gates and the patch of paper at its west (top) end (reduced).

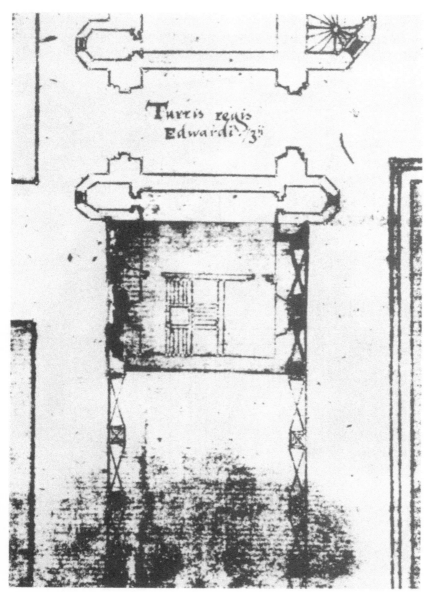

Turris regis
Edwardi 3⁵

14 A detail of the 1555 plan (see fig. 12) photographed by transmitted light to show the drawing of the staircase at the west end of the Library under its later patch of plain paper (enlarged).

north end of the extended Master's Lodge towards the west end of the Chapel that was completed as the New Library (figs. 15, 16). Exactly when this took place is not known – there are gaps in the accounts – but the main building work was probably done in the period 1599–1601, at the end of which the façade of the King Edward Gate was moved back to fill the gap

15 A detail from Loggan's view of Trinity, 1688, showing the New Library (marked 'B') on the top floor of the range between the King Edward Gate and the Master's Lodge. Loggan appears to have drawn the Library roof with too steep a pitch. (TCL X.18.41; enlarged.)

16 A detail from West's view of the Great Court of Trinity College in 1739, showing the site of the New Library on the top floor of the range between the King Edward Gate and the Master's Lodge and the Master's Lodge looking much the same as it does today. The pair of two-light windows as its east (right-hand) end lit the top of the main Library staircase, which emerged at the doorway below them; and there was another stair to the Library in the north-west turret next to the Master's Lodge. The other two two-light windows on the top floor may have been put instead of three-light windows when the New Library was converted to rooms in the late 1690s. (R. West del., Thos. Bowles sculps., July 1739; in TCL; enlarged.)

between the Library range and the Chapel.[1] Work was going on in the
interior of the Library in 1600–1, and perhaps afterwards,[2] but there are
indications that it was not brought into use until about 1604. These are,
first, that Stanhope's will, signed on 28 February 1603, implies that the
books had not yet been placed in the New Library;[3] secondly that the
construction of the Hall and Kitchens, begun in the spring of 1604, may
have resulted in the destruction of the old Michaelhouse Library which is
likely to have served as the Old Library of Trinity College;[4] and thirdly
that nearly all the books from the Old Library were rebound, apparently in
connection with the move to the New Library, in about 1605.[5]

The new library apartment measured 108ft × 24ft inside, running from
a staircase next to the King Edward Gate (similar to the one planned, and
possibly built, on the other side of the same Gate in 1555) to a gable-end
overlooking the Master's garden,[6] with another entrance from the turret
stair next to the Lodge. It was 'a lofty Room, with a vaulted and curiously
wrought roof',[7] about 13ft high, the vault being a shallow one of plaster.
There were six windows at 10–11ft intervals in the part of the south wall
that overlooked the Great Court (the rest of the south wall abutted the
garret floor of the Master's Lodge); there were presumably ten windows at
10–11ft intervals in the north wall of the Library; and probably three
windows in the western gable-end which lit the south-west corner.[8]

[1] Willis and Clark, ii, pp. 480–6.
[2] Willis and Clark, ii, p. 482, quoting the JB's accounts for 1600–1; the accounts for 1601–2 to
1604–5 are missing.
[3] 'if the Librarie in the sayde Colledge bee new erected, and finished beefore my Death' (TC
Mun., Box 31, no. 2, p. 1); 'yf it [the New Library] bee finished and desked with in six
months . . . fitt to receiue Bookes . . .' (ibid., p. 8); the *Memoriale* to 'bee one of the first
Bookes which should be perfected, bound vp chained, & affixed to there Librarie' (ibid.,
p. 10).
[4] Willis and Clark, ii, pp. 489–94; on the position of Michaelhouse Library, see p. 21.
[5] See pp. 69, 96, 101.
[6] The west end of the Library extended over the first floor of the north end of the Lodge
(Sinker, *Librarians*, p. 53).
[7] Sinker, *Librarians*, p. 52, quoting a document by Colbatch and Parne in a Bentleian
controversy of 1728. Loggan 1688 gave the Library a roof of steeper pitch than that of the
roof in West's drawing of 1739 (engraving in TCL), which shows the building essentially as
it is now. The roof may have been lowered when the Library was converted into rooms at
the end of the seventeenth century; but traces of a shallow plaster barrel-vault at the west
end of the range (which appear to represent the original Library ceiling) show that the pitch
of the roof did not have to be as steep as Loggan drew it, and he may have exaggerated. Few
of the present roof timbers are original, and they may have been replaced when the lead
covering shown by both Loggan and West was replaced by tiles.
[8] Loggan 1688 shows that the Library windows in the south wall corresponded to the
first-floor windows beneath them; they still do, but in an asymmetric arrangement of two-
and three-light openings which is shown in West's drawing of 1739, and which may
have been introduced in the conversion of the 1690s, for there is no obvious reason why the

There is no direct evidence of how the New Library was originally furnished, but it was still the normal practice in college libraries to set two-sided book-cases of some sort at right angles to the long walls, one case between each pair of windows, with seats and desks for the readers on each side of the cases; and there were usually four half-cases against the walls at the ends of the rows of full cases. Furnished in this way, the New Library would have had nine full cases along each side of the long walls, making – with four half-cases – a total of twenty-two units. This appears to be confirmed by the mid-seventeenth-century Library catalogues. Although the cases had by then been added to and some of them had been rebuilt, *1640*, *1645*, and *1667* suggest that there was an original equipment of twenty-two cases, of which the first, eleventh, twelfth, and twenty-second were half-cases.[1] These cases – which were called 'classes' in the catalogues and 'seats' in the Junior Bursar's accounts – were apparently numbered anti-clockwise round the room, class 1 being the half-case to the right of the main entrance at the east end, and class 22 being the half-case to its left.[2]

Examination of the surviving books from the Old Library shows that they were nearly all re-covered early in the seventeenth century. The accounts tell us that this was done by a binder named William Hamond, who in 1605–6 removed the roll-stamped calf and wooden boards of the Old Library books, trimmed and coloured their edges, and covered them with plain dark-brown calf on mill-board.[3] Running numbers were written on the newly trimmed fore-edges, which shows that the books were now placed upright on the shelves, fore-edges outwards; which in turn indicates what was probably the main reason for re-covering the books: more books bound in thin mill-board could be stood on a shelf than if they had been bound in thick wooden boards.[4]

Library should not have had six three-light windows matching those of the first floor. The windows on the north side have been altered beyond recall in a series of conversions. The gable-end overlooking the Master's garden was also altered when the floor levels were changed at the beginning of the eighteenth century, but it still shows traces of three west windows at the Library level.

[1] See pp. 92–3 and Appendix B.
[2] See p. 70. For the arrangement of the cases, see p. 115 n. 1.
[3] TC Mun., JB accounts 1605–6: 'Laide out in yᵉ Library . . . to William Hamond for binding books': six payments totalling £21.11s.6d., dated 19 Dec. 1605 to 2 Aug. 1606. See pp. 96, 101.
[4] It may be that books bound in mill-board were also preferred because they were easier to handle than books bound in boards. Sir Thomas Tresham wrote in a letter of 1598, in connection with the re-foundation of the Library of St John's College, Oxford: 'The binding vp of yoʳ Library bookes is spetially to be respected for the well preseruing of them and reddier vse of them. first wheather in wad or in paste bords I prefer the past bords, if

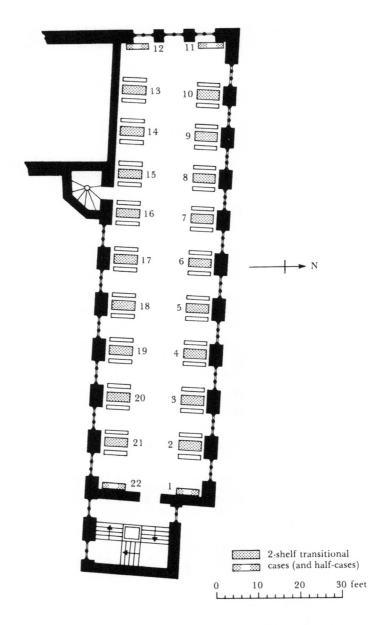

1 *Plan of the New Library and possible arrangement of the cases c.1604*

These running numbers, moreover, correspond to the order of the entries in the OL list in the *Memoriale*, which is thus seen to be a shelf-list of the books as they were arranged in the New Library in 1612–14, when this part of the *Memoriale* was copied out. Each shelf contained about 23 folio volumes, and was therefore about five feet long;[1] and the later catalogues show that there were two such shelves in each of the original full cases and one in each of the half-cases. The lack of chain-staple marks on the new covers of the books proves that they were not chained to the cases.

It is just possible that the New Library cases were single-decker versions of the two-decker book-cases that were introduced at Oxford from 1589,[2] but this is not a form that is otherwise known and it is perhaps more likely that in 1601–4 Trinity was building transitional lectern-cases of the sort that were being made at just this time by Trinity's next-door neighbour Trinity Hall for its own new Library. Trinity Hall's new Library, which was probably built in 1600–5, was furnished with ten handsome lecterns, with back-to-back bench seats fixed between them (fig. 17).[3] Each lectern had a pair of sloping desks at the top for the use of standing readers, under which a flat shelf 2ft wide and 6ft 5in long accommodated two rows of about 27 folio volumes standing upright, fore-edges outwards.[4] Boards could be pulled out on each side from housings under the flat shelves to make desks for readers sitting on the benches. Chain-rods, locks, and keys were fitted to the lecterns, but the bindings of books that were in the Library in the early seventeenth century show that they were not in fact chained.[5] Trinity's new cases could have been very like those of Trinity Hall, except that they were apparently a little shorter and that they were probably set too far apart for back-to-back seating (fig. 18).

they be such dooble past bords as we receaue from Paris binding.' (Quoted in N. R. Ker's Sandars lectures of 1955, *Bodleian Library record*, vi, 1959, p. 515; by 'dooble past bords' Tresham is likely to have meant mill-board.)

[1] The first eight shelves of the OL list contained 22, 26, 23, 20, 23, 22, 26, and 22 folio volumes respectively; the shelf of quarto and octavo books (the tenth) contained 32 volumes. The number of folio volumes to the foot, average 4½, is taken from the books themselves.

[2] See pp. 9–10.

[3] Willis and Clark (ii, pp. 222, 226) think that Trinity Hall Library was built by 1603; Charles Crawley (*Trinity Hall*, Cambridge 1976, p. 35) suggests a date soon after 1604. The cases were original equipment; Streeter (*The chained library*, pp. 35–41) shows that Willis and Clark are wrong in suggesting that they were added later.

[4] Fore-edge numbering shows here, as at Trinity, that this was the original arrangement. Since the early seventeenth century further rows of books have been added at floor level under the cases, and also under the benches.

[5] Streeter, generalising from isolated instances, says that 'scars on old books show that the chains were here attached to the fore-edge of the cover' (op. cit., p. 38); but most of the old books at Trinity Hall show no chain scars at all, and the isolated instances may have been chained at other libraries before coming to Trinity Hall.

17   A lectern of c.1600–5 in the Old Library of Trinity Hall, Cambridge (see fig. 6). Each double-sided lectern originally had two rows of books standing upright and with the fore-edges outwards on each side of the shelf which ran the full width of the unit immediately below the reading desks. (The lower shelf seen here is a later addition.) The lock on the lectern end secured a chain rod, but it appears that Trinity Hall's books were never actually chained to these lecterns.

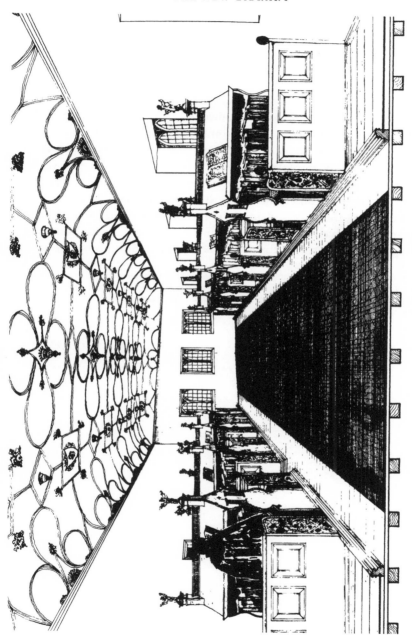

18 A conjectural drawing of the west end of the New Library, Trinity College, in c.1605–10, showing 'a vaulted and curiously wrought roof', and lecterns similar to those at Trinity Hall but more widely spaced. (Drawing by Martin Morris.)

The total capacity of forty five-foot shelves in eighteen full and four half-cases of this sort would have been from about 900 folio volumes (at $4\frac{1}{2}$ volumes to the foot) to about 1300 quarto and octavo volumes (at $6\frac{1}{2}$ volumes to the foot), plus perhaps a few more volumes kept on the lectern desks.[1] The actual contents of the College Library in 1600 was about 325 volumes, of which 266 were folios and 59 – 18 per cent – were quartos and octavos; so that they would have occupied only seven full cases. The order in which the OL books were placed on the shelves of the New Library, while not wholly self-consistent, shows traces of a scheme of classification that was commonly employed in monastic and academic libraries of the fifteenth and sixteenth centuries;[2] and it may be that the books in the Old Library had been classified according to this traditional scheme.

At first, then, there were plenty of empty shelves in the New Library, but benefactions were to fill them within a decade; and it was during this exciting but difficult period that the College Librarianship was endowed.

[1] This is much the same as the estimated capacity, using traditional lectern desks, of the three Library schemes of the 1555 plan: 800, 1200, and 1000 folio volumes respectively.

[2] This traditional scheme of classification, which was adopted in Trinity's New Library in the 1660s, will be described later (see pp. 109, 112–13).

# CHAPTER 10

# STANHOPE'S LIBRARIANSHIP

In 1603 Sir Edward Stanhope[1] provided in his will for the support of a Librarian and a Sub-Librarian at Trinity. His initiative was timely, for the College Library was about to expand faster and to receive finer gifts than at any other time in its history. Stanhope may have had some foreknowledge of these developments, though his first aim seems to have been to increase the usefulness of the existing collection following its move to the new library apartment. Hindsight also suggests that some of the early seventeenth-century donors were encouraged to give generously by the establishment of the Librarianship.

Having already given the College £100 towards the cost of building the New Library,[2] which was now almost completed, Stanhope decided to bequeath a further £700, the income from which was to provide for the Librarian and Sub-Librarian.[3] A transcript of part of his will, which was intended for use as a College Ordinance, is given in Appendix D. It directed that the Librarian, appointed for life by the Master and Seniors, was to be a Scholar or former Scholar of the College, of good character, and at least a BA but not of higher degree than MA. He might not hold or accept any fellowship, office, or preferment, inside the College or out of it, so long as he continued Librarian. But, although not a Fellow, he was to

---

[1] The best biography of Stanhope (who has already appeared in this account as the donor of the *Memoriale*, see p. 34) is in Cooper, C. H. and T., *Athenae Cantabrigienses*, ii, Cambridge 1861, pp. 470–3. Stanhope was elected Scholar of Trinity in 1560 and Fellow in 1564; he graduated BA in 1562–3, MA in 1566, and LLD in 1575, and he served as College Lecturer, 1567–70, and Third Bursar (not a statutory post), 1571–2. Stanhope resigned his Fellowship in 1572 and went to London to practise the law, where he became successively Advocate, Master in Chancery, Chancellor of the diocese of London, and Vicar-General of the province of Canterbury. He became an MP in 1586, and was knighted in 1603. He died on 16 March 1608.

[2] For vaulting and joinery work (*Memoriale*, p. 63).

[3] Normally called the Library Keeper and the Under Library-Keeper in the seventeenth century but, since the sixteenth-century Library cleaners and the nineteenth-century Sub-Librarians were often called Library Keepers, I use the modern terms to avoid confusion.

enjoy a Fellow's privileges, having Fellows' commons, a room near the Library, and a money wage totalling £8 a year (which put him on a level with the junior College officers).[1] The Sub–Librarian was to be an under-graduate pensioner, sizar, or sub-sizar of the College, who was to be of six months' standing and aged fifteen or over on appointment by the Master and Seniors; but he was to vacate the post on graduating BA or on reaching the age of twenty-five. He was to have sizars' commons, to lodge in the Librarian's room, and to be paid a money wage of £4 a year. Not being a Scholar, the Sub-Librarian would not be eligible for succession to the Librarianship.[2]

The duties of the Librarian, specified in Stanhope's will in a form to which each incumbent was required to subscribe, were to keep the keys of the Library and to be responsible for its security; to maintain the catalogue; to see that the Sub-Librarian cleaned the books; to attend the Fellows and their guests in the Library; and to supervise the loan of books for up to fourteen days on the written order of the Master or Vice-Master. On first taking office the Librarian was to accept responsibility for the actual contents of the Library; after which there was to be an annual inspection by senior officers of the College who, if they found any books to be missing, mutilated, or defaced which the Librarian had not reported in time for action to be taken against the offenders, might fine him up to £1.10s. a year towards the cost of repairs.[3] It was not suggested that the Librarian should be responsible for stocking the Library; and later evidence indicates that, when the College bought books for the Library, they were chosen either by the council of Master and Seniors or by a committee of College officers not including the Librarian.[4] The Sub-Librarian was to assist the Librarian in general; and in particular he was to sweep the library apartment and staircase, to dust the books and the furniture, and to clean the windows.

[1] He was to be treated as a Minor Fellow so long as he remained a BA, and as a Major Fellow after graduating MA. A Major Fellow who was also a College Lecturer of middle grade received board, lodging and a money wage of £7 but he – unlike the Librarian – might supplement his income by taking pupils, etc.

[2] The only Sub-Librarian to succeed to the Librarianship was the eighteenth-century pluralist Nicholas Claggett (see Gaskell and Robson, p. 28); he matriculated as a sizar, but was elected a Scholar in the year that he became Sub-Librarian.

[3] That is, up to one quarter of his 'wages' of £6 per annum (the other £2 of his annual emolument being 'livery').

[4] There are many references in the seventeenth-century Bursars' accounts to books 'bought by order of a Meeting'. In 1669 John Hackett asked that the library books bought with the rents of the Bishop's Hostel should be chosen by the Master, the Vice-Master, the Senior Dean, and the Senior and Junior Bursars, or by any three of them (TC MS R.17.6²).

This foundation, which was unparalleled in any other Oxford or Cambridge college, put the Library in the care of a man of education whose sole duty was to administer it for the benefit of the Society. The arrangement offered notable advantages to the Library and thus to the academic development of the College. A full-time Librarian would not only enhance the utility of the collection by keeping it in good order and cataloguing it, but he might also be able to improve its quality by encouraging and directing donations, and by advising the College's purchasing committee what to get with money given for buying books. Incidentally the foundation provided the only academic post at Trinity for a scholar other than a lawyer or a physician who wished to continue his college career without taking holy orders.

There were eight Librarians of Trinity in the period 1609–95. Little is known about the first three: William Hickes, Librarian from 1609 to 1612; Nicholas Parker, 1612–25; and Peter Hersent, 1625–31.[1] All three had been Scholars of the College, as Stanhope's will required, and all were appointed to the Librarianship at about the time they graduated MA at the age of twenty-four or twenty-five. Although we have a few biographical details of these men – Hickes later obtained a benefice, and Hersent while still a BA was admonished for hitting the Manciple[2] – we have no details of their activities in the Library, and no idea of how far they were personally responsible for its development.

William Clutterbooke,[3] Librarian 1631–41, was again a former Scholar of the College who became Librarian at the age of twenty-four; and he was also a poet, who had sets of verses published in four collections of gratulatory poems in the late 1630s. In 1638 a fellow Trinity poet, Samuel Turbervile MA, attempted to have Clutterbooke deprived of the Librarianship on the grounds that he had accepted certain other offices and had failed to keep his nights, contrary to the terms of Stanhope's will.[4] Turbervile actually managed to involve Archbishop Laud in the plot, the Archbishop being tempted by the possibility that he might obtain the presentation of the Librarianship, for which Turbervile was himself a candidate. Fortunately the Master and Seniors were able to deflect Laud, and Clutterbooke was continued in office with no more than an admonition for failing to sign the exit and redit book.[5] His Librarianship then had only three more

---

[1] See Sinker, *Librarians*; *TC Admissions*; Venn; and Appendix E below.
[2] Sinker, *Librarians*, pp. 1–6.
[3] Or Clotterbooke, the spelling of his signature.　　　　[4] Sinker, *Librarians*, pp. 7–11.
[5] The admonition, signed by Clutterbooke, is in TC Mun., *Conclusion book A*, p. ²16.

years to run – he departed for a benefice in 1641 – but during this time Clutterbooke wrote out the earliest surviving catalogue of the Library, the alphabetical finding list of c.1640 which will be described later.[1]

Nothing at all, apart from what may be gleaned from Stanhope's will, is known about what the seventeenth-century Sub-Librarians did in the Library, for not one of the forty-odd lads appointed in the period 1609–95 has left an identifiable trace of his activities.[2] The surviving Senior Bursars' accounts tell us the names of thirty-three of them – there were probably another seven or eight in the periods for which the accounts are lost – and indicate that their average term of office was only $2\frac{1}{4}$ years (with a normal distribution of some 9 months to $3\frac{1}{4}$ years);[3] their average age on appointment was about $19\frac{1}{2}$.[4] It may be that the youth of the Sub-Librarians and the brevity of their appointments was prejudicial to the efficiency and continuity of the administration of the Library, but Stanhope's regulation that they should be undergraduates of the College was observed until 1772.

Seventeen of the known Sub-Librarians of this period were sub-sizars of the College at the time of their appointment, twelve were sizars, and three were pensioners; none was simultaneously Sub-Librarian and a Scholar of the College, although thirteen of them were elected into Scholarships later. The only plain breach of Stanhope's regulations in the seventeenth century was that three of the Sub-Librarians continued to hold office for periods of up to a year after graduating BA.[5] Most of the Sub-Librarians, however, were replaced before they graduated, while six of them did not graduate BA at all. As a group they were not undistinguished in later life. Seven former Sub-Librarians of the period became Fellows of the College, three of them being appointed to senior college offices; and twenty-one were ordained. Also amongst them were a Fellow of another College, a country gentleman, a headmaster, a Fellow of the Royal Society, and two Court Chaplains whose biographies are included in the *DNB*.[6]

---

[1] See pp. 108–9 and Appendix B.

[2] See Appendix E and the references given therein.

[3] The average term of the 30 appointments of which the length is certainly or probably known was 2.2 years (standard deviation 1.34 years); the figures in the text are rounded to the nearest three months, which is the shortest period accounted for.

[4] This is the average age of the 16 men whose age on appointment is certainly or probably known.

[5] See Appendix E, footnotes.

[6] See Appendix E, sidenotes. The country gentleman was Robert Barcroft; Lawrence Ormrod became Headmaster of Rochdale Grammar School in 1638; the royal Chaplains noticed in the *DNB* were David Jenner and Jeremy White.

# CHAPTER 11

# COLLECTIONS OF
# MANUSCRIPTS

In 1600 Trinity did not possess a single one of the superb medieval manuscripts which it now counts amongst its greatest treasures, the only manuscript books in the College Library then being the humanistic manuscript of Athanasius given by Christopherson in the 1550s, and possibly a copy of Nicholas Trivet's *Annales*, of unknown provenance.[1] Then all of a sudden the College was presented with about 330 manuscripts of outstanding quality, in two large collections given by Whitgift and Nevile, and two small ones given by Stanhope and Willmer. These gifts were not of workaday academic and liturgical manuscripts such as Trinity is likely to have inherited from Michaelhouse and the King's Hall and to have lost or discarded between 1546 and 1600, but chiefly of splendid books dispersed from the great monastic libraries at the dissolution, books which had been deliberately preserved by sixteenth-century collectors.

In preserving books from the monastic libraries, Leland, Bale, Matthew Parker, and other sixteenth-century antiquaries were especially concerned to save individual texts which, they saw, were in danger of being lost for ever;[2] and Parker wanted in particular to preserve the texts of historical works that would justify the Elizabethan Church Settlement.[3] There were other reasons, too, for collecting monastic manuscripts. Some must have survived simply because they seemed beautiful or curious; others, apparently, because book-collectors of the sixteenth century, like those of other periods, were sometimes motivated by the urge to accumulate books just for the sake of acquiring and possessing them. Thus the four collections of monastic manuscripts that were given to Trinity during the ten years

---

[1] See p. 40 n. 2. The manuscript of Trivet's *Annales* was not in the Library when the *Memoriale* lists were made in about 1614.
[2] Such as the *Sermones* of William of Bath, of which Trinity owned a copy in the 1540s, but of which no text is now known to survive; see p. 28 n. 3.
[3] See McKisack, M., *Medieval history in the Tudor age*, Oxford 1971, ch. 2.

following the move to the New Library in about 1604[1] included books of textual importance, books of rare beauty, and books that were no more than ordinarily representative of the great libraries from which they came.

The first and largest of the collections of monastic manuscripts to be given to the Library was that of John Whitgift, Archbishop of Canterbury and formerly Master of Trinity. At the time of his death in 1604 Whitgift's private library numbered close on 6,000 volumes, of which at least 200 were manuscripts.[2] Most of Whitgift's books remained at Lambeth, where they were incorporated in the Palace Library established by his successor Archbishop Bancroft, but he bequeathed 150 of his finest manuscripts, 100 of them written in the thirteenth century or earlier, to Trinity.[3] Ninety per cent of these admirable books were theological – mostly patristic and other biblical commentaries – but there was also a small group of chronicle histories; and, although the collection did not include anything as extraordinary as Nevile's Canterbury Psalter or Anne Sadleir's Apocalypse, the overall standard was very high. Fifty-two of Whitgift's 150 manuscripts came from Christ Church, Canterbury (that is, his own cathedral library); two came from St Augustine's, Canterbury; and fifteen from Buildwas Abbey in Shropshire.[4] In removing Canterbury manuscripts to Cambridge, Whitgift followed the example of Archbishop Parker.[5] No doubt the two archbishops – and Dean Nevile after them – believed that Canterbury's monastic books would be safer in academic libraries at Cambridge than exposed in the cathedral library to the possible bigotry or carelessness of their successors; they may have been right, though in fact some other cathedral libraries succeeded in preserving large numbers of their medieval manuscripts.[6] Whitgift may have obtained his Buildwas manuscripts – much the largest surviving group of books from that house – when he was Bishop of Worcester and Vice-President of the Marches of Wales in

---

[1] Whitgift's manuscripts were given in 1604; Stanhope's in 1608; and Nevile's in about 1611. The date of Willmer's gift is uncertain, but the position of the entry which describes it in the *Memoriale* suggests a date in the period 1608–14.

[2] Whitgift's library catalogue is now at Trinity College, Dublin (MS 3); see O'Sullivan, W., 'Archbishop Whitgift's library catalogue', *The times literary supplement*, 1956, p. 468.

[3] The *Memoriale*, pp. 89–91, lists 149 volumes; but James identifies 150 volumes given by Whitgift.

[4] Ker, N. R., *Medieval libraries of Great Britain*, London 1964, pp. 31–3, 41, 14.

[5] There was also another connection with Parker in that five of Whitgift's manuscripts (James 241, 369, 397, 401, and 723) had belonged to John Parker, the Archbishop's son; see Strongman, S., 'John Parker's manuscripts', *Trans. Cam. Bib. Soc.*, vii, 1977, pp. 1–27.

[6] McKisack, M., loc. cit., puts the case for removing the Canterbury manuscripts to Cambridge. For other cathedral libraries, see Ker, N. R., op. cit., especially p. xiv; Durham still has over 300 of its medieval manuscripts, and Worcester has over 250. Nearly 300 Canterbury manuscripts are known, but only 21 of them are still at Canterbury.

1577–83. Whitgift's manuscripts were uniformly bound for him in dark brown calf with a gold fillet and his arms, also gilt, on each cover; and the edges of the books, although often very rough, were not trimmed, presumably in order to preserve marginalia.[1]

Next came fourteen manuscripts bequeathed by Edward Stanhope in 1608 along with his much larger gift of printed books.[2] It was a heterogeneous collection of mostly late-medieval books, but it did include two thirteenth-century Psalters, one of them very fine.[3]

Stanhope's bequest was closely followed by a second great donation of monastic books, the 126 manuscript volumes given, along with 94 printed books, by Thomas Nevile, Master of Trinity and Dean of Canterbury.[4] 'In one day', says the *Memoriale*, 'he put a hundred manuscripts and as many printed books into the New Library.'[5] This can be dated about 1611–12, for a payment was made in 1612–13 to Henry Moody, book-binder, for 'coullering w$^{th}$ virmilion and burnishing 222 bookes of o$^r$ M$^{rs}$ gyfte'.[6] Nevile's manuscripts, though less numerous than Whitgift's, were perhaps even more distinguished. The proportion of theological books was smaller – two-thirds of the collection rather than nine-tenths – and the balance was made up with, amongst other things, seventeen volumes of chronicles and other histories, and a further seventeen volumes of philological, philosophical, and scientific works. Outstanding in a very rich collection were the Canterbury Psalter and the Winchester Gospels (also from Canterbury); and, for the first time in the College Library, three volumes of English poetry: Chaucer, Langland, and Gower. Twenty-four of Nevile's manuscripts had belonged to the Cathedral Library at Canterbury, and two to St Augustine's, Canterbury. One of the Cathedral

---

[1] The *Memoriale*, p. 73, confirms that Whitgift's manuscripts were already bound when they were given to the Library, so it was presumably Whitgift himself who prevented the trimming of their edges. Nevile also preserved the edges of his manuscripts untrimmed, while allowing his binder to trim the edges of his printed books. This restraint, which was unusual for the period, made it difficult for the College Library staff to number the fore-edges of the manuscripts; see p. 97.

[2] *Memoriale*, p. 94, which lists fifteen manuscript volumes; but one of them, James 803, is a printed book.

[3] James 220, 243. James's identification of these books with Stanhope's two Psalters is hesitant, but the similarity of their fly-leaf inscriptions to the form of the *Memoriale* entries for Stanhope's gift appears to confirm it.

[4] *Memoriale*, pp. 91–3. James was able to identify 122 of Nevile's manuscripts.

[5] 'Praeterea nè Bibliothecae nouiter structae & libris iam quam plurimis auctae defuisse videretur, ipse, vt Librorum numerum adaugeret, vno die Manuscriptos Centum, totidem*que* impressos in eam invexit' (*Memoriale*, p. 49).

[6] TC Mun., JB accounts 1612–13, Library account. Moody's task was to colour and burnish the edges of the books, for which he was paid 6d. a volume.

Library books and twenty-three others (including both the St Augustine's books and the Chaucer and the Langland) had previously belonged to Archbishop Matthew Parker or to his son John Parker, or to both of them.[1] Most of these Parker books probably came to Nevile from John Parker, but he may have had a few of them from the Archbishop, either directly or by way of his brother Alexander Nevile who was the Archbishop's secretary. Nevile's manuscripts were bound in plain dark brown calf, with his arms stamped on some of them either in blind or coloured with oil paint. As with Whitgift's manuscripts, the rough edges of the volumes were left untrimmed which, it can be seen, made it difficult for the binder to colour them neatly.

The other early seventeenth-century gift of manuscripts was not a large one compared with those of Whitgift and Nevile, but it too was rich in splendid monastic books. Little is known about the donor, George Willmer, save that he was a Kentish man, born in about 1583, who matriculated Fellow-Commoner of Trinity in 1598 and graduated BA in 1600–1; that he was admitted to the Inner Temple in 1601–2; and that he was a JP for Middlesex at the time of his death in 1626.[2] The entry recording his gift appears to be part of the original draft of the *Memoriale* made in 1612–14; it is placed immediately after the entry for Stanhope's bequest of 1608, so Willmer may have given these books to the College in the period 1608–14, when he was in his late twenties.[3] The *Memoriale* names thirty-nine volumes, of which James identified thirty-seven. There are sixteen fine theological manuscripts, of which ten were written in the thirteenth century or earlier, amongst them a beautiful tenth-century Canterbury manuscript of a commentary on the Acts;[4] four volumes of chronicles; four of scientific works (on mathematics, music, astrology, and medicine); and five important volumes of English poetry, including a fourteenth-century B-text of *Piers Plowman*.[5] They reached the Library bound, uniformly and stoutly but not at Cambridge, in mid-brown calf, with gold fillets and a large block of Willmer's arms, gilt, on each cover. This was a consciously antiquarian collection of fine books from various sources – including four from Canterbury, two each from Christ Church and from St Augustine's – and it is perhaps more likely that Willmer inherited it

---

[1] The twenty-two Nevile manuscripts that had belonged to John Parker are James 22, 38, 40, 42, 61, 288, 342, 594, 595, 624, 628, 645, 653, 704, 716, 717, 725, 751, 752, 770, 819, and 884 (Strongman, S., loc. cit.). The other two Nevile manuscripts, that had belonged to Matthew Parker, are James 711 and 743.

[2] Venn; and a letter preserved in James 883 (quoted by James).

[3] *Memoriale*, pp. 95–6.      [4] James 289.      [5] James 353.

and passed it on to Trinity as an act of piety than that he collected books himself and gave them away while he was still in his twenties.

The 329 manuscript volumes given by Whitgift, Stanhope, Nevile, and Willmer in 1604–14 were followed by at least 206 manuscript volumes received between the late 1620s and 1695 (when the books were moved to the Wren Library) from a total of thirty-nine individual donors and one unidentified source.[1] Most of the later gifts were small ones – nineteen of the thirty-nine donors gave a single volume, and only six of them gave ten or more – and they included a higher proportion of Renaissance and modern manuscripts.

*Manuscript volumes*

| | | 13th cent. and earlier | 14th and 15th cents. | 16th and 17th cents. | Oriental | unidentified | totals |
|---|---|---|---|---|---|---|---|
| 1604–14 (four collections) | vols | 179 | 117 | 24 | 1 | 8 | 329 |
| | % | 55 | 36 | 7 | 0 | 2 | |
| 1620s–1695 (forty collections) | vols | 42 | 43 | 88 | 17 | 16 | 206 |
| | % | 20 | 21 | 43 | 8 | 8 | |
| totals | vols | 221 | 160 | 112 | 18 | 24 | 535 |
| | % | 41 | 30 | 21 | 3 | 5 | |

The most enigmatic of the later accessions is the collection of twenty-four manuscript and eleven printed volumes listed in the *Memoriale* as 'ad Collegium pertinentes', that is 'belonging to the College'.[2] One of the manuscripts has an inscription dated 1611; one of the printed books is dated 1619; and the position of the entry in the *Memoriale* indicates that it was probably made in the period 1633–7.[3] At least fourteen (and probably

[1] The details of the seventeenth-century donors of manuscripts and of their gifts (which are summarised in Appendix F) have been compiled from *Mem* and *Ben*; from James; from Venn and other biographical reference books; and from the manuscripts themselves. The figures given here are minima; there are a number of manuscripts in the Library of unknown provenance, and some of them may have arrived in the seventeenth century without the details being entered either in the books themselves or in the lists of donations.

[2] *Memoriale*, p. 5.

[3] James 361 (not from Warden) is dated 1611 in Irish; the printed book dated 1619 is a Euclid, now T.46.16. The entry in the *Memoriale* comes between those for John Fortho (1633) and Thomas Whalley (1637).

sixteen) of the manuscripts are twelfth- and thirteenth-century monastic books from the Abbey of Warden in Bedfordshire, and an inscription in one of them suggests that in the sixteenth century they belonged to a person named R. Manley.[1] Warden was not College property (though Cardington, near Warden, was), and the only Manley at Trinity was a Fellow-Commoner of 1623 who did not graduate and about whom nothing else is known.[2] It may be that these books came to Trinity in the 1630s in payment of a debt.

Mid-century donations of manuscripts included the spectacular thirteenth-century Anglo-Norman Apocalypse which is one of the splendours of the Library, and which was received from Mrs Anne Sadleir, daughter of Sir Edward Coke, in 1660;[3] four twelfth- and thirteenth-century manuscripts given by Henry Greswold, Fellow, in 1661; nine medieval manuscripts given by Jonathan Dryden, Fellow, in 1663; and twelve Hebrew and other Oriental manuscripts given by Thomas Hill, Fellow, in 1669.[4] About fifteen manuscripts of various periods were received in 1670 and afterwards from John Laughton, who was to be successively Librarian of Trinity and of the University.[5] Five medieval manuscripts and three printed books were found in the study of another Librarian of Trinity, Thomas Griffith, probably following his death in 1674; it was not clear at the time whether these books belonged to Griffith or to the College, but they were added to the Library in any case.[6]

The last major group of manuscripts to reach the Library before the move to the Wren were sixty-one volumes of predominantly modern manuscripts given by Sir Henry Puckering in 1691.[7] Puckering's papers,

---

[1] The inscription is in James 129.

[2] The name is spelled 'Manly' in *TC Admissions* and Venn.

[3] About whom see James, C. W., *Chief Justice Coke, his family and descendants at Holkham*, London 1929, ch. 8. How Mrs Sadleir acquired the Apocalypse is not known, but in 1649 she placed it in the care of her friend Ralph Brownrigg (who had been Master of St Catharine's, Cambridge, and Bishop of Exeter, but who was by then deprived of his preferments), with instructions that he was to pass it on to Trinity when God should have restored the College to its pristine happiness, the vulgar people to their obedience, and King Charles II to his throne (inscription in James 950). Brownrigg died in 1659, but the book did reach Trinity immediately after the Restoration, the College's letter of thanks being dated 10 August 1660 (James 699, item 72).

[4] See Appendix F.

[5] Laughton was still a BA in 1670 when he gave the thirteenth-century Bible that is James 237. James identified eight other manuscripts given by Laughton, but it appears that a further six are listed in *Ben*, p. 108. They were probably given over a considerable period of time.

[6] 'Libri inventi in musæo M[ri] Griffith bibliothecæ nunc vel donati, vel restituti' ('books found in Mr Griffith's study, now either given or restored to the Library'), *Ben*, p. 35.

[7] Though not a Fellow, Puckering, recently widowed, resided in College for the whole or part of the last ten years of his life, 1691–1701. The manuscripts he gave to the Library in

which remained in the College when he died intestate in 1701, apparently included the precious autograph manuscript of Milton's minor poems, unbound and in some disarray; but it was not identified and added to the Library for at least another twenty-five years.[1]

These great seventeenth-century accessions of manuscripts seem to have been appreciated and well cared for from the beginning. They were always shelved and catalogued separately from the Library's printed books, and scarcely any were lost. It is not until 1673, however, that there is any indication in surviving records that there were special restrictions on the borrowing or transcription of the College's manuscripts.[2]

---

1691 are listed in Bernard, E., *Catalogi librorum manuscriptorum*, Oxford 1697, pp. 101–2. James identifies a further nineteen manuscripts given by Puckering after 1691, perhaps at the time after 1695 when the Library received 4,000 of Puckering's printed books.

[1] The Milton manuscript (James 583) was found amongst Puckering's papers by Charles Mason, Fellow of Trinity from 1725, and University Professor of Geology from 1734; it was bound for the Library in 1736. See Aldis Wright's preface to the facsimile of the manuscript, Cambridge 1899, p. 1.

[2] 15 April 1673; 'Ordered by the Master and Seniors, that no Manuscript be let forth out of the library or suffered to be transcribed without leave from the Master and Seniors' (TC Mun., *Conclusion book A*, p. 277).

# CHAPTER 12

# THE GROWTH OF THE WORKING COLLECTIONS, 1601–40

Until quite late in the sixteenth century most dons at Oxford and Cambridge needed the use of no more than about a couple of hundred books whatever their subjects. Areas of study, and the books which covered them, were clearly limited; and in general new subjects and the books associated with them were not added to the old ones but replaced them. College libraries, therefore, usually contained between 250 and 500 volumes, while individual scholars could supply most of their own needs with private libraries averaging about 100 volumes.

During the last quarter of the sixteenth century, however, there was an increasing tendency to add new subjects and books to what was there already, rather than to throw out the old to make way for the new. Thus in the mid-century the teaching of the medieval Schoolmen was superseded in the universities by that of later theologians, and their books were removed from the college libraries; but when in the 1590s interest in the Schoolmen began to revive, their books were reintroduced into the college libraries not as replacements for but as additions to the works of the later theologians. Everywhere learning began to expand, and the need for books to expand with it. The college libraries grew steadily larger, and at the same time increased in importance as the need for books began to exceed the capacity of individuals to own enough of them privately.

Although the humanities and sciences were increasingly studied during the seventeenth century, the central academic interest of the majority of the senior members of Trinity continued to be divinity, and their central function to be the education of future clergymen. In 1600 the College Library had contained about 325 volumes, of which 53 per cent concerned the study of divinity. During the seventeenth century the book stock grew steadily, both by gift and by purchase, until by the 1690s the number of printed volumes had risen to about 3,570 but the proportion of divinity books was still just over half (51 per cent). This growth, which resulted chiefly from gifts of books and of money intended for the purchase of books, can be followed both in the lists of donations kept by the College, and in three seventeenth-century catalogues which describe the Library as it was in about 1640, in 1667–75, and in 1675–95.[1]

In the first period, from 1601 to 1640, the *Memoriale* records the gifts of thirty-seven donors, of whom thirteen gave various sums of money for the purchase of library books by the College, providing for some 646 printed volumes; while the other twenty-four donors, who seem in most but not necessarily all cases to have given actual books, were responsible for about 810 volumes (see Appendix G). The 1,456 volumes given in 1601–40 which are listed in the *Memoriale*, added to the 324 printed volumes that were in the Library in 1600 and the 22 odd volumes added in 1601–17 (see the OL, TS, and OL* lists in Appendix A), make a total for 1640 of 1,802 printed volumes. This seems at first to accord closely with the stock described in the catalogue of 1640, in which 1,819 printed volumes are entered, but inspection reveals that about 100 of the 1,456 recorded as gifts in the *Memoriale* had not yet been entered in the catalogue,[2] and that about 75 volumes entered in the catalogue were not accounted for in the *Memoriale*. However, the discrepancy – which is typical of the lists and catalogues of the seventeenth century – is not a large one, and we can be reasonably sure that the College Library in 1640 contained close on 1,900 printed volumes, and that we know what they were and where most of them came from.

A scheme for arranging the books in the Library by their subjects instead of by their donors was drafted soon after 1640.[3] The scheme is incomplete – amongst others some 225 law books were omitted – and it was probably not carried out, but it does give an indication of how the Library was developing. It lists 1,033 printed volumes of divinity books and 438 volumes of books on other subjects. The main groups amongst the other subjects were philosophy, 70 printed volumes; science (called medicine and mathematics, but including botany, chemistry, cosmography, etc.), 106 volumes; humane letters (including lexicography, classical literature and oratory, and philology), 130 volumes; and history, ancient and modern, 132 volumes.

---

[1] See Appendix B.

[2] The books not entered in the catalogue came from all over the Library, and seem to have been omitted by accident; they were entered in later catalogues.

[3] *1645* in Appendix B.

As with the manuscripts, most of the gifts and purchases of printed books were fairly small ones, only eight of the thirty-seven involving more than about twenty volumes. Of those who gave books rather than money, Peter Shaw, a past Fellow of 1564–72 and an exact contemporary of Sir Edward Stanhope, gave 143 volumes of divinity books in 1601;[1] while Stanhope himself bequeathed his great collection of law books in 1608, which with books on other subjects totalled 238 volumes, the largest single gift of books to be placed in the Library before the move to the Wren at the end of the century.[2] Nevile's printed books, 94 volumes mostly of divinity, arrived with his manuscripts in 1611–12. Silvius Elwes, Chaplain, gave 184 volumes in 1626–30, chosen because he thought that they would be especially useful or that they might be difficult to find;[3] again there was a majority of divinity books, but Elwes included a strong section of books on modern history.

There is no evidence that the College spent much of its own money on books in this period, but it was nevertheless able to choose nearly half the library books it received in spending the money that was given for the purchase of books. Again these were mostly divinity books – especially commentators and other works of biblical exegesis – but the College also bought books on other subjects. A Camden's *Britannia* was bought in 1609, Speed's *History of Great Britain* (one of the first books in English to be bought for the Library) in 1613, and five more history books in English in 1618.[4] The lack of Latin poetry was tackled in 1625 with the purchase of large annotated editions of Catullus, Martial, and Virgil.[5]

[1] *Memoriale*, p. 99. Also TC Mun., SB accounts, 1600–1, Extraordinaries: 'to the Cart[rs] to brought M[r] Shawes books and the porters for unloading, iij[s] vj[d]'; ibid., Receiptes: 'Receaued of M[r] Peter Shawe towards the Cheyning and desking of his bookes given to the newe Liberarie, v[li]'. Shaw's books were not chained when they were eventually placed in the New Library.

[2] Although James Duport bequeathed about 2,000 volumes to the Library in 1679, they were not placed on the shelves until after the move to the Wren.

[3] *Memoriale*, p. 107.

[4] Camden, William, *Britannia*, London 1607, STC 4508 (gift of William Smyth, 1609); Speed, John, *The history of Great Britain*, London 1611, STC 23045 (gift of Richard Wright, 1613, which included William Perkins's *Works*, 1609, and the new Authorised Version of the Bible, 1611).
The five history books in English bought with money given by Sir William Sedley (or Sidley) in 1618 were: Sandys, George, *A relation of a journey*, London 1615, STC 21726; Purchas, Samuel, *Purchas his pilgrimage*, London 1617, STC 20507; Knolles, Richard, *The generall historie of the Turkes*, probably London 1610, STC 15052; Mayerne Turquet, Louis de, *The generall historie of Spain*, London 1612, STC 17747; and Serres, Jean de, *A generall historie of France*, London 1611, STC 22245.

[5] Catullus, Tibullus, and Propertius, *Opera*, ed. J. Scaliger, Paris 1604; Martial, *Epigrammata*, ed. J. Langius, Paris 1617; Virgil, *Opera*, ed. J. L. de la Cerda, 3 vols, Frankfurt and Lyons 1613–18 (all bought with money given by Sir Michael Stanhope in about 1625).

Of particular interest is the rapid growth of the science sections of the Library in the earlier seventeenth century, the period immediately preceding the arrival of Isaac Barrow. In 1600 there had been only five medical and mathematical books in the collection;[1] by the 1640s there were over a hundred. The draft classification scheme of c.1645, the first known attempt to put the contents of the College Library in subject order, listed fifty-three volumes as *Medici*, including writers not only on medicine but also on alchemy, botany, chemistry, metallurgy, pharmacology, and surgery; and then a further fifty-three volumes as *Mathematici*, including besides mathematicians writers on architecture, astrology, astronomy, chronology, cosmography, geography, optics, and perspective. (In addition to these medical and mathematical books the Library contained a few works of natural history – Aldrovandi, Gesner, Pliny, and Wotton – which, together with Bacon's *Instauratio magna*, were classified with *Philosophi*.[2])

The 106 volumes of *Medici* and *Mathematici*, eighty-four of which are still in the Library, are catalogued in Appendix H. Ninety-nine volumes can be traced to individual benefactions, and it turns out that over three-quarters of them were not given as books but were bought by the College in the period 1618 to 1639 with money given for the purchase of books.

The medical section of the Library[3] was given the standard herbals of Fuchs, Turner, and Gerard (S11–S13 in Appendix H), but lacked Clusius, Dodonaeus, L'Obel, and John Parkinson. Agricola's standard handbook of metallurgy (S34) was bought, as was the anatomy of Vesalius (S15). But medicine in general was unevenly covered. The College did not obtain

*Medical and Mathematical books, c.1645*

|  | Medici | Mathematici | total |
|---|---|---|---|
| items | 44 | 60 | 104 |
| items bought | 27 (61%) | 44 (73%) | 71 (68%) |
| volumes | 53 | 53 | 106 |
| volumes bought | 38 (72%) | 41 (77%) | 79 (75%) |

[1] OL68, OL121, OL125, TS51, and TS53.

[2] These books were: Aldrovandi, Ulisse, *Ornithologia* (Frankfurt 1610), and *Historia de animalibus insectis* (Frankfurt 1618), bought 1625; Gesner, = OL198 plus a fourth volume; Pliny, = TS57; Wotton, = OL114; Bacon, Francis, *Instauratio magna (Novum organum)* (London 1620, STC 1162 or 1163), probably bought early 1640s, sold as a duplicate 1784.

[3] This paragraph relies heavily on advice kindly given me by Mr Charles Webster.

such modern medical handbooks as those of Felix Platter and Kaspar Bauhin, or the monographs of Gabriel Fallopius or William Harvey. On the other hand it did buy a good collection of Renaissance commentators who were appreciated for their practical soundness: Solenander, Scholz, Forestus, and Montanus (S18–S20, S22), together with a few more popular works such as the English translation of Guillemeau's book on surgery (S27). Perhaps the most interesting feature of this part of the Library is the group of eighteen volumes of alchemy and iatrochemistry bought by the College in 1637 (S28–S34) as a representative collection of the major medieval and Renaissance writings in this area. They included the heterogeneous *Theatrum chemicum* (S30), and the daringly modern Paracelsus and Sennert (S28–S29). But even the medieval sources were to appear pertinent to the advocates of the new experimental science, and these works were to be read with close attention by Newton and his contemporaries.

On the mathematical side there was perhaps less sense of direction in the Library's policy for accessions. Euclid, Schoener, and Clavius (S41, S55, S35) were included, but some other fairly obvious mathematicians and algebraists (Finé, Bombelli, Vieta) were not. Again, Kepler's *Astronomia nova* (S45) was bought in 1625, and Copernicus (S73) was bought in 1637 along with Brahe's *Astronomiae instauratae mechanica* (S53); but the Library did not have Kepler's *Harmonica mundi* or *Rudolphine tables*; and Galileo is conspicuously absent. Applied mathematics was represented chiefly by architecture, supported by standard works on perspective.

But for all the shortcomings of the Library's science sections, it remains remarkable that Trinity was assembling them at all in the earlier seventeenth century. College libraries elsewhere still relied largely on gifts of books for the improvement of their collections; and, if Trinity's science sections were imperfect, those of the other college libraries were yet more so.[1]

Only seven of the thirty-seven known donors of the period 1601–40 were Fellows of the College at the time their gifts were made, and only one of the Fellows was a major benefactor to the Library: this was Thomas

---

[1] An exception was Christ's College, Cambridge, which received a bequest in 1626 from Henry Burrell which included an annuity of £4 to be spent in buying 'such new books and mathematical instruments as shall . . . be thought fit to be bought, and will every year be coming out' (Peile's *Christ's College biographical register*, i, p. 267). The College's manuscript *Donations book* shows that Burrell's bequest was in fact used for buying science books, but unfortunately dates of accession are not given. (I am grateful to Dr C. P. Courtney and Professor Rupert Hall for information about Burrell's bequest.)

Whalley, who bequeathed about £120 for the purchase of library books in 1637.[1] Of the other major benefactors of the period, one (Nevile) was Master of the College, one (Elwes) was a College Chaplain, two (Shaw and Edward Stanhope) were past Fellows, while the other three (Suckling, Sedley, and Michael Stanhope) had only indirect connections with the College.

It appears, therefore, that in the early seventeenth century, as in the sixteenth, it was not a normal practice for Fellows of Trinity to give or bequeath books to the College Library. The probate inventories of four Fellows of the College who died during the first decade of the seventeenth century – that is at just the time when the New Library was coming into use – show that they owned private libraries numbering about 95, 100, 120, and 70 books respectively, but that none of them bequeathed their books to the College.[2] Few probate inventories survive from the 1620s or afterwards,[3] but what little evidence there is suggests that, as before, Trinity dons in the earlier seventeenth century normally owned a hundred or two academic books, but did not leave them to the College. There were exceptions: Silvius Elwes, Chaplain, gave a selection of 184 of his books to the College in the late 1620s;[4] while some of the much larger collections of books that were bequeathed to the Library in the second half of the century must already have been in course of formation.[5]

---

[1] The *Memoriale* (p. 117) does not say how much money Whalley bequeathed to the Library, but the list of 201 volumes bought with his bequest suggests a sum of about £120.

[2] Probate inventories of John Shaxton (died 1600–1), William Ball (1601), Edward Lively (1605), and Thomas Coaker (1609) (CUA, VCC inventories, bundles 6 and 7). The figure for Coaker's books is speculative since the greater part of it represents a group of 'other bookes', priced but not enumerated.

[3] The only surviving probate inventories which specify books after 1620 are those of Alexander Clugh, MA of Emmanuel (1621, 48 entries for books); Samuel Collins, Provost of King's (1651, 1 entry); and John Nidd, Fellow of Trinity (1659, 289 entries).

[4] *Memoriale*, pp. 107–9.

[5] John Nidd bequeathed about 300 volumes in 1659 (see p. 131); Isaac Barrow about 1,100 volumes in 1677 (see p. 131); James Duport about 2,145 volumes in 1679 (plus two other collections left elsewhere, see p. 141); and Sir Henry Puckering about 3,360 volumes in 1701 (see p. 141). Elsewhere, Richard Holdsworth, Master of Emmanuel, bequeathed about 10,280 volumes to the University in 1649, and William Lucas, MP, bequeathed about 4,000 volumes to the University in 1664 (see Oates, J. C. T., *Cambridge University Library, a historical sketch*, Cambridge 1975, pp. 11–12).

# CHAPTER 13

# THE ARRANGEMENT OF THE BOOKS, 1601–40

It appears that, when the New Library came into use in about 1604, it was equipped with eighteen full and four half-cases of the transitional lectern type, which could accommodate approximately 1,000 predominantly folio volumes on a total of forty shelves.[1] This probably seemed an adequate capacity at the time – the total stock in 1600 was only just over 300 volumes – but then books poured into the Library at such a rate as to fill the estimated capacity of 1,000 volumes by 1610, and to reach a total of over 2,000 volumes by 1640.

*The growth of the Library, 1601–40*[2]

|                                         | MS vols | printed vols | cumulative total |
| --------------------------------------- | ------- | ------------ | ---------------- |
| Old Library, 1600 (OL + TS)             | 1       | 324          | 325              |
| (OL*)                                   | 1       | 22           | 348              |
| Donations, 1601–10                      | 164     | 506          | 1018             |
| 1611–20                                 | 165     | 350          | 1533             |
| 1621–30                                 | 5       | 341          | 1879             |
| 1631–40                                 | 43      | 259          | 2181             |
| Totals, Old Library and Donations       | 379     | 1795         | 2181             |
| Totals, *1640* catalogue                | 353     | 1819         | 2172             |

The first clear account of the arrangement of the New Library is given by *1640*, the alphabetical finding list which gives shelf references for each volume and which can be rewritten as a shelf-list. If I am right in supposing

[1] See p. 69 above.
[2] Figures from Appendix A (Old Library), and Appendixes F and G (Donations).

that the Library was originally equipped with eighteen full and four half lectern-cases of the transitional, two-shelf type, numbered 1 to 22, then it would appear that the extra shelving required by the growth of the collection after 1610 was provided first by adding to the number of the two-shelf cases, and secondly by replacing some of the two-shelf transitional cases with six-shelf book-cases. The additional cases of the earlier type were three full cases (numbered 23, 24, and 25) and one half-case (numbered 26), which provided shelving for a further 175 volumes. There is no indication of where they were placed, but the three full cases could have been set longitudinally, without benches, in the central aisle, with the half-case under the west window between cases 11 and 12 (see pp. 95 and 115 n. 1). They could have been added in 1611–12, when Nevile gave the Library his 126 manuscripts and 94 printed books.

The next stage, the replacement of two-shelf transitional lectern-cases with six-shelf book-cases, may have begun in 1618, when the College bought about 200 volumes with money given by Suckling, Sedley, and Bennet (fig. 19). By 1640 eight full cases (nos. 2–6 and 19–21) and two half-cases (nos. 1 and 22) had been replaced – or possibly converted – which made room for 100 extra volumes per full case, or 900 extra volumes in all. With a new total of 83 shelves, the theoretical capacity of the Library in 1640 was 2,075 large volumes; and we know that it actually contained 2,172 volumes, most but not all of them large.

None of the New Library furniture survives, but it seems likely that the new six-shelf book-cases were similar to those made for Clare College Library in 1626, which have elaborately carved face-ends, and were originally fitted with desks on each side and with back-to-back seats like those at Trinity Hall.[1] At Trinity, as at Clare, the books were not chained. They were placed upright on the shelves with the fore-edges outwards, the running number of each volume being written in ink on the paper of the fore-edge. We can assume that shelf-lists were pasted in special emplacements carved or mounted on the case-ends.

If the alphabetical finding list of 1640 is reorganised as a shelf-list it shows which books stood in which cases, and from this we can see that the books which came into the New Library up to 1640 were shelved in order of accession, not in subject order. Although some reclassification must

---

[1] See Streeter, B. H., *The chained library*, London 1931, pp. 64–9. The Clare book-cases were basically similar to the less elaborately ornamented cases introduced at eight Oxford colleges between 1590 and 1611 (Streeter, op. cit., ch. 3; and Ker, N. R. in *Bodleian Library record*, vi, 1959, pp. 510–11).

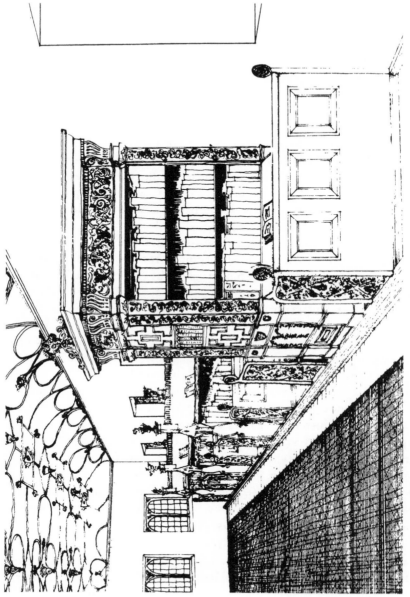

19 A detail from the conjectural drawing of the New Library, Trinity College (see fig. 18), showing the replacement of a lectern with a six-shelf book-case similar to the book-cases made for Clare College, Cambridge, in 1626. (Drawing by Martin Morris.)

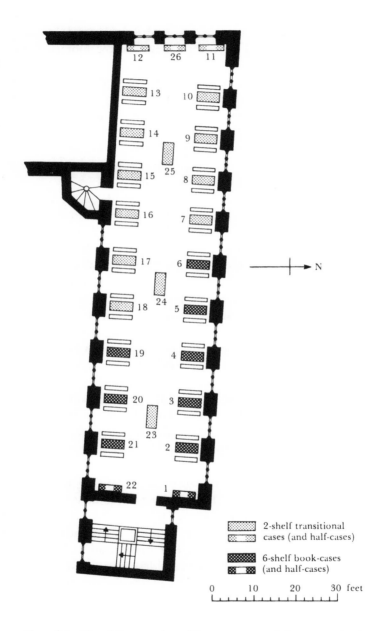

2 *Plan of the New Library and possible arrangement of the cases in 1640*

have taken place as the two-shelf cases were replaced by six-shelf cases, we may guess from the order of the books in 1640 that originally the small cases containing the books from the Old Library and Sir Edward Stanhope's books ran from the main entrance to the Library along the south, or left-hand, wall; and that those containing Peter Shaw's books and Nevile's printed books ran along the north wall to the right of the entrance door. Whitgift's manuscripts may have been placed originally next to the entrance, where most of them remained, while the bulk of the other manuscripts went into the additional cases 23, 24 and 26. (See p. 98.) As more and more printed books were acquired, the OL and Shaw books were reshelved along with more recent accessions in the new six-shelf cases at the east end of the Library. (See p. 99.)

The classification of the books by donors, besides being easy for the librarians, had the advantage that, by drawing attention to the generosity of individual benefactors, it encouraged others to do likewise; but it must have been very inconvenient for the readers, for books on a particular subject or by a particular author might be distributed all over the library. No doubt lists were pasted on to the case-ends which inventoried the contents of each shelf, but there must also have been a need for a general index or catalogue. The earliest surviving index – though not necessarily the first to have been made – is the alphabetical finding list of about 1640.[1] Even this list, though much better than nothing, did not index everything in the Library, for it was in fact an inventory in alphabetical order, listing only the first tract in each volume and even then giving no bibliographical details such as date or place of printing. If a Fellow wanted to consult a work that was bound in the body of a volume that contained several items, it appears that he could neither have found it nor even have known whether it was in the Library unless the Librarian happened to recall its existence and location.

It has already been mentioned that, soon after the books were moved from the Old Library to the New in about 1604, they were nearly all rebound by a binder named William Hamond.[2] The characteristics of Hamond's style of binding, which are found in many early seventeenth-century bindings (not necessarily by Hamond) in other Cambridge libraries,[3] were these (figs. 20, 21): a cover of dark brown calf on mill-board, unlettered and undecorated except for a blind fillet round the edges, and

---

[1] See Appendix B, *1640*.    [2] See p. 69.
[3] Notably in the University Library and Trinity Hall Library; but most of the older college libraries contain examples.

sometimes the arms or initials of the donor in gilt on the upper cover; raised bands; the edges cut and coloured; the endpapers reinforced with two strips, a narrow one from a vellum manuscript and a wide one of plain paper; the endpapers made from early printed books or from printers' waste, and not pasted down to the boards. These simple, workmanlike bindings were perfectly appropriate to the New Library. Once the books were unchained and stood side by side on the new shelves, they no longer needed the thick wooden boards which had withstood the pull of the chains and the tendency of covers to warp when the books lay flat on the old lectern desks; and since wooden boards take up more shelf space than mill boards, it was sensible to discard them along with the chains. Having got so far, there was no point in decorating the new calf covers of the mill boards since, unlike the roll-stamped covers of the wooden boards, they were not going to be laid out on lecterns where they could be seen. This new style of binding continued to be used for covering the books in the New Library for more than fifty years with only slight changes, the chief ones being that by the mid-century the calf was stained a paler brown than before; that the vellum reinforcing strips were generally omitted; and that the endpapers were made of plain, not printed, paper.

Although the volumes were not chained to the shelves of the New Library, they stood with their fore-edges outwards, probably because it was traditional to mark the edges rather than the spines of library books. At Trinity the marking took the form of running numbers – that is, numbers corresponding to the order of the books on a shelf – written in pen and ink on the fore-edges (fig. 22). The earliest of these numbers, written in small figures near the top of the fore-edge, follow the order given in the lists of 1612–14 in the *Memoriale*, and probably date from the period of rebinding c. 1605. They were then crossed out and replaced with another set of running numbers, also written in small figures, which do not correspond to any surviving list or catalogue. Next the second set of numbers was replaced with a third set, written in larger figures near the middle of the fore-edge, which followed the shelf order of the reclassification of the 1660s.[1] Numbering directly on to the fore-edge was superseded, finally, by numbering on small paper tabs pasted inside the top half of the upper cover of each volume so as to project in front of it (fig. 23);[2]

[1] TC Mun., JB accounts, 1666–7: 'to Wisdome Junr for figuring the bookes in the Library' £1.0s.6d.; 'to Henry Dickenson [binder] for figuring 4 classes'. See pp. 113, 115.

[2] Similar but not identical marking systems by means of fore-edge tabs were used in the seventeenth century at other Cambridge college libraries (for instance at Queens' and St John's, where the tabs did not project but were pasted round the fore-edges of the boards).

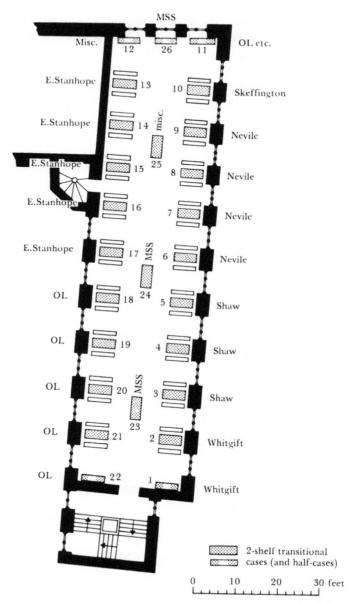

3 *Possible classification of the New Library by donors, c.1612–18; and possible arrangement of the cases*

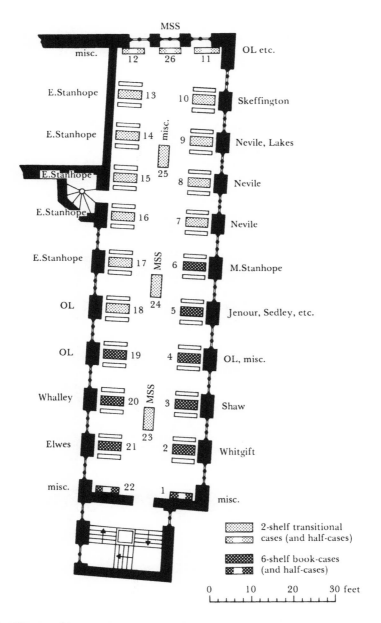

4 *Classification of the New Library by donors, 1640; and possible arrangement of the cases*

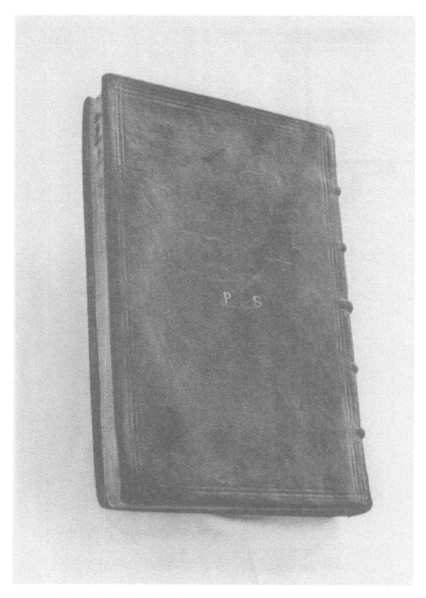

20 A plain calf binding for Trinity College Library, probably by William
Hamond, c.1605–6. Gilt initials in the middle of each board mark the book as the
gift of Peter Shaw, 1601. (TCL E.10.14.)

21 Inside the front cover of a plain binding made for Trinity College c.1605–6 (see fig. 20). Usually there were two reinforcing strips, but here there are three, made from a vellum manuscript, a piece of plain paper, and an early printed leaf respectively. The endpapers were not pasted down, and on the leather at the top left-hand corner of the upper cover can be seen the remains of a fore-edge tab (see fig. 23). (TCL E.10.17, OL14.)

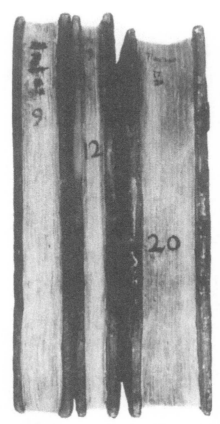

22  Running numbers written on the fore-edges of Trinity College Library books
in the seventeenth century. The small upper numbers are earlier than the large
numbers lower down, which were the numbers allotted in the reclassification of
the 1660s. (TCL E.10.14; I.17.5; K.17.15.)

traces of tab-stubs pasted one on top of another in some volumes indicate
several amendments, and suggest that tabs may have been used in parallel
with fore-edge numbering during the mid-century.

   Running numbers indicate only the positions of the books on the
shelves, not which shelves and which cases they belong to. Although
Trinity's books were certainly known in the seventeenth century by
class-marks which gave the case and shelf to which each volume belonged,[1] there is no indication that class or shelf numbers were marked

[1] The alphabetical finding lists of *1640* gave class, side, and shelf; the class lists of *1645, 1667,*
   and *1675* gave class, shelf, and running number.

23 Here the running number of a book written in the 1660s on the fore-edge is supplemented by the same number written on a paper tab pasted to the inside of the upper cover. Writing on the fore-edge was then given up, and tabs alone were used from the 1670s to the 1690s. (TCL M.1.25.)

anywhere in or on the books themselves. How a displaced book – one returned, say, by a borrower – was assigned to its proper place in the library is another unsolved puzzle. In the early days the donor's mark (see below) would have indicated the area from which a book came, but this would not have helped after the books were reclassified according to subject, and there must have been some other method of placing the books, possibly one connected with the borrowing system.

The most usual donors' marks for New Library books during the first half of the seventeenth century were the arms or initials of the donor stamped on both covers of the books he gave (fig. 20). At the same time inscriptions might be written on the title-pages (as they had been on the title-pages of Skeffington's books in 1593 (fig. 11); and from 1607 printed donors' labels were occasionally used, stuck at first on the title-page and later inside the upper cover (fig. 24).[1] Another way of distinguishing the books (though it was not consistently applied) was to colour the trimmed edges of the books differently for each benefaction, which showed as blocks of colour in the rows of exposed fore-edges. Later in the century donors' marks were usually confined to inscriptions on title-pages and printed labels stuck inside the covers.

As to objects in the New Library other than books – 'the Mapps, Globes ore other ornaments' referred to in Stanhope's will of 1603 – the pair of great Mercator globes given to the College by John Dee in 1548 would have been thoroughly out of date by the early seventeenth century.[2] New terrestrial and celestial globes were bought in 1628 with £40 bequeathed for the purpose by Sir John Doddridge, who was not a Trinity man but was a judge who had enjoyed the hospitality of the College while on circuit;[3] these were probably the pair of globes by 'Janssonius' – that is Willem Janszoon Blaeu of Amsterdam – which were still in the Library in the early eighteenth century but which have since disappeared.[4] Another terrestrial globe of unknown make was given to the College by John

---

[1] Initials were used from about 1605 when the Old Library books were rebound. The earliest use of arms appears to have been on the covers of Whitgift's manuscripts, received in 1604, but probably executed for Whitgift rather than the College. A printed label, dated 1607, was stuck on the title-pages of Kenelm Jenour's books (which also had 'K I' stamped on the covers).

[2] See p. 33 above.

[3] *Memoriale*, p. 113, which refers to the nights passed by Doddridge 'sub hac ipsâ Bibliothecâ' in the Judge's Room at the north end of the Master's Lodge.

[4] Blaeu was selling his globes at Amsterdam until his death in 1638. The pair of globes by 'Janssonius' is included in an 'Inventory of all the Rarities &c besides Books in Trinity Colledge Library' (undated but c.1700) in Add. MS a.106, ff. 218–19.

TOMVS
PRIMVS OMNI-
VM OPERVM RE-
VERENDI DOMINI MAR-
TINI LVTHERI DOCTORIS THEO-
logiæ, Continens scripta primi Triennij, ab eo tempo-
re, quo primùm controuersia de Indulgentijs mota
est, videlicet ab anno Christi M. D. XVII.
vsq; ad annum XX.

CATALOGVM AVTEM SINGVLARVM PARTIVM
inuenies post Præfationem Philippi Melanthonis. Ac conti-
net hic primus Tomus, non solùm multas enarrationes &
Disputationes, Euangelij doctrinam illustrantes, sed etiam
historica pleraq, Epistolas Imperatoris Maximiliani, Leo-
nis x. Ro. Pontificis, Ducis Saxoniæ Electoris Friderici, Car-
dinalis Caietani, & aliorum Principum, Quas si conferet
Lector, intelliget varijs modis Ro. Pontificem conatum esse
opprimere emergentem Euangelij lucem. Et agnoscet im-
mensam bonitatem Dei, qui voluit instaurare &
colligere sibi Ecclesiam, & depulsis tenebris
rursus veram & salutarem doctri-
nam monstrare.

VVITEBERGAE
Typis Zachariæ Lehmani
M. D. LXXXII.

Ex dono KENELMI IENOVR de Dunmow Magna
in Comitatu Essex. 1607.

24 A printed label pasted on the title-page records the donation of a book by
Kenelm Jenour in 1607. (TCL I.16.57; reduced.)

Fortho, probably in the period 1616–33.[1] There is no record, however, that the Library acquired either mathematical instruments or museum curiosities during the first half of the seventeenth century.

[1] *Memoriale*, p. 81. Fortho's globe may have been bequeathed with his books in 1633, but it is perhaps just as likely that he gave it to the College on vacating his Fellowship in 1616.

# CHAPTER 14

# ADMINISTRATION AND REORGANISATION, 1641–74

Substantial changes in the organisation of the College Library took place during the Librarianship of Thomas Griffith, 1641–74. Griffith (or Mutton, as he was probably called when he matriculated in 1633[1]) was elected Librarian at an especially troubled time in the history of the College. By 1645 the Master (Comber) and forty-seven Fellows of Trinity had been ejected on account of their royalist activities or for refusing the Covenant, and only one of the governing body of eight Seniors remained in office.[2] Not surprisingly Griffith, who appears to have been a royalist,[3] came close to losing the Librarianship. Perhaps he thought it prudent to withdraw from Cambridge while the troubles were at their height, for in the winter of 1645 the key of the Library was held, not by the Librarian, but successively by Thomas Archer MA and John Davies BA.[4] Then the following summer it was agreed by the new Master (Hill) and Seniors that 'M^r Griffith be wholy remooved from y^e Library keepers place for: his long neglect thereof: etc.';[5] and a fortnight later it was further agreed that Thomas Holloway BA 'should be elected into y^e Library keepers place'.[6]

All ended well for Griffith, however. Holloway the substitute received the Librarian's stipend for the year 1646 only, after which Griffith was reinstated, the orders which had deprived him and appointed Holloway being erased from the Conclusion book. This was fortunate for the Library; far from neglecting his work, Griffith proved to be a notably diligent College officer; and he also received several payments in addition to his

---

[1] Sinker, *Librarians*, pp. 12–13, 17–18. Mutton's signature also appears in TC Mun., *Admissions and admonitions*, p. 262 (admissions of Scholars, 3 May 1633).

[2] Mullinger, iii, pp. 308–12.

[3] Royal letters were issued in 1666 to enable Griffith to be appointed College Registrary as well as Librarian (Sinker, *Librarians*, pp. 16–17).

[4] 'Agreed then by the Master & present seniority that Mr Archer be required to deliver up the key of the Library for sir Davies, & that he shall have the wages for the present wch is due quarterly to the Library keeper' (TC Mun., *Conclusion book A*, p. 179).

[5] TC Mun., *Conclusion book B*, p. 187.     [6] TC Mun., *Conclusion book B*, p. 187.

stipend on account of special work done for the College.[1] Griffith acted as a Tutor for eleven years from 1646, and he was appointed 'Register', or College scribe, in 1666.[2]

During the 1640s books continued to come into the Library at a rate which increased its contents by an average of about 25 volumes a year.[3] The more books there were, the more difficult it must have been for the Library staff to make them available to the Fellows since they were neither arranged in order of subjects nor fully catalogued. Clutterbooke, Griffith's predecessor, had made an important start on cataloguing by writing out an alphabetical author-index to the collection in about 1640 (fig. 25); but this index, although it was far better than nothing, was limited in usefulness both by the brevity of its entries and by the fact that it listed only the first items in volumes which contained several tracts.[4] There was as yet no classified index.

A scheme for classifying the Library by subjects was drawn up in the period 1645–8.[5] The surviving copy of the scheme is not in Griffith's hand, and it may have been written out by Thomas Pockley BA who was given a gratuity of £5 in 1649 for having done 'something wch is usefull in the Library'[6] (fig. 26). It is incomplete, Classes 12–16 and 22–6 being omitted, so that a total of only 1,669 volumes are classified out of a probable total in 1645–8 of 2,300–2,400 volumes; and it was probably not actually carried out.[7]

The intention was to begin with the manuscripts already in Classes 1 and 2, and then to go round the room in numerical order of classes – that is, anticlockwise – following a traditional order of subjects which will be discussed in a moment. After Class 11, however, there is a break in the sequence, Classes 12–16 being missed out; and if, as seems likely, these classes contained the law books which are otherwise unaccounted for, the omission was probably deliberate, for the law books were not included in

---

[1] Griffith received £10 in 1649, reason not stated (TC Mun., *Conclusion book B*, p. 13); £13.6s.8d. in 1657 for writing out 'a Copie of the Founders originall grant' (loc. cit., p. 362); £8.4s.4½d. in 1662, reason not stated (loc. cit., p. 70); and £10 in 1666 'for his Charges & paines extraordinary in yᵉ Library upon yᵉ firing of it' (loc. cit., p. 99).

[2] 'Mr Griffith' was a Tutor from 1646 to 1657; this was presumably Thomas Griffith the Librarian for, although there was a George Griffith who became a Fellow in 1646, he left the College in 1649 (Sinker, *Librarians*, p. 15; *TC Admissions 1546–1700*, p. vii; Innes, p. 33). Griffith, who was a notable calligrapher, was appointed 'Registrarius' in 1666 (TC Mun., *Conclusion book B*, p. 103, and p. 107 n. 3 above); the total emoluments of this post were approximately equal to the stipend of the Librarian.

[3] Though only 32 of them were recorded as gifts.

[4] See Appendix B, *1640*.

[5] See Appendix B, *1645*.                        [6] TC Mun., *Conclusion book B*, p. 19.

[7] See p. 111. The reason for supposing that the *1645* scheme was not carried out is that its running numbers were not written on the fore-edges of the volumes concerned.

| | | |
|---|---|---|
| Mayro in Sententias | 2ʃ. 2. 3. |
| Matthiolus in Dioscoriden | 9. 0. 0. |
| Medina de Penitentia | 2ʃ. 1. 2. |
| Idnia paranesis | 2ʃ. 1. 2. |
| Melanchton — bo͡l. 4 | 4. 2. 1 |
| Melanchtoni Loci Communes | 19. 1. 1. |
| Enochij — bo͡l 3ˢ | 16. 0. 1. |
| Mercatoris Chronologia | 2ʃ. 2. 3. |
| Mercatoris Cosmographia | 1. 2. 1 |
| Mercati — bo͡l — 2ᵒ | 5. 2. 2. |
| Merceri — bo͡l. 2ᵒ | 3. 2. 2. |
| Meterani Historia Belgica | 17. 0. 1. |
| Meterani Histori Belgica | 8. 0. 0. |
| Meursij — bo͡l. 10. | 2ʃ. 2. 2. |
| Mŝfai Dictionarium | 2. 0. 2. |
| Mŝfai Dictionarium | 12. 0. 0. |
| Missale Romanum | 9. 0. 1. |

25  An extract from the alphabetical finding list of c.1640, probably written by the Librarian William Clutterbooke. Entries give authors and short titles only, while the figures on the right give the numbers of the case, the side of the case, and the shelf respectively. (TC Add. MS a.103; reduced; see Appendix B.)

any of the seventeenth-century Trinity catalogues after 1640. The scheme then continues with Classes 17–21; but the last five Classes (22–6), which apparently contained the rest of the manuscripts and some miscellaneous printed books, are omitted from the surviving copy. The scheme shows that the classes were numbered and shelved in the same way as they had been in 1640, except that Classes 7, 8, 17, and 18 are entered as six-shelf, not two-shelf, cases.

The practice of classifying large institutional libraries by subjects was already a very old one. By about the year 1200 the library of Corbie Abbey near Amiens was arranged in the order: Church Fathers; commentators; Church history; Church councils; canon law; grammar; and poetry:[1] an arrangement of theology followed by the liberal arts that continued to be typical of large monastic libraries.[2] An alternative, 'academic', arrange-

[1] Delisle, L., *Recherches sur l'ancienne bibliothèque de Corbie*, Paris 1860, pp. 49–61. Bibles were not catalogued, but would presumably have been placed first.
[2] For instance, in England, the library of Dover Priory; its classification of 1389 is printed in *The Library*, viii, 1927–8, p. 81.

*Classis 10. 2. fide*

Medici

1 Vesalij Anatomia
2 Horatij Eugenij epia
   & consultationes
3 Idem de Febribus
4 Solenandri Concil: Med:
5 Scholzij Concil: Med:
6 Foresti observationes
7 vol. 2.
8 Herculis Saxonici Praxis
9 Montani opa
10 Mercati opa vol. 1.
11 vol. 2.
12 Vitalis de furno
13 Swicksii tabulæ
14 Paræi chirurg:
15 The French Chirurg:
16 Senerti opa vol. 1
17 vol: 2
18 vol. 3
19 vol. 4
20 vol. 4

26 An extract from the draft class catalogue of c.1645–8, possibly written by Thomas Pockley BA; it gives author and short title entries for the 'Medici' in Class 10, Side 2. (BL MS Sloane 78, f. 148 (reproduced by courtesy of the Trustees of the British Museum); reduced; see Appendix B, and Appendix H, S15 ff.)

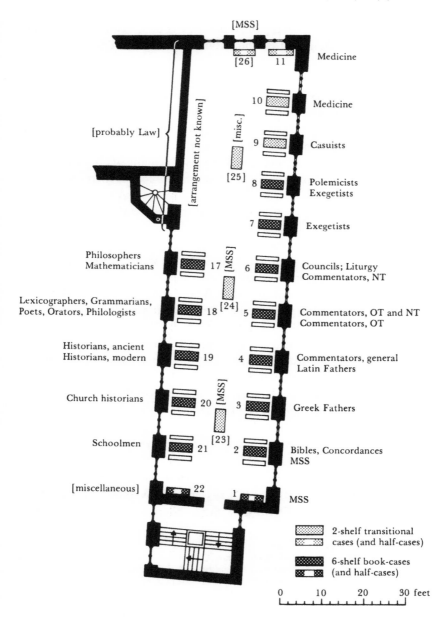

5 *Proposed classification of the New Library by subjects, 1645–8; and possible arrangement of the cases*

ment was that of the Sorbonne, which by the late thirteenth century had classified its substantial library the other way round, beginning with the subjects of the trivium and the quadrivium, and placing theology after them.[1]

Although both the monastic and the academic schemes of classification were used in a few Oxford and Cambridge libraries before the Reformation,[2] most of the collections were too small to need the aid of a traditional arrangement for the books, and private schemes were common. When these libraries began to expand in the later sixteenth century, however, many of them adopted the traditional monastic scheme of classification of theology followed by the liberal arts, a natural choice for their users, who were primarily concerned with the study of divinity. A typical case was that of King's College, Cambridge. In the mid-fifteenth century the 175 volumes of the Library were arranged in the order (which was peculiar to King's): philosophy; theology; medicine; astrology and mathematics; canon law; poetry; and grammar.[3] The Library was almost entirely dispersed in the mid-sixteenth century, but when it was built up again the monastic classification was introduced. A note attached to the catalogue of 1612, which appears to precede the arrangement actually adopted, proposes the order: Bibles; Greek and Latin Fathers; Church councils; modern theologians; controversialists; Schoolmen; mathematics; medicine; and law.[4] The same note adds an interesting 'Ratio Dispositionis' which explains that the theological books concern the soul; that the medical books concern the body; and that the law books concern worldly goods; hence the order of their arrangement in the Library.

It appears that classification by subjects was begun at Trinity College Library in the sixteenth century, a version of the monastic scheme being used in the Old Library. The shelf order of the OL books[5] when they were moved over to the New Library in about 1604 shows clear traces of this traditional arrangement: Bibles (OL2–5) are followed by Church Fathers (OL8–27), Schoolmen (OL36–45), and modern – chiefly Protestant –

---

[1] Franklin, A., Les anciennes bibliothèques de Paris, i, Paris 1867, pp. 227–9, 304–11.

[2] Of two fifteenth-century lists of the contents of Cambridge University Library, the first (c. 1424) is an inventory of 122 volumes in 'monastic' order; the second (1473) is a shelf-list of 330 volumes in 'academic' order (CAS Com., ii, 1864, pp. 239–76).

[3] James, M. R., A descriptive catalogue of the manuscripts in the Library of King's College, Cambridge, Cambridge 1895, pp. 72–83.

[4] King's College MS Lib. 1, f. 4. The 'monastic' scheme of classification actually used at King's according to the shelf-list of 1612 was an expansion of the scheme shown in this note.

[5] That is, the order of the OL list in the Memoriale, confirmed by the running numbers written on the fore-edges of the volumes themselves.

commentators (OL29–32, 49–65); with a mixture of philosophers, his-torians, poets, orators, and lexicographers towards the end (OL73–4, 86 onwards). But, although most of the OL books were arranged in the New Library in subject order, many were out of place, and it cannot be sup-posed that the collection was newly classified when it was moved in; therefore it must have been classified well before the move, the anomalies resulting presumably from the subsequent insertion of additional books where there happened to be space for them. The books would then have been transferred to the New Library without rearrangement, the shelf-lists in the *Memoriale* being taken from copies of the case-end 'catalogues' in the Old Library.

From 1604 to 1640, as we have seen, new accessions were kept in donor order. For the proposed subject classification of 1645–8 a monastic scheme was drawn up, omitting law, and with the Schoolmen placed oddly at the end. There is no evidence that this scheme was carried out, although running numbers on the fore-edges of some of the books which cannot be matched with any surviving catalogue suggest that reclassification of some sort may have been attempted at about this time.[1] Finally in the 1660s Griffith reclassified all the printed books according to a monastic scheme basically similar to that proposed in the 1640s, but with the Schoolmen placed near the end of theology, and with the order of philosophy, humanities, and history reversed; law was again omitted, and the manu-scripts stayed where they were in order of donation (p. 114). The New Library remained in this order until 1695; and the same scheme was used again as the basic classification of the Wren Library.[2]

In Griffith's scheme the cases for printed books (which had by now all been converted from the two-shelf to the six-shelf form) were designated with roman capital letters from A to Q in place of the old arabic figures, and the six shelves of each unit were given the lower-case Greek letters from alpha to zeta.[3] The books in their new locations had running num-bers written in large figures near the middle of the fore-edge,[4] but there was still apparently no indication in the books themselves of their class or

[1] These unidentified running numbers are written in small figures near the OL running numbers at the top of the fore-edge. They were written after the OL numbers and before the reclassification of the 1660s; but they are not the numbers proposed in 1645–8.

[2] The original classification of the Wren Library was the New Library scheme of the 1660s, with law at the end and gaps left for additions (see Add. MS a.109). Despite later reclassification, traces of Griffith's scheme may still be seen in the Library today.

[3] This system of class marking was introduced at Cambridge University Library when the Lambeth Library was received in 1649.

[4] See p. 101 n. 1.

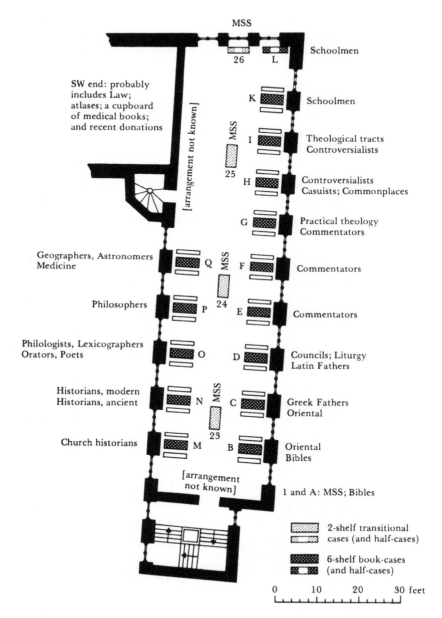

MSS

Schoolmen

26   L

SW end: probably
includes Law;
atlases; a cupboard
of medical books;
and recent donations

[arrangement not known]

MSS

K   Schoolmen

I   Theological tracts
Controversialists

25

H   Controversialists
Casuists; Commonplaces

G   Practical theology
Commentators

Geographers, Astronomers
Medicine

Q   MSS   F   Commentators

24

Philosophers   P   E   Commentators

Philologists, Lexicographers
Orators, Poets

O   D   Councils; Liturgy
Latin Fathers

Historians, modern
Historians, ancient

N   MSS   C   Greek Fathers
Oriental

23

Church historians   M   B   Oriental
Bibles

[arrangement
not known]

1 and A: MSS; Bibles

2-shelf transitional
cases (and half-cases)

6-shelf book-cases
(and half-cases)

0   10   20   30 feet

6 *Classification of the New Library by subjects, 1667–95; and possible arrangement of the
cases*

shelf letters. The manuscript cases 1 and 23 to 26 seem not to have been altered, and they retained their old designations.

It seems likely that the sequence ran from east to west on the north side (classes B to L), then returned to the east end to run from M to Q which would have been half-way along the south side. The manuscript cases 23–6 may not have been moved; but it is hard even to guess at the arrangement of cases 1 and A, which may both have been in the north-east corner, or of the law books, atlases, and recent accessions which were probably housed in the south-west end of the Library in furniture which included a cupboard and cases lettered R, S, and T.[1]

Griffith's reclassification was accompanied by a new catalogue of all but the law books, which Griffith wrote out himself in his fine scribal hand (fig. 27).[2] The new catalogue, which is dated 1667, is still an entirely inadequate guide to the College's manuscripts, which are neither well described nor indexed (fig. 29); but the part which deals with the printed books is some improvement on Clutterbooke's finding list of 1640. Where necessary Griffith has supplied short titles as well as authors, and there is an alphabetical index of authors. The entries rarely include place or date of publication, and they seldom list more than the first tracts of volumes which contained several items, but at the time 1667 probably seemed an adequate guide to what was still a pretty small collection of books.

The troubled years of the mid-century also saw a marked reduction in the flow of books into the Library. The College had received over 250 printed volumes as gifts in the 1630s, but only 32 volumes were recorded as gifts in the 1640s, and – apart from the gift of £100 bequeathed for the purchase of books in 1653 by Robert Metcalfe, Fellow – fewer still in the 1650s.[3] That there was nevertheless a serious need for more library books is indicated by a College order of 29 October 1658 in which it was

[1] The evidence for the placing of the classes in my plans of the New Library is slight and ambiguous. The manuscript classes 1 and A were apparently on the right at the east (entrance) end of the room, and I have supposed that the classes from 2(B) ran westward along the north wall to class 11(L), which was a half-case. The numerical scheme may then have continued anticlockwise round the room, but it seems more likely that in the 1660s the five six-shelf cases M to Q ran westwards along the south wall from the east end (an arrangement to be paralleled later in the Wren Library), leaving room for classes R, S, and T to be added in the south-west corner. (For the placing of 1 and A, see John Laughton's catalogue of MSS in 1675 and in Bernard, E., *Catalogi librorum manuscriptorum*, Oxford 1697, p. 93. Laughton also said that the manuscript classes 23–6 were 'in parte bibliothecae australi', which is obscure, since the Library did not really have a 'southern part'; my suggestion that they were placed in the central aisle of the Library is no more than a guess.)

[2] See Appendix B, *1667*.

[3] Metcalfe bequeathed the money for the purchase of theological books; the *Memoriale* (p.124) records the gift but does not list the books bought.

*Medici &c.*

α.

1  Mercati Opa vol. 1
2  _____ vol. 2
3  Foresti Opa vol. 1
4  _____ vol. 2
5.6  Augenij Opa vol. 1. 2.
7  Scholzij Concilia Medic.
8  Herculis Saxonici Pantheon.
9  Montanus
10  Vitalis de Furno.
11  Gorræi Definicões Medic.
12  Veccheci Tabula
13  Reyneri ........ Consil. Medic.
14  Ardoynus de Venenis.
15  Parkinson's Herbal vol. 1
16  ── vol. 2 Flowers.
17  Remberts Herbal, Dodonæus
18  Icones Stirpium.
19  Loniceri nralis hist.

27 An extract from the indexed class catalogue of 1667–c.1675, written by the Librarian Thomas Griffith. The entries (which are in a different order from the one proposed in the draft scheme of 1645) give authors and short titles, and occasionally dates, but are scarcely more informative than those of the *Memoriale* (see fig. 10). (TCL Add. MS a.101, p. 61; reduced; see Appendix B.)

Q. 2. medici.

1. Lud. Mercati opera. ┐
2. vol. 2. ─ ─ ─ ─ ┘ Francof. 1608.
3. Petri Foresti opera. ┐
4. vol. 2. ─ ─ ─ ─ ┘ Francof. 1619.
5. Horatij Augenij epistolæ, & consultationes
   medicinaliy. Franc. 1597.
6. ─ Idem de febribus, & ratione curandi; p
   sanguinis missionem.
7. Laurentij Scholtzij consilia medicinalia.
   Hanoviæ 1610.
8. Herculis Saxoniæ pantheum medicinæ,
   & tractatus de pulsibus.
9. Johan. Bapt. Montanus. Francof. 1587.
10. Vitalis de Furno. Moguntiæ 1531.
11. Jo: Gorræi definitiones medicæ. Par. 1564.
12. Jacobi Weckeri medicinæ syntaxis. Bas. 1576.
13. Reineri Solenandri consilia medicinalia.
    Francof. 1596.
14. Ardoynus de veneniy. Bas. 1562.
15. J. Parkinson's herbal. Lond. 1640.
16.
17. Rembert Dodoens herbal translated by H. Lyte.
    1619.
18. Mat. de l'Obel ─ icones stirpium ex officina
    Plantiniana.
19. Adami Loniceri naturalis historia. Fran. 1559.

28 An extract from the indexed class catalogue of c.1675–95, written by the Librarian James Manfeild. Entries, which give not only authors (with first names) and short titles but also dates and usually places of printing, are a great improvement on those of 1667 (see fig. 27). (TCL Add. MS a.104. Q.γ; enlarged; see Appendix B.)

*M. S.*

A

&

1   Dionysius de sacris Nominibus

2   Figura Bibliorum.

3   Gesta rerum Angliæ Gallicè,

4   Heraclides de vitâ sctoꝝ Patꝝ

5   Dionysij Hierarchia

6   Petrus de Eliacho

7   Beda in Eptas Canonicas

8   Malmsb. de gestis Pontific Angliæ

9   Augustin' de Moribus Ecclia

10  Hieronymus de hebræis Quæstiõibꝫ

11  Exposiõ Decal. & Oraõis Dõicæ

29 An extract from the shelf-list of manuscripts written by Griffith in *1667* (see fig. 27). The inadequacy of these inventory entries, which derive from the donations lists in the *Memoriale*, is apparent when they are compared with Laughton's catalogue of the same books in *1675* (see fig. 30, p. 136). (TCL Add. MS a.101, p. 11; reduced; see Appendix B.)

concluded that each Fellow should 'bee desired' to give the College Library a book of his own choice worth twenty shillings or more, a priced register of such donations to be kept in the Library.[1] It appears from the surviving donations lists that this order was not put into effect for another four years, when a further Conclusion dated 27 August 1662 read:

Agreed by yᵉ Master & Seniors that they for themselves will each of them give a Booke to yᵉ College-Library, & doe expect that every one for yᵉ present in actuall

[1] TC Mun., *Conclusion book B*, p. 356.

Fellowships shall doe yᵉ like, as also every one who shall hereafter be admitted Major Socius, & that yᵉ Booke or Bookes by each person so given shall not be of lesse value than twenty-shillings.[1]

This time a new register book for the Fellows' gifts was written out by the Librarian, beginning with the roll of the Master and Fellows as they were in 1663, the names of new Fellows being added later as they were elected; it was later known as the *Benefactions book*, and it was to remain in use until the mid 1680s, largely superseding the *Memoriale*.[2]

The *Benefactions book* eventually contained entries for 150 donors or potential donors of printed books in the period 1662–c.1685, mostly Fellows but including 25 benefactors who were not Fellows.[3] Many of the Fellows listed, 52 out of the 125, including three of the Seniors who were responsible for the Conclusion of 1662,[4] appear not to have given books to the Library. Of the 98 Fellows and others who did give printed books, 83 gave from 1 to 10 volumes; 7 gave from 11 to 20 volumes; and 8 gave over 20 volumes.[5] The Conclusion of 1662, unlike that of 1658, did not say that the choice of these books should be left to the donors, and it may be that in some cases Fellows gave money for the purchase of books rather than the books themselves. The values of the gifts were not entered in the *Benefactions book*.

The total number of printed volumes given to the Library between 1641 and about 1685 was, according to the *Memoriale* and the *Benefactions book*, about 995; but the actual number is likely to have been greater than this. Added to the 1,819 printed volumes listed in the catalogue of 1640, the 995 volumes of recorded donations give a total of only 2,814 volumes; but it appears from the catalogue of 1675 and other lists that the actual stock of the Library in about 1685 was around 3,450 printed volumes.[6] Thus it

---

[1] TC Mun., *Conclusion book B*, p. 66.

[2] *Ben*, now bound in Trinity Add. MS a.106.

[3] Donors of items other than printed books (manuscripts, curiosities, etc.) are omitted from these figures. The 25 donors who were not Fellows included two Masters, two Librarians, a Chaplain, and a variety of other members and well-wishers of the College.

[4] Cheyney Rowe, Herbert Thorndike, and Nathaniel Willis.

[5] The donors of more than 20 volumes were John Pearson (Master 1662–73), c.34 vols, *Ben*, p. 5; George Chamberlain (Fellow 1627–1701), 102 vols; *Memoriale*, p. 131, *Ben*, p. 11; Abraham Cowley (Fellow 1640–67), 40 vols, *Ben*, p. 16; George Seignior (Fellow 1664–79), 73 vols, *Ben*, pp. 24–5, 36, 44; Isaac Barrow (Fellow 1649–72, Master 1672–7), c.65 vols, *Ben*, pp. 33–4, 45; Charles Fraser (Fellow 1673–83), 31 vols, *Ben*, p. 37; Edmund Vintner (Fellow of King's) c.77 vols, *Ben*, pp. 49–50; and Thomas Whincop (Fellow 1618–21), 23 vols, *Ben*, pp. 57, 59.

[6] By 1685 the number of printed books listed in *1675* had reached about 2,820, to which must be added about 630 volumes of bound pamphlets and law books which were not entered in *1675* (see pp. 127–8, and Appendix B).

appears that during these years, 1641–85, the College acquired some 650 printed volumes that were not accounted for in the donations books. Entries in the College accounts (described at the end of this section) suggest that an average of 8–9 volumes a year were bought for the Library during this period, which would account for 350–400 of them. No doubt the rest were given but not recorded. One such unrecorded gift was a collection of 126 medical and other books bequeathed to the College by John Nidd, Fellow, in 1659.[1]

The College did not normally keep duplicate copies of its library books until the eighteenth century, counting as duplicates not only extra copies of the same edition of a work, but also extra copies of any edition of the same work. In the sixteenth century, when the capacity of the College Library is likely to have been limited to a few hundred volumes, and when it would still have been a common practice to discard old library books when new ones were acquired,[2] duplication would have been out of the question; and duplicates continued to be rejected in the New Library. Although some donors gave the College only such of their books as were not already in the College Library, others gave their books without this provision, so that duplicates were occasionally received. When this happened the less desirable copy of the pair was put aside and sold.[3] If the two copies were of different editions the later one was kept; otherwise the Library would keep the copy that was in better condition.[4]

Although the College had owned pairs of globes since very early days,[5] the Library was not used as a general repository for scientific instruments and museum objects until the later seventeenth century. Then, however, a growing interest in coins, curiosities, and instruments was reflected in a variety of gifts made from the 1660s onwards; which, for the want of specialist museums in either the College or the University, were placed in the New Library. The first recorded gift of objects other than books or

---

[1] See p. 131 n. 1.      [2] See pp. 4 ff.

[3] TC Mun., JB accounts, 1648–9, Chamber rents: 'Rec⁴ for part of yᵉ Supernumery bookes in the Library', £12.14s.6d.

[4] See also Sir Edward Stanhope's will of 1603 (TC Mun., Box 31, no. 2, pp. 8–10). Having said that he bequeathed to the College only those books which it 'hath not alreadie belonginge to there Publike Librarie', Stanhope went on:

And yf there bee anie of my Bookes aboue set down which Trenitie Colledge in Cambridge alreadie hath, yf they desier to change anie of there Bookes with mine as beeinge of a later impression [i.e. edition] ore more fitly bounde for them My Will is that the saide Colledge may exchange all such Bookes with anie of mine which I shall die possessed of.

[5] See pp. 33, 104 above.

globes consisted of 'many old coins' given (along with the Trinity Apocalypse) by Anne Sadleir in 1660–9;[1] and this was followed by twelve more donations of objects made before the move to the Wren (see p. 122). They included two scientific instruments (Morland's speaking trumpet, and a quadrant); nine coins and medals; and a variety of curiosities, most of them wonderful rather than soberly instructive.[2] During the same period the Library also received its portrait of Bishop John Hacket; and the College bought a Castlemaine's globe made by Moxon. For the most part these objects were of little academic interest, and it was not until the eighteenth century that the College Library housed collections of instruments and specimens that were of value for research.[3]

The regulations which governed the use of the Library in the seventeenth century were based on provisions in the will of Sir Edward Stanhope, which came into effect in 1608. It was implicit in the will that Fellows, and Fellows only, might have free use of the Library;[4] and this central restriction was amplified in the only full set of Library regulations which have survived from the period of the New Library, and which were ordered by the Master and Seniors in February 1651.[5] Here it was laid down that Fellows of the College might work in the Library in their own right, and that Fellow-Commoners and MAs of the College might also work in it provided that each one was sponsored by a Fellow. But no BA or undergraduate of the College (unless he were a Fellow-Commoner), nor any stranger, might work in the Library or even enter it unless he was accompanied by a Fellow throughout, or unless he had been specially authorised to do so by the Master or Vice-Master.

With regard to borrowing books, Stanhope's will had stipulated that no book might be lent out of the Library to anyone except by written order of the Master or Vice-Master in each case, and then for not more than fourteen days.[6] This regulation was repeated in Conclusions of the Master

[1] 'Anna Sadler . . . Bibliothecam . . . Nummisque plurimis vetustis locupletavit' (*Memoriale*, p. 130).

[2] Most extraordinary were the seventeen curiosities given by William Mainstone of Woodberry Hall, twelve of which were objects of ethnological interest from the Far East, and the other five were zoological specimens (*Ben*, p. 53).

[3] Notably the astronomical instruments, including some given by Thomas Scattergood in the seventeenth century, which were brought into the Library in 1703; the coin cabinet which grew enormously during the eighteenth century; the Greek and Romano-British inscriptions presented in 1750 and 1766; and the ethnological collection deriving from Cook's voyages presented in the 1770s (see Gaskell and Robson, pp. 27–8).

[4] '[The charge of the Library Keeper shall be] to attend anie of the fellowes of the Colledge when they do either goe into the Librarie to Studie; or bringe in any stranger with them and to continue in the Librarie soe longe as anie doe stay in it' (TC Mun., Box 31, no. 2, p. 4).

[5] See Appendix I.        [6] TC Mun., Box 31, no. 2, p. 4.

## Accessions of objects other than books, 1548–1693

| Date | Donor | Description and reference | Location |
|------|-------|--------------------------|----------|
| 1548 | John Dee, Fellow 1546–8 | 2 Mercator globes; astronomer's staff and ring (p. 33 above) | unknown |
| ? 1616 | John Fortho, Fellow 1589–1616 | 1 terrestrial globe (*Memoriale*, p. 81) | unknown |
| 1628 | Sir John Doddridge, Judge | 2 Blaeu globes (*Memoriale*, p. 113) | unknown |
| 1660–9 | Anne Sadleir | Many old coins (*Memoriale*, p. 130) | unknown |
| 1674–9 | Thomas Boteler, Fellow 1664–92 | Sir S. Morland's speaking trumpet (*Ben*, p. 24) | Whipple Museum |
| ? 1680 | ? Henry Frere, Fellow 1640–51 | Oriental bracelets (Add. MS a.106, f.85a) | unknown |
| ? 1680 | John Laughton, Librarian 1679–83 | Part of an Egyptian mummy; a scarab (Add. MS a.106, f.85a) | unknown |
| ? 1680 | Sir Andrew Hacket | Portrait of Bishop John Hacket (*Ben* p. 44) | Wren Library |
| 1680 | Dudley North (bro. of the Master) | A magic cup, probably Yemeni; a Greek coin (*Ben*, p. 44) | cup in Fitzwilliam Museum |
| 1681 | bought | Castlemaine's globe, by Moxon 1679 (Add. MS a.106, f.88b) | Whipple Museum |
| 1681 | Thomas Turner of Essex | A brazen quadrant (*Ben*, p. 52) | unknown |
| 1681–8 | Henry Firebrace, Fellow 1674–1709 | 5 medals (*Ben*, p. 39) | 4 in Fitzwilliam Museum* |
| 1682 | William Mainstone of Cambridgeshire | 17 assorted curiosities, mostly Oriental (*Ben*, p. 53) | 1 in TCL† |
| 1688 | Daniel Skinner, Fellow 1674–85 | 1 medal (*Ben*, p. 54) | unknown |
| 1688 | 'M—' | 'A petrified Figg' (*Ben*, p. 54) | unknown |
| by 1690 | Benjamin Pulleyn, Fellow 1656–90 | 1 medal (*Ben*, p. 20) | unknown |
| 1693 | Hon. Robert Montague, Nobleman 1684 | 1 medal (*Ben*, p. 54) | Fitzwilliam Museum‡ |

* Hawkins, E., *Medallic illustrations of British history*, ed. Franks and Grueber, London 1885, p. 605 no. 5; p. 608 no. 12; p. 489 no. 111; p. 630 no. 51.
† 'An excrescency upon the head of a Deer' (*Ben*, p. 53).
‡ Hawkins, E., op. cit., p. 662 no. 25.

and Seniors of August 1646 and February 1660,[1] but the fuller Library regulations of 1651 allowed Fellows to take books out of the Library in their own right for forty-eight hours on filling in and signing the borrowers' register.

Besides laying down borrowing rules, the orders of 1646, 1651, and 1660 all demanded the return of books that were absent from the Library, which indicates that a good deal of illegal borrowing took place in spite of the regulations and of the fines that were supposed to enforce them.[2] Indeed the Master and Seniors were so concerned about the problem in 1660 that they threatened to chain the books, and chains were actually bought for the purpose;[3] in the event, however, the book-cases were not adapted for chaining and the scheme was dropped.

It will be remembered that the surviving accounts of the Senior and Junior Bursars do not include a complete record of Library expenditure in the sixteenth and seventeenth centuries.[4] There are sporadic entries in the building and extraordinary accounts for Library repairs and equipment, and regular entries for payments to a cleaner in the 1580s and 1590s, and to Stanhope's Librarian and Sub-Librarian after 1608; but a good deal of expenditure which certainly took place – for books, binding, stationery, etc. – is simply not accounted for. In 1647–8, however, and for five years afterwards, an account for 'Chamber Rent' was drafted in the Junior Bursar's book after the Auditor's certificate, from which it appears that a

---

[1] TC Mun., *Conclusion book A*, p. 188 (3 August 1646); ibid., p. 261 (24 February and 1 March 1659–60).

[2] 1646: 'That the Librarie-Keeper shall not deliver forth any Booke out of the Librarie, till those be returned which are allready in the hands of the Fellowes or others in the Colledge' (TC Mun., *Conclusion book A*, p. 188).
 1651: 'That every person belonging to this Colledge who hath now in his Custodye any booke or bookes formerly borrowed or taken out of $y^e$ Library shall forth with send in the same . . .' (TC MS 0.11a.2$^{51}$).
 1660: 'Ordered that all the Librarie bookes w$^{ch}$ are now out of the Librarie bee brought in within foureteene dayes, and that the Librarie keepers shall not presume to take or lend out any booke without such licence as is aboue mentioned [i.e. the written order of the Master or Vice-Master]' (TC Mun., *Conclusion book A*, p. 261).
 The fines are specified in the Library regulations of 1651 (see Appendix I).

[3] 'Ordered that the bookes in the Librarie bee chained, & that M$^r$ Blackfall's Legacie of fiftie pounds bee that way employed. this to bee done in case it bee not found that the Charge of doing it will bee too great, or some greater inconvenience appeare then is yet discovered' (TC Mun., *Conclusion book A*, p. 261, 24 February 1659–60).
 'Pd Richard Wakeman for chaines by order', £8.18s.0d. (TC Mun., JB accounts, Library, 1659–60).

[4] See pp. 25–6, 27. For the period 1601–95 the accounts to Michaelmas in the following years are missing: *Senior Bursar*: 1603, 1605, 1607, 1611, 1613, 1617, 1619, 1620, 1622 to 1636 inclusive, 1638, 1639, 1641, 1649; *Junior Bursar*: 1602, 1603, 1604, 1605, 1607, 1608, 1609, 1610, 1611, 1612, 1614, 1616, 1617, 1618, 1619, 1622 to 1643 inclusive, 1645, 1661, 1662, 1663. For the accounts missing in the period 1547–1600, see p. 25 n. 3.

variety of Library expenditure was paid for out of undergraduates' room rents, which were paid to the Junior Bursar by the Tutors but were not entered in his main account. We cannot be sure, but it is possible that undergraduates' room rents had always been used to finance ordinary expenditure on the College Library.[1]

The room rent accounts for the six years from 1647–8 to 1652–3 show an expenditure for the Library totalling £75.16s.5d., of which £29.5s.6d. was for books. The other items were: furnishings and maintenance, £18.0s.0d.; binding and stationery, £6.2s.2d.; an inspection supper, £3.12s.5d.; and for unspecified purposes, £18.16s.4d.

There were then two other groups of Library accounts in the Junior Bursars' books of the later seventeenth century, both entered in the audited parts of the accounts. These were, first, brief Library accounts for the four years 1656–7 to 1659–60 totalling £54.8s.0d., of which £38.16s.0d. was for books, the remainder being for binding, stationery and maintenance. Secondly, charges for Library books and a few other items were made against a small part of the Bishop's Hostel room rents for the five years from 1681–2 to 1685–6; they totalled £44.14s.10d., of which £41.17s.10d. was for books.[2]

These three groups of Library accounts referred chiefly to the purchase of books, other items being in a minority in the second and third groups. Of the total of £174.19s.3d. which they record as Library expenditure during the whole fifteen years, £109.19s.4d. (63 per cent) was spent on books. This gives an average of about 8–9 volumes bought per annum; although the books were not actually acquired at an average rate, but by means of occasional large purchases with a trickle of books in between. Thus £20 was spent on law books in 1648–9;[3] £26 on books bought by William Lynnet 'by order of a meetinge' in 1659–60;[4] and £20 on a set of Calvin's works and some other books in 1681–2. These three large purchases made up 60 per cent of all the books bought during the fifteen years.

[1] See pp. 25–6, 76 n. 4.
[2] The Bishop's Hostel room rents, which totalled £50 per annum, were received from 1671–2, but only a fraction of the income was used for ordinary Library expenditure in the seventeenth century. From 1679–80 the greater part of it was credited to the Wren Library building account.
[3] 'Paid Mr Winne for ye Civill law bookes', £20 (Chamber Rent account 1648–9); this may have been Richard Whynn, a Trinity man who became a Barrister in 1639 (Venn, iv, p. 483).
    Compare the Conclusion of 11 January 1648 'that ther shall be twenty pounds issued out of the bursars office to buy books into the Library in consideration of the Chamber rent swallowed up in the Colledge accounts till audit 1647 scil. Those 3 Chambers wch formerly the Master challenged, one in the Ostle, the 2 other in the Queenes Tower' (TC Mun., Conclusion Book B, p. 7).
[4] No Conclusion to this effect was recorded.

Expenditure on furniture and maintenance recorded both in the Library accounts and elsewhere in the Junior Bursars' books was mostly for new or altered book-cases (or 'seats' as they were called in the accounts). Two new cases were bought in 1647–8; cases were raised, and shelves and desks removed, in 1648–9; and further new cases were bought in 1654–5, 1655–6, and 1658–9.[1] Other items of Library equipment were occasionally referred to: the fixing of wooden crests,[2] the renewal of the matting on the floor,[3] the provision of a 'Booke-Wheele',[4] and repairs to a weather glass.[5]

There were regular payments for binding and stationery made to local stationers.[6] The cost of an inspection supper was also charged from time to time, sometimes at rates that considerably exceeded the ten shillings allowed in Stanhope's will for the entertainment of the College officers who had the duty of making an annual check of the contents of the Library.[7]

[1] Chamber Rent account 1647–8; Carpenters' and Chamber Rent accounts, 1648–9; Extraordinaries, 1654–5, 1655–6, and 1658–9. Each case cost from £6 to £9.

[2] 'To Woodruf the Joyner for gluing & nayling cresses in the Library', 1s. These may have been donors' arms, anticipating the Grinling Gibbons carvings in the Wren Library. (Carpenters' account, 1620–1.)

[3] Following a Conclusion of 5 October 1663 (*Conclusion book B*, p. 79), 392 yards of new matting were bought and laid in 1663–4 (Extraordinaries).

[4] 'paid M$^r$ Henson for y$^e$ Booke-Wheele in the Library', £2.10s. (Chamber Rent account, 1651–2). A book-wheel was a revolving desk similar to those later fitted in the Wren Library (see Clark, J. W., *The care of books*, Cambridge 1901, pp. 294–5, 304–8).

[5] 'For mending the Weather Glass in the Lybrary', 3s. (Extraordinaries, 1672–3).

[6] For instance in the Chamber Rent account for 1648–9 there are entries for books bought from Richard Ireland, bookseller at Cambridge 1634–52; for binding and stationery from William Graves, bookseller at Cambridge 1641–67; and for unspecified work done in the Library by 'Holden', who is probably the John Holden who bound books for the Library in 1657–8 and 1658–9, and who may be the John Holden who was freed of his stationers' apprenticeship in 1651 (McKenzie 4039).

[7] 18s. was paid for the supper in 1644 (Extraordinaries, 1643–4); £3.12s.5d. in 1652 (Chamber Rent account, 1651–2); 10s. 2d. in 1670 (Extraordinaries, 1669–70); and 12s. in 1671 (Extraordinaries, 1670–1). For the provisions of Stanhope's will, see Appendix D, p. 224.

# CHAPTER 15

# THE BOOK STOCK, 1667–95

The structure and development of the Library's book stock in the period
1667–95 can be followed in detail in the two indexed class catalogues of the
later seventeenth century (*1667* and *1675* in Appendix B). The earlier and
more abbreviated of these catalogues was copied out by Thomas Griffith
the Librarian in 1667, and was then added to until about 1675, when it was
superseded by a more detailed class catalogue written by James Manfeild,
Griffith's successor in the Librarianship. Manfeild's catalogue was added
to in turn until 1695, when the whole collection was transferred to the
Wren Library and the old class catalogues were replaced.

An analysis of the library books by classes shows both the general
characteristics of the collection and the tendency of its development in the
later seventeenth century. The following tables show that the Library still
had a preponderance of divinity books during the third quarter of the century, but that the proportion of books on subjects other than divinity was
steadily rising. It appears from the draft class catalogue of c.1645 that there
were then about 56 per cent of divinity books and 44 per cent of books on
other subjects;[1] but by 1667 there were only 52 per cent of divinity books
to 48 per cent of others; while by 1695 the percentage of divinity books
was down to 51, scarcely more than half the total book stock. The stock of
divinity books did continue to grow, increasing from 1667 to 1695 by 20
per cent, but it grew more slowly than the stock of humanities books,
which increased by 51 per cent during the same period, or the stock of
science books, with an increase of 44 per cent.

Each of the four major sections of the book stock – divinity, humanities,
science, and law – is now considered with a view to assessing its general

---

[1] This is assuming that the Würzburg law books (see p. 132 below) were in the Library by
1645; if they were not, the proportion would have been 61 per cent divinity and 39 per cent
others. (*1645* listed 1,033 volumes of divinity books and 438 volumes of books on other
subjects; but the law section was omitted, which probably consisted of 375 volumes
including the Würzburg books, or 215 volumes without them.)

| Class | | Volumes | |
|---|---|---|---|
| | | 1667 | 1695 |
| A | Atlases; miscellaneous | 19 | 23* |
| A,B | Bibles | 72 | 81 |
| B,C | Oriental | 125 | 142 |
| C | Greek Fathers | 94 | 110 |
| D | Latin Fathers | 73 | 78 |
| D | Church Councils | 34 | 141 |
| D | Liturgy, ritual | 33 | 35† |
| E,F,G | Commentators | 352 | 349 |
| G | Practical theology, sermons | 78 | 90 |
| H | Casuists | 19 | 30 |
| H | Commonplaces | 54 | 59 |
| H,I | Controversy | 198 | 255 |
| I,K | Theological tracts | 72 | 109 |
| K,L | Schoolmen | 168 | 184 |
| L | Cowley bequest‡ | 32 | 28 |
| M | Church history | 131 | 147 |
| N | Ancient history | 37 | 66 |
| N | Chronology | 28 | 36 |
| N | Modern history | 95 | 141§ |
| O | Historical collections | 23 | 24 |
| O | Greek and Roman orators | 23 | 38 |
| O | Greek and Roman poets | 15 | 39 |
| O | Philology | 70 | 133 |
| O,P | Lexicography | 42 | 45 |
| P | Ancient philosophy | 57 | 68 |
| P | Modern philosophy | 28 | 41 |
| P,Q | Natural philosophy, Medicine | 107 | 118 |
| P,Q | (in the press) Medicine | 92 | 93‖ |
| Q | Geography, Astronomy, Mathematics | 76 | 185¶ |
| R | Atlases; miscellaneous | – | 49 |
| Q,S | Bound pamphlets** | 253 | 258 |
| | Law†† | 375 | 375 |
| | Total | 2,875 | 3,570 |

*Notes*
* In *1675* listed in the index but not in the shelf-list.
† Includes one shelf from Class M of *1675*.
‡ Miscellaneous books bequeathed by Abraham Cowley in 1667.
§ Includes Byzantine history from Class O, and Modern history from Class T, of *1675*.
‖ In *1675* Nidd's small medical books in the press (or cupboard) were listed in the index but not in the shelf-list.
¶ Includes the Barrow mathematical books from Class G of *1675*.
** Figures from the draft lists in Add. MS a.101A, 105; not listed in *1667* or *1675*.
†† Uncatalogued; the Skeffington, Edward Stanhope, and Würzburg law books.

*The printed book stock from 1667 to 1695, by subject groups*

| | 1667 | | 1695 | | |
| --- | --- | --- | --- | --- | --- |
| | vols | % of stock | vols | % of stock | % increase 1667–95 |
| Divinity (classes from Bibles to Church history, excluding Cowley bequest) | 1,503 | 52 | 1,810 | 51 | 20 |
| Humanities (classes from Ancient history to Modern philosophy) | 418 | 14 | 631 | 18 | 51 |
| Law (uncatalogued; the Skeffington, E. Stanhope, and Würzburg law books) | 375 | 13 | 375 | 10 | 0 |
| Science (classes from Natural philosophy and medicine to Mathematics | 275 | 10 | 396 | 11 | 44 |
| Miscellaneous (Atlases, Cowley bequest, and bound pamphlets not in *1667* or *1675*) | 304 | 11 | 358 | 10 | 18 |
| Total | 2,875 | 100 | 3,570 | 100 | 24 |

quality, and to seeing whether it included particular authors and works of the period 1600–75 that proved to be especially influential.

The divinity section was wide-ranging in its scope, but was strongest in biblical commentators (backed up by a notable group of books in Hebrew and other Oriental languages), and in works of doctrinal controversy. Coverage of the more important seventeenth-century works of theology, however, was patchy. The College bought the works of William Perkins in 1613, and those of Francisco de Suarez in 1625;[1] and it may also have bought its copies of Richard Baxter's *Saint's everlasting rest* (in the 1654 edition), of William Chillingworth's *Religion of Protestants* (in the 1674 edition), and of Cornelius Jansen's *Augustinus* (in the 1652 edition).[2] Donations supplied John Selden's *De jure naturali* (1640), and the works of Henry More (1675–9).[3] On the other hand the College did not buy or

[1] Perkins's works (2 vols, Cambridge 1609, now C.2.34, 34A) were bought with money bequeathed by Richard Wright in 1613; Suarez's works (13 vols, Mainz 1620, now F.17.8–) were bought with money bequeathed by Michael Stanhope in 1625.

[2] Baxter: G. $\zeta$.15 in *1667, 1675*, now absent. Chillingworth: H. $\zeta$.31 in *1675*, now absent. Jansen, I.$\beta$.4 in *1667, 1675*, now K.17.2, no donor's mark.

[3] Selden: O.$\delta$.2 in *1667*, O.$\zeta$.21 in *1675*, now *Grylls.32.105, given by Thomas Hill before 1667, probably alienated before being acquired by Grylls. More: I.$\delta$.40– in *1675*, now T.11.19–, given by John North in 1680.

otherwise acquire William Ames's *Medullae theologiae* (1627); anything by Jakob Boehme or Tommaso Campanella; Pierre Charron's *De la sagesse* (1601); Ralph Cudworth's *Intellectual system of the universe* (1678); the *De veritate religionis Christianae* (1622) of Hugo Grotius; any of the theological works of Marin Mersenne; Samuel Pufendorf's *De jure naturae et gentium* (1672); or Edward Stillingfleet's *Rational account of the grounds of the Protestant religion* (1664). Valuable sets added to this section after 1667 included two great collections of Church councils in 55 folio volumes.[1]

The humanities section of the Library consisted chiefly of history, classics, and philosophy.

The secular history books, which totalled 267 volumes in 1695, made an effective group. There were not only the Greek and Roman historians, but also a good selection of modern writers, including amongst the English historians Bacon, Camden, Holinshed, Raleigh, and Speed;[2] a number of modern European histories; and the Parisian Corpus of Byzantine history.[3] In addition to this the College owned 147 volumes of Church history, and 141 volumes of Church councils, including for example such important modern works as Sarpi on the Council of Trent.[4] There were a few gaps – the Library had not yet acquired Jean Bodin's *Methodus ad facilem historiarum cognitionem*, 1566, or Richard Hakluyt's *Divers voyages*, 1582, or Abraham Whelock's *Chronologia Saxonica*, 1643 – but altogether the history sections at the end of the seventeenth century were well-considered and comprehensive.

In classics some improvement was made to the Library's holdings of Latin literature and philology, which had been almost wholly neglected before 1625.[5] Even so it was not until 1676, with the accession of 21 volumes of variorum editions of Latin authors given by George Seignior that the College Library contained, for instance, the works of Caesar, Horace, Ovid, or Sallust;[6] Seignior also gave a collection of the writings

---

[1] *Conciliorum generalium et provincialium collectio regia* (37 vols, Paris 1644, now M.4.1–) given by George Chamberlain 1673–7; *Sacrosancta concilia ad regiam editonem*, ed. P. Labbe and G. Cossart (18 vols, Paris 1671–2, now M.17.1–) given by George Seignior in 1675 (*Ben*, p. 36).

[2] Bacon, F., *The history of the reign of K. Henry VII*, London 1622, given by Elwes 1626–30, now VI.6.134; Camden, W., *Britannia*, London 1607, now VI.3.79; Holinshed, R., *Chronicles*, London 1577, = OL129; Raleigh, W., *The history of the world*, London 1614, N.β.18–19 in *1667*, now absent; Speed, J., *The history of Great Britain*, London 1611, N.ε.22 in *1667*, now absent.

[3] Fifteen volumes of *Corpus Byzantinae historiae*, Paris 1648–; O.η.1–5 in *1675*, now absent.

[4] Sarpi, P. (Paolo, Servita), *Historia del Concilio Tridentino*, London 1619; D.ε.11 in *1667*, now absent.

[5] See Appendix A and p. 88.

[6] These editions were mostly octavo Elzeviers of late 1650s and early 1660s; they are listed at O.ε.14–34 in *1675*, and identified in the index.

and editions of Johannes Meursius in 39 volumes.[1] However these substantial gifts were not matched by any systematic attempt by the College to acquire other major seventeenth-century editions of the Latin classics, such as those of Johann Friedrich Gronovius or Nicolas Heinsius. The small collection of Greek authors which was in the Library at the end of the sixteenth century was not much improved in the seventeenth, though it seems that the College bought a copy of Stanley's Aeschylus in the edition of 1664.[2] The College also appears to have bought the *Germania, Italia*, and *Sicilia antiqua* of Philippus Cluverius (1616–24), Janus Gruterus's *Inscriptiones antiquae* (1602), and the variorum Tacitus and Velleius Paterculus with Lipsius's commentary (1608).[3] Coverage was again patchy, however, for amongst the more important works of classical scholarship that appeared between 1600 and 1675 but which were not acquired for the College Library were (for instance) John Selden's *De dis Syris* (1617), Ezechiel Spanheim's *De praestantia et usu numismatum antiquorum* (1664), Orazio Torsellino's *De particulis Latinae orationis* (1602), and the *De praecipuis Graecae dictionis idiotismis* of Franciscus Vigerus (1627).

Ancient philosophy was by this time well covered, but modern philosophy was not. Up to 1695 there was nothing in the Library by Cumberland, James Harington, Leibniz, Malebranche, Pascal, or Spinoza, though major works by all of them were available by 1675.[4] Herbert of Cherbury's *De veritate* (1645 edition) came as a donation, as did the Latin translation of Hobbes's philosophical works in 1677.[5] It was also in 1677 that the College bought Barrow's copies of Descartes' *Principia philosophiae* and *Meditationes de prima philosophia*;[6] but the Library had no copy of the *Discours de la méthode*.

We have already looked in detail at the science sections of the Library as they were in 1645.[7] The only important additions made to them during the

---

[1] Listed at O.δ.1–39 of *1675*, and identified in the index.

[2] O.γ.23 in *1667* (added) and *1675*; now II.3.28.

[3] The three items by Cluverius, and the Gruterus, were bought in 1625 from Michael Stanhope's bequest; the *Sicilia* and the *Germania antiqua* are respectively U.5.18 and 19 (the *Italia antiqua* has been exchanged for another copy); the Gruterus is now W.18.11.

[4] Neither was there anything in the Library by Locke, but this is understandable since his major works were published in 1690 and afterwards.

[5] Herbert's *De veritate* (P.δ.22, 21 in *1667, 1675*, now T.9.88) was given by Thomas Hill before 1667. Hobbes's *Opera philosophica latine*, 2 vols, Amsterdam 1668 (P.δ.34–5 in *1675*, now T.51.26–7) was given by William Perry in 1677.

[6] *Principia philosophiae*, Amsterdam 1644, and *Meditationes de prima philosophia*, 3rd ed., Amsterdam 1654, 1656. These two books, both now absent, were bought together with Descartes' *De homine* (Leyden 1662, now S.3.44) and *Lettres de M' Descartes* (2 vols, Paris 1663, 1659, now T.36.23–4) from Barrow's estate in 1677 (*Ben*, p. 45).

[7] See pp. 89–90, and Appendix H.

next fifty years came as gifts, the most substantial of which were a fine collection of over a hundred medical books bequeathed by John Nidd, Fellow, in 1659,[1] and about sixty mathematical books given by Isaac Barrow, Fellow and Master, in the 1670s.[2] There were also a few gifts of individual science books, including Hooke's *Micrographia* given by Thomas Gale in 1665, and Newton's *Principia* given by the author in 1687.[3] Scarcely any science books were bought by the College during the later seventeenth century, however, and there were some remarkable gaps in the collection. It was still the case in 1695 that the Library did not contain (amongst the 'Mathematici') Gilbert's *De magnete* (1600), Galileo's *Sidereus nuncius* (1610), his *Dialogo* (1632), or his *Discorsi* (1638),[4] Napier's *Logarithms* (1614), or Kepler's *Harmonices mundi* (1619); or (amongst the 'Medici') anything by Boyle, anything by Ray,[5] or Borelli's *De motu animalium* (1680–1); and, although there was a copy of Harvey's *De motu cordis* (1628), it had been acquired in 1660–74 as one of a volume of tracts, and it was not catalogued.[6] There was not even a set of *The philosophical transactions of the Royal Society*, which had started publication in 1665, but which was not taken for the College Library until after the move to the Wren.[7]

The law section of the Library was not included in the *1667* or *1675*

[1] Nidd's probate inventory (CUA) lists about 300 volumes, of which 126 were left to Trinity (92 of them being placed in the 'press' near Q, and later in class 25); most of the rest of Nidd's books were bequeathed to his friend and contemporary William Lynnet (Fellow 1647–1700) who in turn bequeathed them to Trinity.

[2] Barrow (Fellow 1649–72, Master 1672–7), gave about 35 books before he became Master and a further 25 afterwards; and about 10 more were bought from his library after his death in 1677 (*Ben*, pp. 19, 33–4, 45; *1667*, pp. 35, 64). A catalogue of the 1,099 volumes left by Barrow is now Bodleian MS Rawl. D.878, ff. 39–59; it is worth remembering that these books were in the Master's Lodge at Trinity in the 1670s.

[3] Now Q.10.39 and Adv.b.1.5 respectively. Newton also gave Nehemiah Grew's *Musaeum Regalis Societatis*, 1681, now Q.11.67.

[4] While Newton is believed to have read Galileo's *Dialogo* while working towards his *Principia* – though neither Barrow nor Newton owned a copy at the time of their deaths – he seems not to have known Galileo's *Discorsi*. The College Library never owned either book in Newton's time; would the course of his work have been affected if it had? (See Cohen, J. B., 'Newton's attribution of the first two laws of motion to Galileo', *Atti del simposio su Galileo*, Florence 1964, pp. xxiii–xlii; and Harrison, J. R., *The library of Sir Isaac Newton*, Cambridge 1978.)

[5] Ray, who was a Fellow from 1649 until he was ejected in 1662 for refusing the religious tests, gave the College five volumes of John Ogilby's topographical folios in 1673 (*Ben*, p. 32, and inscriptions in U.6.29–32), but he did not give any of his own works of systematic biology.

[6] It was in a volume of a series of mainly religious tracts (see p. 133) which, with some of the tracts removed, is now S.10.111.

[7] Vols i–xix (1665–97) of the TCL set of *The philosophical transactions of the Royal Society* originally belonged to Thomas Kirke (see *DNB*), who matriculated pensioner of Trinity in 1668, was elected FRS in 1693, and died in 1706.

catalogues, but it appears from *1640* and from the first Wren catalogue of c. 1700 that during the second half of the century it consisted of about 375 volumes in three groups. There were, first, Thomas Skeffington's law books given in 1592, originally 55 volumes but reduced by 1640 to about 40 volumes, some of them having been replaced or otherwise alienated.[1] Next there were 175 volumes of law books received in 1608 with the rest of Sir Edward Stanhope's bequest.[2] The third group of about 160 volumes of law books was not catalogued in *1640* (as were the Skeffington and Stanhope law books), but was first recorded in the Wren Library catalogue of c.1700;[3] nevertheless there is some likelihood that these books, which had once belonged to the sixteenth-century Prince-Bishop Echter of Würzburg, were in the Library by 1650. Bishop Echter's library was still in Würzburg castle when it was sacked by the Swedish army of Gustavus Adolphus in 1631. Most of the books were eventually sent to Sweden, but before this happened a consignment of Würzburg books reached England, and appear to have been sold in Cambridge in 1632–3; and it seems likely that the Würzburg books that were in Trinity College by 1700 formed the major part of this consignment.[4] There is no record of how the College came by these books, which are splendid folios bound in the 1580s in roll-stamped pigskin with coloured armorial stamps on the covers and gilt lettering on the fore-edges. Perhaps it is most likely that the College bought a good many of them in 1632–5, a period for which no bursars' accounts survive; and that it bought the rest in 1649, when £20 was spent on civil law books[5] (a sum that was too small to pay for all the Würzburg books – which were on canon as well as on civil law – but which cannot otherwise be accounted for).

Why, finally, were the Skeffington and Stanhope law books not recatalogued, and why were the Würzburg law books allowed to remain uncatalogued, in *1667* and *1675*? We cannot be sure, but a possible explanation is that these great collections and digests of canon and of Roman civil law, mostly printed in Italy, France, and Germany during the second half

---

[1] See pp. 42, 44 and Appendix A.
[2] See p. 88; they filled classes 13–16 in *1640*.
[3] Add. MS a.109, in class '2'.
[4] Fechner, J. U., 'English holdings from the library of Julius Echter von Mespelbrunn, Prince-Bishop of Würzburg', Cambridge University M.Litt. b.312 (1975). Fechner identified 163 Würzburg books at Trinity, which he describes in detail on pp. 264–344 of his dissertation; another Würzburg book, not described by Fechner, is now VI.15.65. At least three, and probably four, of these books came into the Library after the move to the Wren.
[5] TC Mun., JB accounts 1648–9, Allowances for chamber rent and Library, 6 July 1649: 'Paid M$^r$ Winne for y$^e$ Civill law bookes', £20.

of the sixteenth century, were of so little interest to the Fellows of Trinity a hundred years later that the Librarians who made the catalogues could not be bothered to include them.

The final miscellaneous section of the Library consisted, first, of atlases and other large books which, with a handful of recent donations, were placed in Classes A and R; and secondly of a great collection of some 3,000 pamphlets bound in 253 volumes which were kept in Classes Q and S. These pamphlets, though they ranged in date from the beginning of the sixteenth century to 1660, were mostly of the 1640s and 1650s, and they were in two series: 175 volumes of mainly Civil War tracts, and 78 volumes of mainly religious tracts.[1] The two series appear to have been the private collections of two individuals who wrote press marks and lists of contents – but not unfortunately their names – on the front paste-downs of each bound volume. There is no indication of how these two collections came to the Library, but they must have arrived – possibly together – after 1660, the date of the last pamphlets included in them, and before 1674, when a note about a missing volume was entered in the shelf-list.[2] These pamphlets were not catalogued in *1667* or *1675*, but there was a separate chronological index to the more important items.[3]

To sum up: the book stock of the College Library developed in a more haphazard way during the second half of the seventeenth century than it had done during the first. From the 1650s to the 1680s the College solicited small gifts of books from the Fellows, and it also received a few larger gifts of books;[4] but it did not solicit – or at any rate it did not receive – large gifts of money for the purchase of Library books such as those which had enabled it to plan the development of the Library up the the 1640s. Neither, it appears, did the College spend enough of its own money on Library books to make up for the lack of donated funds. As a result the book stock in the later seventeenth century lacked a variety of important – in some cases central – texts; lacunae which must have been apparent to at least some of the Fellows.

---

[1] A shelf-list for both series, which gave the title of the first tract in each volume, was written out by Griffith at the end of Add. MS a.101A, the Civil War series preceding the religious series. By the time they were listed in the Wren catalogue of c. 1700 there remained 238 volumes containing about 2,900 pamphlets in classes Z.7–8 (religious) and Z.14–17 (Civil War). Some of the volumes from the religious series, in smooth calf, are now in class I; and some of those from the Civil War series, in rough calf, are in class Y.

[2] Add. MS a.101A, f. 31.     [3] Add. MS a.105.     [4] See p. 119 n. 5.

# CHAPTER 16

# THE LAST YEARS OF THE NEW LIBRARY

Thomas Griffith died in his late fifties in March 1674, and was succeeded as Librarian by James Manfeild, a Scholar and MA of the College then aged about twenty-six.[1] Five years later, in 1679, Manfeild exchanged the Librarianship for a College Chaplaincy held by John Laughton; then in 1684 he was elected University Librarian; and he remained both College Chaplain and University Librarian until his death in 1686.[2] In about 1675, when he was Librarian of Trinity, Manfeild made an efficient new class catalogue of the printed books (*1675*) (fig. 28). This was a considerable improvement on Griffith's catalogue of 1667, for it included more accurate headings, the individual cataloguing of multi-item volumes, and the addition of places and dates of publication. It was also during Manfeild's Librarianship that the College decided to build the Wren Library, a matter to which we shall return.

John Laughton, Manfeild's successor as College Librarian, was a Scholar and MA of the College who had been appointed College Chaplain in 1678 and who then gave up his Chaplaincy in favour of the Librarianship in 1679, when he was aged thirty.[3] Four years after that he exchanged offices with Thomas Rotherham, another of the Chaplains, Rotherham becoming Librarian and Laughton taking Rotherham's Chaplaincy. Finally Laughton was elected University Librarian in 1686 in succession to Manfeild, holding both the Chaplaincy and the University Librarianship until his death in 1712. Laughton's major work at Trinity Library was to make a new and greatly improved catalogue of the manuscripts, which he copied out at the end of Manfeild's class catalogue (*1675*), and which was

---

[1] Sinker, *Librarians*, pp. 18–19.
[2] The date of Manfeild's death from CUA, VCC administration and inventories, 1685–6.
[3] Sinker, *Librarians*, pp. 19–25. Uffenbach, writing in 1710, said that Laughton's name was pronounced '*Laffton*' (Mayor, J. E. B., *Cambridge under Queen Anne*, Cambridge 1911, p. 140); but the alternative spelling 'Lawton' was commonly used in contemporary documents such as the TC JB accounts, and Uffenbach may have been mistaken.

later printed in Bernard's manuscript catalogue of 1697 (fig. 30).[1] Laughton went on to become a well-known classical scholar as well as a diligent University Librarian; and he made Trinity a substantial gift of books in 1700–12.[2]

Thomas Rotherham, the Chaplain who took over the College Librarianship from Laughton in 1683 was at about forty-six the oldest man ever to be appointed Librarian of Trinity; and, although he was an MA of the College, he had never been a Scholar, so that his appointment was in breach of Stanhope's regulations for the Librarianship.[3] The catalogues now being in a satisfactory condition, there is little remaining evidence of Rotherham's tenure of the Librarianship, but it was during the last of his thirteen years in office, in 1694–5, that the Wren Library was sufficiently near completion for it to be brought into use, and for the New Library – now to be known in its turn as the Old Library – to be emptied of books. Having overseen the move, Rotherham exchanged the Librarianship for a Chaplaincy with James Banks in January 1696; and he died at the age of sixty-six in 1702.

It appears that the idea of building what became the Wren Library originated in dissatisfaction with the existing library building. Concern about the structural condition of the Great Court Library may have been felt in the winter of 1665 when, between Michaelmas and Christmas, the roof caught fire and was extensively damaged.[4] Fortunately the books were unharmed, but there was considerable disruption, and the episode probably prompted the College to look critically at the library building. Then in 1670 John Hacket, Bishop of Lichfield, bequeathed £1,200 for the

---

[1] Bernard, E., *Catalogi librorum manuscriptorum*, Oxford 1697, pp. 93–101.

[2] TC Mun., JB accounts, New Library account, 1700–1, records the payment of 4s. for the 'Portridge for M[r] Laughtons Books to y[e] Library'; this probably refers to the bulk of Laughton's donation to the Library. *Don*, pp. 234–318, lists 1,625 printed volumes given by Laughton, but a few of them bear dates after 1700. Laughton also gave TCL some antiquities (Add. MS a.106, f.85[a]), and about 10 MS volumes (*Ben*, p. 53; Add. MS a.106, f.54[b]; James, i. p. xxii, and ii, p. xxvi). It is clear however from contemporary accounts that he still possessed notable collections of manuscripts and coins in the period 1700–12 (Mayor, J. E. B., *Cambridge under Queen Anne*, Cambridge 1911, pp. 117, 194).

[3] Sinker, *Librarians*, pp. 25–8. This Thomas Rotherham was descended from the brother of Archbishop Thomas Rotherham, the fifteenth-century benefactor of Cambridge University Library.

[4] TC Mun., JB, SB, and Steward's accounts, 1665–6, 1666–7; cf. Willis and Clarke, ii, p. 531. The bills of glaziers, plumbers, carpenters and joiners, and bricklayers for repairing the Library roof after the fire totalled £54.6s.8d. of which the largest item was the plumbers' bill for £37.14s.3d. 'for lead, soader & worke over the Library'. It is not clear how much damage was done to the plaster vault, but windows were broken, and books were removed. A gratuity of £10 was given to the Librarian, and tips totalling £2.4s.6d. were given to others, for helping to cope with the fire and for reorganising the Library afterwards.

1 (1) Dionysius de Hierarchia
(2 Homiliæ Gregorij super extremam
partem Ezechielis
(3 Liber de Xtianâ disciplinâ secundum Augustinum

2   Figura Bibliorum cum varijs Tabb: in
Augustinum Isiodorum &c

3   Historiæ rerum Angliæ a Bruto ad annum
1356 Gallicè. In finie quædam sunt de
pestilantiâ & carmina. In eodem volumine
continentur res gestæ Edwardi III per
Robertum de Avesbury.

4   Heraclides de vitis SS. PP: ad Lausum
Præpositum Palatij

5   Dionysius Areopagita quem Joannes
Eriugena transtulit de Græco in Latinum
jubente ac postulante Rege Carolo Ludovici
Imp: filio

6 (1 Richardi Ullerston Oxoniensis A D. 1408
tractatus qui intitulatur petitiones quoad
Reformationem Ecclesiæ militantis
(2 Ejusdem tractatus de Officio militari.
(3 Petrus de Eliaco de Ecclesiastica Potestate
(4 Egidius Romanus de peccato Originali.
(5 Tractatus de Adoratione Imaginum.

30 An extract from the shelf-list of manuscripts entered in the class catalogue of
c.1675–95 by the Librarian John Laughton. This first attempt to make a descriptive
catalogue rather than an abbreviated inventory of Trinity's manuscripts was
printed in Bernard's *Catalogi librorum manuscriptorum* of 1697. The six volumes
listed here, which were all given by Whitgift, are now B.2.28, B.2.29, R.5.32,
B.2.30, B.2.31, and B.15.23. (TCL Add. MS a.104, MSS p. 1; reduced; see
Appendix B.)

construction of a new residential block on the site of the Garret Hostel, which was to be called the Bishop's Hostel, and of which the rents – some £50 a year – were to be 'expended yearely upon the College library, either for bookes, or desques [book-cases], or for the fabrick and structure of the said library'.[1] Hacket's bequest, which if it had all been spent on books would have more than doubled the Library's average rate of accession,[2] was apparently the turning point. The Library in the Great Court, the College now believed, was scarcely strong enough to carry the books that were already in it, and it was certainly not strong enough to take any more. 'Whereas the present Library', Isaac Barrow wrote in the first appeal circular for the new Library (fig. 31),

notwithstanding much cost laid out in Supporting and Repairing it, is found too weak a Fabrick for the great weight of Frames and Books, already contained in it; so, that its failing for a time hath been feared, that fear growing with frequent accessions of New Books thereto: However, assuredly it cannot either for Strength or Capacity be fit to receive the Addition of Books intended by our Noble Benefactour [Bishop Hacket], (whose Intentions we resolve exactly to perform) and by other Donations constantly accruing to it.[3]

But this was not all: the College saw that it had the opportunity to complete Nevile's Court with a new library building of unprecedented nobility, and was eager to take it. The appeal circular continued:

We the Master and Fellows of the said College have entertained a design of Erecting a new Library in a place very convenient for use, and for the grace of the College, intending to inlarge the *New Court*, called *Nevile's Court*; and by adjoyning the Library, to make it up a fair Quadrangle: The accomplishment of which design,

---

[1] Hacket's letter to the College dated 11 August 1669 (TC MS R.17.6, f.1ᵃ). Hacket, who was a member but not a former Fellow of Trinity, and who left his own books to the University Library, specified in a codicil to his will dated 31 August 1669 that the rents of the Bishop's Hostel were to 'bee Yearelie Imployed to furnish the Publique Librarie of the said Colledge wᵗʰ Bookes at the Discrecion of the Master Vice-Master Senior Deane & Senior Bursar of the saide Colledge' (TC Mun., Wills and charters, pp. 206–7). The College believed nevertheless that he was content for the money to be spent on the 'fabrick and structure' of the Library as well as on Library books. (The Library referred to by Hacket was of course the Library in the Great Court, not the Wren Library.)

[2] The stock of the Library grew from about 325 volumes in 1600 to about 3,730 volumes (3,220 printed, 510 MS) in 1675, an average rate of accession of about 45 volumes a year. The Bishop's Hostel rents of £50 might have bought up to 75 volumes a year.

[3] Printed leaf catalogued as TC MS O.11.a.4ᵇ. The argument was reiterated in the second appeal circular dated 10 July 1677: 'The present *Library* of *Trinity College* in *Cambridge* is a Fabrick very weak, and although it hath been supported with great Charge, yet it continually gives suspicion of failing. So that it cannot possibly serve for the Ordinary Accession of Books, much less for that arising out of the Annual Revenue of the Hostle erected by Doctor *Hacket*, late Lord Bishop of *Lichfield* and *Coventry*; Nor indeed besides the Weakness, is the *Library* of Capacity to receive many more Books' (second printed leaf catalogued as MS O.11.a.4ᵇ).

Hereas the Right Reverend Father in God, D⁻ *John Hacket*, late Lord Bishop of *Lichfield* and *Coventrey*, out of his great kindneſs to *Trinity College* in *Cambridge* (of which Society he ſome time was a moſt worthy Member and Ornament) did inlarge the ſame with a fair Building, the Yearly Rents whereof, he did out of his great Wiſdom, Aſſign to be imployed in Buying Books for the Library of the ſaid College: And whereas the preſent Library, notwithſtanding much coſt laid out in Supporting and Repairing it, is found too weak a Fabrick for the great weight of Frames and Books, already contained in it; ſo, that its failing for a time hath been feared, that fear growing with frequent acceſſions of New Books thereto: However, aſſuredly it cannot either for Strength or Capacity be fit to receive the Addition of Books intended by our Noble Benefactour, (whoſe Intentions we reſolve exactly to perform) and by other Donations conſtantly accruing to it. We the Maſter and Fellows of the ſaid College have entertained a deſign of Erecting a new Library in a place very convenient for uſe, and for the grace of the College, intending to inlarge the *New Court*, called *Nevil's Court*; and by adjoyning the Library, to make it up a fair Quadrangle: The accompliſhment of which deſign, beſide the advantages from it to this Society, will as we conceive, yield much Ornament to the *Univerſity*, and ſome honour to the Nation. Wherefore, as we our ſelves have not been wanting by a free Contribution of Money, according to the Abilities of each one, to ſet it on foot; ſo we do earneſtly recommend the furtherance of it to all Generous Perſons, Favourers of Learning, and Friends to the *Univerſities*, eſpecially to thoſe, who have had any part of their Education in this College, Humbly requeſting and hoping from them, That now, upon ſo needful and worthy an occaſion, they will expreſs their Affections to Learning, and to this Royal Nurſery thereof: Whereby, as they will at preſent injoy the ſatisfaction of having in ſo noble a way benefited the Publick and Obliged Poſterity; ſo they ſhall certainly perpetuate their own Memory with Honour, by ſo conſpicuous and durable a Monument of their Benefaction. To which end, we promiſe that our moſt careful endeavour ſhall concur, in recording their Names with the beſt advantage, as in the Duty of Gratitude we are bound.

*Jan.* 3. 167¾.

ISAAC BARROW *Maſter.*

---

Maſter Tho. Boughey *Merchant*, *in* Token-houſe Yard, Lothbury, *is appointed, under the Common Seal of the College, to be the Receiver of all ſuch Sums of Money as ſhall be Paid, or Returned in or about* London.

31 The first appeal circular for building the Wren Library, dated January 1676. (TCL O.11a.4⁹; reduced.)

beside the advantages from it to this Society, will as we conceive, yield much Ornament to the *University*, and some honour to the Nation.[1]

The decision to build the Wren Library was made by January 1675, in which month James Duport, Dean of Peterborough, Master of Magdalene, and formerly Fellow of Trinity, signed his will in which he bequeathed 'to the new Library in Trin: Coll: one Hundred pounds And to the building of Saint Paules one Hundred pounds'.[2] In addition to this bequest, with its significant association of Wren's two masterpieces, Duport left to Trinity his private library at Magdalene which totalled 2,144 volumes and which was far too large to be fitted into the Great Court Library as it was then equipped.[3] The first appeal circular was dated 3 January 1676, and the main work of constructing the new Library went on until 1694–5.

In fact, as far as the size of the room was concerned, the Library in the Great Court was large enough to take many more books than the approximately 3,500 volumes which filled it in 1675. If, for instance, the six-shelf book-cases had been replaced with taller, twelve-shelf, cases, and if the number of cases had been increased from twenty to thirty (at intervals of 7ft 4in rather than of 11ft), the capacity of the Library would have been tripled to about 10,500 volumes. But there remained the practical argument that the Library in the Great Court was not strong enough to take any more books without structural failure, and the enthusiastic one that the College wanted to build a splendid new Library at the end of Nevile's Court. It is our good fortune that these arguments prevailed, and also that Wren was encouraged to build a Library that would accommodate, not 10,000 but 50,000 volumes.

Meanwhile the Library in the Great Court continued to function though with its intake of books considerably reduced. From 1675 to 1695 the Library acquired only about 250 volumes altogether, an average rate of accession that was little more than a quarter of the average rate from 1600 to 1675.[4] This was a deliberate policy, for rents which had been intended for the purchase of books were spent instead on building, while actual donations of books were kept out of the Library until the Wren was ready for them.

The cost of building the Bishop's Hostel, which was completed in 1671, exceeded the Bishop's bequest by £206.17s.6d. and, having consulted

---

[1] TC MS O.11.a.4⁹.     [2] PRO Prob. 11/360.     [3] See p. 141 below
[4] From 1600 to 1675 the average rate was about 45 volumes a year (see p. 137 n. 2 above); from 1675 to 1695 it was about 12 volumes a year (additions to *1675*).

Hacket's heir and taken legal advice, the College applied the first four-and-a-half years' rents to paying off the excess.[1] By the time the deficit was cleared it had been decided to build the Wren, whereupon the College applied the Bishop's Hostel rents to the costs of the new building. By 1700, when the Wren Library building accounts were closed, Bishop's Hostel rents totalling £1,440 had been spent as follows: £207 on building the Bishop's Hostel and £35 on maintaining it; £920 on building the Wren Library; and only £85 on books, etc., for the College Library.[2] The balance of just under £200 was credited to the Junior Bursar's account.

Gifts that paralleled Hacket's bequest were made soon afterwards by Thomas Sclater and Humfrey Babington. Sclater, a former Fellow who had been ejected in 1649–50 and who later became MP for the University and a Baronet, gave £800 in 1676 to pay for an extension of the north side of Nevile's Court that would join it to the north end of the Wren Library; and he stipulated that, any claim to the use of the rooms in the extension by a member of his family having first been met, they should be let and their rents be spent on Library books.[3] Humfrey Babington, another of the Fellows ejected in 1649–50, but one who was reinstated in 1660 and who was to become Vice-Master in 1690, agreed to pay for a similar extension of the south side of Nevile's Court in 1681, providing that he himself might occupy rooms in the extension during his lifetime and that, family claims having been met, the rents should be applied thereafter to the purchase of library books.[4] As with the Bishop's Hostel rents, the greater part of the income from the Sclater and Babington rooms during the seventeenth century was spent not on books but on building: of £617 received in rents from 1679 to 1700, £11 was spent on maintenance of the rooms, £109 was applied to the augmentation of Scholarships, £470 was transferred to the Wren Library building account, and the balance of £27 was credited to the Junior Bursar's account.[5]

Soon after his appointment to the Mastership of Trinity, in 1701, Bentley was to challenge the disposition of the Bishop's Hostel, Sclater and Babington rents, arguing that by spending them on building the Wren

[1] TC MS R. 17.6, f.3 ᵃ is a legal opinion dated 25 June 1672 to the effect that the College might properly use the Bishop's Hostel rents for meeting the deficit on the Hostel building account.

[2] Figures from TC Mun., JB accounts, 1671–2 to 1699–1700. Of the £85 spent on the College Library, £73 went for the purchase of books in the two years 1680–2. There is also a separate Bishop's Hostel rent account in TC MS R.17.6, ff. 4–5.

[3] TC Mun., Wills and charters, pp. 210 ff.

[4] TC Mun., Wills and charters, pp. 217 ff.

[5] TC Mun., JB accounts, 1678–9 to 1699–1700.

rather than on library books the College had been 'robbing the library'.[1] In fact it is not clear that the College was legally entitled to spend £1,390 of these rents on the cost of building the Wren, and it is even more doubtful that the credit balance of £220 should have been transferred to the Junior Bursar's account for general purposes. At all events, Bentley carried his point and forced the College to spend £360 from endowment income on library books.

It has already been mentioned that in 1674 James Duport, the Master of Magdalene, willed his private library at Magdalene to his old College.[2] Duport died in 1679 and Trinity duly received 2,144 volumes of his books, of which it kept 1,950 volumes after the disposal of duplicates.[3] There was no room in the College Library for this magnificent gift, which was much the largest donation of books that the College had ever received, and it appears to have been kept elsewhere until the Wren Library was ready to house it.[4]

Two more great gifts of books came to the College at the end of the seventeenth century. A collection of 3,359 volumes of printed books was given by Sir Henry Puckering (alias Newton) at some time between 1691, when his manuscripts were received into the College Library, and his death in 1701;[5] but, unlike his manuscripts, Puckering's printed books were not entered in the catalogue before the move to the Wren. The third of these large donations was of 1,625 printed volumes given by James Laughton, Chaplain of Trinity, University Librarian, and formerly Librarian of Trinity; most of them appear to have reached the College in 1700.[6]

The gifts of Duport, Puckering, and Laughton, which totalled almost

[1] Monk, J. H., *The life of Richard Bentley, D.D.*, 2nd ed., London 1833, i, pp. 163–4; and Monk's references.

[2] Duport, who was Dean of Peterborough as well as Master of Magdalene, left his library at Magdalene to Trinity; his library at Peterborough to Magdalene; and his library at Boxworth to two of his nephews (PRO Prob. 11/360).

[3] *Ben*, p. 7 gives the number bequeathed as 2,144; *Don*, pp. 332 ff., lists the 1,950 volumes that remained after the disposal of duplicates in 1679 (concerning which see TC Mun., *Conclusion book B*, p. 150; JB accounts 1679–80, Extraordinaries).

[4] The Junior Bursar had Duport's books moved in 1679–80, presumably to Trinity (TC Mun., JB accounts, 1679–80, Extraordinaries). An entry in Newton's commonplace book appears to show that he had access to a Duport book after it was received by the College but before it was catalogued in the Library, probably in the period 1679–95 (Harrison, J. R., *The library of Isaac Newton*, Cambridge 1978, p. 6).

[5] The 3,359 volumes given by Puckering are listed in *Don*, pp. 1 ff.; TC Add. MS a.107 is an earlier author-catalogue of the collection. Duplicates may have been disposed of before these lists were made.

[6] See p. 135 n. 2. Again, duplicates may have been disposed of.

7,000 volumes, tripled the Library's stock of printed books (3,220 volumes in 1675). No doubt they were prompted by the planning and execution of the great new Library in Nevile's Court; certainly they justified the vision of the College in building on so ample a scale.

The contents of the Library in the Great Court were eventually moved into the Wren during the academic year 1694–5, the books being shifted by the College Porters and the whole operation being overseen by the Librarian.[1] There they were arranged on the middle shelves of Wren Classes C to L and S to Y in approximately the same subject and shelf order as before.[2] The bound pamphlets were placed in Class Z, the law books in II, and the manuscripts were locked up at the south end in B and R. When the great donations made by Duport, Puckering, and Laughton were added to the Library in 1695–1701 they were not classified with the other books but were kept as separate collections in Wren Classes III, IV, and V (Duport), M, N, and O (Puckering), and A, C, VI, and VII (Laughton).[3] Thomas Rotherham was succeeded as Librarian early in 1696 by James Banks,[4] and it was Banks who, by about 1700, completed the first class catalogue of the Wren Library.[5]

The Library in the Great Court was converted forthwith into sets of rooms. About two-thirds of it, from the main staircase at the east end to the turret stair at the angle of the Master's Lodge, was turned into commodious apartments at the expense of the Duke of Somerset (a major contributor to the Wren Library building account), which were at first occupied by members of his family; this part of the room is now the site of C3 and A3 Great Court. The western third of the Library was converted into garret rooms over the north end of the Master's Lodge; later the

---

[1] TC Mun., JB accounts 1694–5, Extraordinaries: 'To the Porters for Removing the Books into the New Library', £3.6s.0d.; *Conclusion book B*, p. 192, 24 July 1696: 'Agreed then by y[e] M[r] & Seniours that ten pounds be given to M[r] Rotherham as a Gratuity for his trouble in removing the Books out of y[e] old Library into ye New'.

[2] The original Wren classification is established both by the shelf-lists written on the case-ends and by the first Wren class catalogue of c. 1700, now Add. MS a.109. Before 1747 the classes did not coincide with the bays (as they do now), but consisted of both sides of one projecting book-case plus the wall case to the right of it (Add. MS a.111, f.143).

[3] It is possible that the Duport bequest, and perhaps also Puckering's gift, were shelved in the north end of the Wren before the rest of the books were brought across from the Great Court.

It must have been the arrangement of the Duport, Puckering, and Laughton collections by donors which caused Uffenbach to complain in 1710 that the classification of Trinity Library was 'not at all good', being by benefactions rather than by subjects (Mayor, J. E. B., *Cambridge under Queen Anne*, Cambridge 1911, p. 126); in fact about a third of the stock was still arranged by subjects.

[4] Sinker, *Librarians*, pp. 28–9.

[5] Add. MS a.109.

ceilings of the first-floor rooms at this end of the Lodge were raised into what had been the west end of the Library, with what is now A1 Great Court above them.[1] None of the seventeenth-century Library furniture has survived, and there is no evidence that it was re-used elsewhere.

[1] There is no record of these conversions in the College accounts. What appears to be the earliest mention of them is quoted in Sinker, *Librarians*, p. 53.

# APPENDIXES

# A CATALOGUE OF THE COLLEGE LIBRARY IN 1600

The catalogue is based on the OL and TS lists in the *Memoriale*,[1] and it follows the order of the entries in those lists. Each catalogue entry consists of: (1) An OL or TS serial number, starred if the book appears to have reached the Library after 1600. (2) The original entry transcribed from the *Memoriale*, in italics. (3) Descriptions of each item, giving: heading (following Adams); short title; format; place, printer, date; Adams, Goff, or STC number. (4) Classification, from the mid-seventeenth-century class catalogues. (5) Present class mark; or, if the book is absent, what appears to have happened to it.

The catalogue is followed by a combined alphabetical index to the headings.

Degrees of probability in the catalogue entries are indicated as follows: doubtless (virtually certain, but formal proof is lacking); probably (highly likely); possibly (more likely than not).

OL1 *Athanasij opera graecè*
  ATHANASIUS, Abp of Alexandria, St
  Tractatus, *Greek*
  2°, paper manuscript; James 203

  Manuscripti (Patres Graeci)

  B.9.7; given by John Christopherson by 1558

OL2 *Biblia hebræa vatablj vol: 2*
  BIBLE, Latin
  Biblia utriusque testamenti, *annot.* F. Vatablus, *etc.*
  2 vols, 2°, [Geneva], R. Stephanus, 1557; Adams B1055

  Biblia

  A.13.33–34

[1] *Memoriale*, pp. 87–9, 98.

OL3   *Biblia Gallicè*
BIBLE, French
La saincte bible, *French*
2°, Antwerp, M. Lempereur, 1534; Adams B1127

Biblia

A.11.11

OL4   *Biblia Munsterj*
BIBLIA, O.T., polyglot
Hebraica biblia, latina planeque nova, *Hebrew and Latin, trs.* S. Münster
2°, Basle, M. Isingrinius and H. Petri, 1546; Adams B1241

Biblia

A.14.8

OL5   *Biblia Hieronymi Latinè*
(unidentified)

Biblia

(probably absent; apparently not allotted an OL running number, OL4 being '4' and OL6 being '5')

OL6   *Conciliorum vol: 3*
COUNCILS
Conciliorum omnium tom I(–III)
3 vols, 2°, Cologne, J. Quentel, 1551; Adams C2770

Concilia

M.2.1–3

OL7   *Conciliorum Canones*
COUNCILS
Canones conciliorum omnium
2°, Basle, J. Oporinus, 1553; Adams C2771

Concilia

M.2.4

OL8    *Theophilactus in Euang: græ.*
       THEOPHYLACTUS, Abp of Ochrida
       Ἑρμηνεία εἰς τὰ τέσσαρα Εὐαγγέλια, Greek
       2°, Rome, [A. Blado], 1542; Adams T594

       Patres Græci

       Y.19.1


OL9    *Oecumenius in Euang: lat:*
       OECUMENIUS, Bp of Tricca
       Commentaria in quatuor evangelia
       2°, Louvain, R. Rescius, 1543; Adams O119

       Patres Graeci

       E.3.19


OL10   *Cyrilli opera*
       CYRIL, Abp of Alexandria, St
       (doubtless Operum tomi quatuor
       2°, Basle, J. Hervagius, 1546; Adams C3168)

       Patres Graeci

       absent (probably sold as a duplicate, 1784)


OL11   *Augustini operum vol: 9*
       AUGUSTINE, Bp of Hippo, St
       Opera omnia
       10 vols in 9, 2°, Basle, Froben, 1528–9; Adams A2157

       Patres Latini

       K.18.17–25


OL12   *Gregorij Magni vol: 2*
       GREGORY I, Pope, the Great
       Opera omnia
       2 vols, 2°, Basle, H. Froben and N. Episcopius, 1551; Adams
       G1170

       Patres Latini

       E.10.60–61

OL13   *Epiphanius Latine*
EPIPHANIUS, Bp of Constantia
Contra octoaginta haereses
2°, Basle, R. Winter, 1545; Adams E253

Patres Latini

E.16.54


OL14   *Gastij Collectanea vol: 2*
AUGUSTINE, Bp of Hippo, St
Commentarii ex omnibus lucubrationibus passim, *ed.* J. Gast
2 vols, 2°, Basle, J. Hervagius, 1542; Adams A2186

Patres Latini

E.10.17–18


OL15   *Historia sacra multorum patrum*
(unidentified)

Historici ecclesiastici

(probably absent; apparently catalogued in 1675 as 'Historiæ sacræ, diversis autoribus'; cf. OL151, OL181)


OL16   *Antidotum contra hæreses*
SICHARDUS, Johannes
Antidotum contra haereses
2°, Basle, H. Petri, 1528; Adams S1065

Patres Graeci

Y.19.2


OL17   *Lactantij opera*
LACTANTIUS FIRMIANUS, Lucius Coelius
Opera omnia
2°, Basle, H. Petri, 1563; Adams L27

Patres Latini

E.16.15

OL18 *Philo Judæus*
PHILO, Judaeus
(doubtless In libros Mosis de mundi opificio, *etc.*, *Greek*
2°, Paris, A. Turnebus, 1552; Adams P1033)

Historici ecclesiastici

absent (probably alienated between 1675 and 1700)

OL19 *Jrenæi opera*
IRENAEUS, Bp of Lyons, St
Opus eruditissimum in 5 libros digestum
2°, Basle, H. Froben and N. Episcopius, 1548; Adams I153

Patres Graeci

E.16.6

OL20 *Basilius Latine*
BASIL, Abp of Caesarea, the Great, St
Omnia opera
2°, Basle, H. Froben and N. Episcopius, 1551, 1552; Adams B340

Patres Graeci

E.3.17

OL21 *Tertullianus*
TERTULLIANUS, Quintus Septimius Florens
(probably Scripta
2°, Basle, H. Froben and N. Episcopius, 1550; Adams T410)

Patres Latini

absent (probably alienated after 1800)

OL22 *Nazianzenus græce*
GREGORY, Patriarch of Constantinople, Nazianzus, St
(probably Ἅπαντα, τὰ μεχρὶ νῦν μὲν εὑρισκόμενα, *Greek*
2°, Basle, J. Hervagius, (1550); Adams G1133)

Patres Graeci

(possibly Adv.a.3.14, but if so the book was temporarily alienated from the Library during the second half of the seventeenth
century; more likely absent)

OL23    *Justinus Martyr græce*
        JUSTIN, Martyr, St

(23¹)   (possibly Opera omnia
        2°, Paris, J. Dupuys, 1554; Adams J495)

(23²)   (possibly [Works], *Greek*
        2°, Paris, R. Stephanus, 1551; Adams J494

        Patres Graeci

        (possibly E.16.12$^{1-2}$, but early marks lost in 18th–cent. rebinding)

OL24    *Hylarius*
        HILARY, Bp of Poitiers, St
        Lucubrationes quotquot extant
        2°, Basle, H. Froben and N. Episcopius, 1550; Adams H555

        Patres Latini

        E.16.22

OL25    *Dionysius Areo=pagita*
        DIONYSIUS, the Areopagite
        (probably Opera, *Latin*, edition unidentified; cf. Adams G524,
        G525)

        Patres Graeci

        absent

OL26    *Oecolam=padius*
        OECOLAMPADIUS, Joannes
        Commentarii omnes in libros prophetarum
        2°, (Geneva), J. Crispinus, 1553, 1558; Adams B1281

        Commentatores

        D.15.29

OL27    *Oecumenius græcè*
        OECUMENIUS, Bp of Tricca
        (doubtless Expositiones antiquae, *Greek*
        2°, Verona, S. Nicolini, 1532; Adams O111)

        Patres Graeci

        absent (probably alienated after 1800)

OL28   *Catalogus testium veritatis*
FLACIUS, Mathias, Illyricus
Catalogus testium veritatis
2°, Strassburg and Basle, J. Oporinus, 1562; Adams F553

Historici ecclesiastici

K.17.15


OL29   *Brentij Commentaria vol: 2 ('2' altered to '3')*
BRENZ, Johannes

(29$^1$)   In exodum
2°, Halle, P. Brubach, 1544; Adams B2763

(29$^2$)   In leviticum
2°, Frankfurt a. M., P. Brubach, 1542; Adams B2766

(29$^3$)   Job cum piis commentariis
2°, Halle, P. Frentzius, 1546; Adams B2779

(29$^4$)   In prophetam Amos
2°, Halle, P. Brubach, 1544; Adams B2785

(29$^5$)   In acta apostolica homiliae
2°, Frankfurt a. M., P. Brubach, 1541; Adams B2802

(29$^{6*}$)  In evangelii secundum Lucam homiliae
2°, Halle, P. Brubach, 1537; Adams B2788

Commentatores
I.12.18$^{1-4}$ (29$^{1-4}$), I.12.21 (29$^5$), I.12.19 (29$^{6*}$). (The third volume, I.12.19, was given to the Library in 1612.)


OL30   *Petrj Martyris vol: 4$^r$*
MARTYR, Peter, Vermilius

(30$^1$)   Defensio doctrinae de eucharistiae sacramento adversus S. Gardineri librum
2°, (Zurich, C. Froschouer, 1559); Adams M760

(30$^2$)   In librum Judicum commentarii
2°, Zurich, C. Froschouer, 1565; Adams M772

(30³)   In duos libros Samuelis commentarii, ed. 2
        2°, Zurich, C. Froschouer, 1567; Adams M777

(30⁴)   (unidentified)

        Protestantes (30¹); Commentatores (30²⁻⁴)

        K.17.24 (30¹), D.1.27 (30²), D.2.9 (30³); the fourth volume is
        absent (probably alienated in the early seventeenth century).

OL31    *Bucerj Commentaria vol: 2*

  (31¹)   BUCER, Martin
          Metaphrases et enarrationes epistolarum D. Pauli
          2°, Strassburg, W. Rithelius, 1536; Adams B3043

  (31²)   OECOLAMPADIUS, Joannes, and ZWINGLI, Ulrich
          Oecolampadii et Zuinglii epistolarum libri quatuor
          2°, Basle, B. Lasius and T. Platter, 1536; Adams O107

  (31³)   BUCER, Martin
          Scripta Anglicana fere omnia
          2°, Basle, P. Perna, 1577; Adams B3049

          Commentatores (31¹⁻²), Protestantes (31³)

          Y.19.3¹⁻² (31¹⁻²), I.17.6 (31³)

OL32    *Musculj vol: 5*
        MUSCULUS, Wolfgang

  (32¹)   In Mosis Genesim commentarii
          2°, Basle, J. Hervagius, 1554; Adams M2007

  (32²)   In psalterium commentarii
          2°, Basle, J. Hervagius, 1551; Adams M2010

  (32³)   In Esaiam commentarii
          2°, Basle, J. Hervagius, 1557; Adams M2014

  (32⁴)   In Matthaeum commentarii
          2°, Basle, J. Herbagius, 1562; Adams M2019

  (32⁵)   Commentariorum in Joannem Heptas prima
          2°, Basle, B. Westhemer, 1545; Adams M2022

          Commentatores

          D.3.18, D.17.21, D.15.32, D.10.87, D.10.92

OL33 *Marlorati thesaurus*
MARLORAT, Augustin
Propheticae et apostolicae scripturae thesaurus
(probably 2°, London, T. Vautrollier, 1574; STC 17409)

Systematici

absent (probably replaced c. 1624–40 by the 2nd 2° edition,
Geneva, P. and I. Chouët, 1624)

OL34 *Justiniani opera theologica*
JUSTINIANUS, Laurentius
Opera, vita auctoris
(doubtless 2°, Basle, H. Froben and N. Episcopius, 1560; Adams
J705)

Theologi practici

(doubtless E.3.18, but early marks lost in 18th-century rebinding)

OL35* *Sayri vol: 2*
SAYRUS, Gregorius

(35¹*) Clavis regia sacerdotum, casuum conscientiae, sive theologiae
moralis thesauri
2°, Venice, B. Barezzi, 1607

(35²*) Casuum conscientiae, sive theologiae moralis thesauri
2°, Venice, J. B. Colosinus, 1606

Causuistae

F.16.54, D.46.13

OL36 *Henriquez summa theologiæ*
HENRIQUEZ, Henricus
Summa theologiae moralis
2°, Venice, D. Zenarus, 1600; Adams H242

Scholastici in Thomam

E.10.25

OL37*   *Toletus in Lucam*
TOLETUS, Franciscus
Commentaria in evangelium secundum Lucam
2°, Venice, G. Varisco, 1601

Commentatores

D.10.90

OL38   *Rich: de Media = Villa vol 2*
MIDDLETON, Richard

(38¹)   In primum sententiarum questiones
2°, Venice, L. de Soardis, 1507; Adams M1419

(38²)   In secundum sententiarum questiones
2°, Venice, L. de Soardis, 1509; Adams M1420

(38³)   In tertium sententiarum questiones
2°, Venice, L. de Soardis, 1509; Adams M1421

(38⁴)   In quartum sententiarum questiones
2°, Venice, L. de Soardis, 1509; Adams M1422

Scholastici in sententias

$F.16.57^{1-2}$, $F.16.58^{1-2}$

OL39   *Henricus Agandauo*
GOETHALS, Hendrik, of Ghent
Quodlibeta
2°, Paris, J. Badius, 1518; Adams G822

Scholastici

F.16.49

OL40   *Albertj Magni vol: 3*
ALBERTUS, Magnus, Bp of Ratisbon
Scriptum primum (-quartum) super primum (-quartum) sententiarum
4 vols in 3, 2°, Basle, J. de Pfortzheim, 1506; Adams A542

Scholastici in sententias

F.16.7–9

OL41* *Ocham vol. 2*
OCKAM, Gulielmus

(41¹*) Decisiones viii questionum super potestate summi pontificis
2°, Lyons, J. Trechsel, 1496; Hain *11952

(41²*) Quaestiones et decisiones in IV libros sententiarum
2°, Lyons, J. Trechsel, 1495; Goff O–15

(41³*) Dialogorum libri septem adversos haereticos *with* Compendium errorum
2°, Lyons, J. Trechsel, [after 1493]; Goff O–9

(41⁴*) Opus nonaginta dierum et dialogi
2°, Lyons, J. Trechsel, 1495; Goff O–13

Scholastici in sententias

VI.15.8$^{1-2}$ (41$^{1-2}$), VI.15.6$^{1-2}$ (41³), VI.15.6³ (41⁴) (probably bought in 1610)

OL42* *Vasquez in Thomam*
VASQUEZ, Gabriel
Commentariorum ac disputationum in tertiam partem S. Thomae, vol. 1 only of 4, 2°, Ingolstadt, A. Angermarius, 1610

Scholastici in Thomam

F.17.32 (probably bought in 1610)

OL43 *Caietani vol. 3*
AQUINAS, Thomas, St
Summa, *comment.* T. de Vio Cajetanus
3 vols, 2°, Lyons, G. Rouille, 1588; Adams A1441

Scholastici in Thomam

E.6.10–12

OL44 *Nicholai Lyræ vol: 6*
BIBLE, Latin
Biblia sacra, *comment.* N. de Lyra
6 vols, 2°, Lyons, G. Trechsel, 1545; Adams B1035

Commentatores

A.O.21–26

OL45　*Durandus in Sententias*
DURANDUS, Gulielmus, Bp of Meaux
In sententias comment. libri quatuor
2°, Lyons, G. Rouille, 1595; Adams D1187

Scholastici in sententias

E.18.14

OL46\*　*Pinedæ in Job vol: 2*
PINEDA, Joannes de, of Seville
Commentariarum in Job libri tredecim
2 vols, 2°, Cologne, A. Hierat, 1605

Commentatores

D.3.21–22

OL47\*　*Villalpandi in Ezechielem vol. 3*
PRADUS, Hieronymus, and VILLALPANDUS, Joannes
Baptista
In Ezechielem explanationes
3 vols, 2°, Rome, A. Zanettus 1596 (i), C. Vulliettus 1604, 1605
(ii), C. Vulliettus 1602 (iii); Adams P2050

Commentatores

D.18.24–26

OL48　*Alfonsus de Castro*
CASTRO, Alfonsus de
Adversus contra omnes haereses
2°, Cologne, M. Novesianus, 1549; Adams C968

Tractatus theologici

D.37.5

OL49　*Dionisius a Rickell in psalmos*
DIONYSIUS, Carthusianus, à Rickel
In psalmos omnes
2°, Cologne, P. Quentell, 1531; Adams D557

Commentatores

D.16.71

OL50    *Thomas Stapletonus*
        STAPLETON, Thomas
        (probably Universa justificationis doctrina hodie controversa,
        libris duodecim tradita
        2°, Paris, M. Sonnius, 1582; Adams S1663)

        Pontificii

        absent (probably alienated by the mid-seventeenth century)


OL51    *Hosij opera*
        HOSIUS, Stanislaus
        Opera
        2°, Paris, G. Desboys, 1562; omitted by Adams

        Pontificii

        F.11.23


OL52    *Latomj opera theologica*

   (52¹)    LATOMUS, Jacobus
            Opera
            2°, Louvain, B. Gravius, 1550; Adams L264

   (52²)    COCHLAEUS, Johannes
            Commentaria de actis et scriptis M. Lutheri
            2°, Mainz, F. Behem, 1549; Adams C2252

            Pontificii

            E.10.21¹⁻²


OL53    *Marloratus in nouum Testament:*
        MARLORAT, Augustin
        Novi testamenti catholici expositio
        (edition unidentified)

        Commentatores

        absent (probably discarded as a duplicate between 1640 and
        1667)

OL54  *Gualtherj vol: 2*
GUALTHERUS, Rodolphus, Senior
Homiliarum in evangelia dominicalia pars I (II)
2 vols, 2°, Leyden, (n.d.), 1585; Adams G1368

Commentatores

I.12.8–9

OL55  *Zuinglij vol: 4*
ZWINGLI, Ulrich

(55¹)  Opera
3 of 4 vols, 2°, (Zurich, C. Froschouer, 1546); Adams Z216

(55²)  In evangelicam historiam annotationes
2°, Zurich, C. Froschouer, 1539; Adams Z236

Commentatores

I.17.14, 13, 12 (55¹); I.17.15 (55²)

OL56  *Pellicanus in vetus testament*
PELLICANUS, Conradus
(unidentified commentary on the Old Testament)

Commentatores

absent (probably discarded c.1640–67)

OL57  *Whitgiftus contra Cartwright*
WHITGIFT, John, Abp
(probably The defense of the aunswere, to the admonition against
the replie of T.C., *English*
2°, London, H. Binneman, 1574; STC 25430)

Tractatus theologicae

absent (probably sold as a duplicate, 1784)

OL58  *Melancthonis loci communes*
MELANCTHON, Philipp
Tabulae locorum communium
2°, Basle, J. Oporinus, 1560; Adams N391

Commentatores

I.17.5

OL59　*Aretius felinus in psalmos*
BUCER, Martin
(probably Sacrorum psalmorum libri quinque, *ed.* 'Aretius
Felinus', *i.e.* Martin Bucer
2°, Basle, J. Hervagius, 1547; Adams B1426)

Commentatores

absent (probably alienated by 1645)

OL60　*Clauis Scripturæ*
FLACIUS, Mathias, Illyricus
Clavis scripturae
2°, Basle, J. Oporinus and N. Episcopius, 1567; Adams F556

Theologi practici

D.15.11; given by Michael Meade c.1595–7

OL61　*Defensor pacis*
MARSILIUS, of Padua
Opus insigne cui tituli fecit autor defensorem pacis
2°, (?Basle, V. Curio), 1522; Adams M675

Tractatus theologici

D.37.2

OL62　*Dryedonis vol: 2*
DRIEDO, Johannes
Opera, tom. I(–IV)
4 vols in 2, 2°, Louvain, B. Gravius, 1550 (i), 1552 (ii, iii.1), 1548
(iv); Adams D904, 907, 909, 911

Systematici

F.16.30–31

OL63　*Anselmi opuscula*
ANSELM, Abp of Canterbury
Opera
2°, (Strassburg, G. Husner, after 1496); Goff A–760

Patres Latini

VI.14.39

OL64    *Soto in Epistolam ad Roma:*
SOTO, Domingo de
In epistolam Pauli ad Romanos
2°, Antwerp, J. Steelsius, 1550; Adams S1501

Commentatores

D.10.15


OL65    *Gorran in Epistolas* +
GORRAN, Nicolaus de
(unidentified edition of Postilla super epistolas Pauli)

Commentatores

absent (probably alienated before 1640, and possibly not allotted
an OL running number)


OL66    *Erasmi Ecclesiastes*
ERASMUS, Desiderius
(unidentified edition of Ecclesiastae libri quatuor)

Concionatores

absent (probably alienated between 1640 and 1667)


OL67    *Tusanj Lexicon*
TUSANUS, Jacobus
Lexicon graecolatinum, *Greek and Latin*
2°, Paris, C. Guillard, 1552; Adams T1208

Lexicographi

IV.4.65


OL68    *Strabo graeco Latinè*
STRABO
(doubtless Rerum geographicarum libri septemdecim, *Greek and
Latin*
2°, (Geneva), E. Vignon, 1587; Adams S1908)

Mathematici

absent (probably alienated after 1800)

OL69    *Thucidides gallice*
THUCYDIDES
LHistoire de la guerre qui fut entre Peloponnesiens et Atheniens, *French*
2°, Paris, J. Badius, 1527; Adams T679

Historici Graeci

II.3.15

OL70    *Cassalius de iustificatione*
CASALIUS, Gaspar, Bp of Coimbra
De justificatione humani generis
2°, Venice, B. Baretius, 1599; Adams C815

Pontificii

E.10.30

OL71*    *Christo: â Castro in Jeremiam*
CHRISTOPHORUS, a Castro
In Jeremiae, Lamentationes, et Baruch
2°, Paris, M. Sonnius, 1608

Commentatores

D.17.33

OL72    *Diodorus Siculus*
DIODORUS, Siculus
(doubtless Bibliothecae historicae libri
2°, (Geneva), H. Stephanus, 1559; Adams D472)

Historici Graeci

absent (probably sold as a duplicate, 1859)

OL73    *Demosthenes graecè*
DEMOSTHENES
(doubtless Λόγοι δύο καὶ ʽεξήκοντα, *Greek*
2°, Basle, J. Hervagius, 1532; Adams D261)

Oratores

absent (probably sold as a duplicate, 1859)

OL74    *Graecorum oratorum orationes*
        ORATORES GRAECI
        (probably Isocrates, Alcidamas, *etc.*, Greek
        2°, Venice, Aldus, 1534; Adams O245)

        Oratores

        absent (probably alienated between 1675 and 1700)

OL75    *Bibliothecæ Concionum vol. 2*
        (unidentified)

        Theologi practici

        absent (probably alienated before 1640; possibly replaced by the
        copy of Truxillo, Thomas de, *Thesauri concionatorum*,
        2 vols, 2°, Lyons, C. Pesnot, 1584, Adams T1009, which was
        given by Peter Shaw in 1601)

OL76    *Titlemannus in Psalmos*
        TITELMANN, Franz
        (doubtless Elucidatio in omnes psalmos
        2°, Antwerp, P. Nutius, 1573; Adams T754)

        Commentatores

        absent (probably sold as a 'duplicate' of T753, 1784)

OL77    *Feri Postillæ*
        FERUS, Johannes
        (probably Postillae sive conciones in epistolas et evangelia
        2°, Cologne, A. Birckman, 1557; Adams F332)

        Concionatores

        (probably I.12.22, but early marks lost in seventeenth-century
        rebinding)

OL78    *Hermanni vol. 2*
        (unidentified 2-vol work by HERMAN, of Wied, Abp of
        Cologne)

        (probably Systematici)

        absent (probably alienated before 1645)

OL79    *Faber in Epistolas Paulj*
        FABER, Jacobus, Stapulensis
        Epistola ad Rhomanos, ad Hebraeos, *comm*. Jacobus Faber
        2°, Paris, H. Stephanus, 1512; Adams B1837

        Commentatores

        D.8.122; given to Michaelhouse by William Filey


OL80    *Cochlæus de Seditionibus*
        (probably a fragment of
        BRUNUS, Conradus
        De seditionibus libri sex, I. Cochlaei appendix triplex
        2°, Mainz, F. Behem, 1550; Adams B2961)

        Tractatus theologici

        absent (probably alienated by 1667)


OL81    *Viguerj institutiones*
        VIGUERIUS, Joannes
        Ad naturalem et christianam philosophiam institutiones
        2°, Paris, C. Fremy, 1554; Adams V766

        Systematici

        F.16.48


OL82    *Pighij vol. 2*
        PIGHIUS, Albertus

  (82¹)    Controversiarum in comitiis Ratisponensibus tractatarum
           explicatio
           2°, Cologne, M. Novesianus, 1545; Adams P1184

  (82²)    Hierarchiae ecclesiasticae assertio
           2°, Cologne, J. Novesianus, 1551; Adams P1193

           Pontificii

           F.16.28–29

OL83   *Peresius de diunis traditionibus*
PEREZ DE AYALA, Martin, Abp of Valentia
De divinis apostolicis, atque ecclesiasticis traditionibus
2°, Cologne, J. Gennepaeus, 1549; Adams P678

Historici ecclesiastici

F.16.59

OL84   *Lindanj Panoplia*
LINDANUS, Wilhelmus, Bp of Roermond
Panoplia evangelica, pars altera
2°, Cologne, M. Cholinus, 1560; Adams L718

Pontificii

E.10.20

OL85   *Breuiarium domesticum*
LITURGIES, Latin rite, breviaries (probably Salisbury)
(probably Breviarium seu horarium domesticum as usum Sarum
2°, Paris, C. Chevallon and P. Regnault, 1531; Adams L939)

Liturgica

(probably C.6.7, but early marks lost in rebinding)

OL86   *Platonis vol. 2*
PLATO
(probably Opera quae extant omnia, *Greek and Latin*
3 vols in 2, 2°, (Geneva), H. Stephanus, 1578; Adams, P1439)

Philosophi Platonici

absent (probably sold as a duplicate in 1784)

OL87   *Sabellici vol. 2*
SABELLICUS, Marcus Antonius Coccius
(doubtless Opera omnia
4 vols in 2, 2°, Basle, J. Hervagius, 1560; Adams S12)

Historici antiquiores

(probably Y.18.21–22, but early marks lost in eighteenth-century rebinding)

OL88    *Poetæ Græci*
POETAE GRAECI
(doubtless Poetae Graeci principes heroici carminis, *Greek*
2 vols in 1, (Geneva), H. Stephanus, 1566; Adams P1699)
Poetae Graeci

absent (probably sold as a duplicate in 1859)

OL89    *Cuspinianus in Aurelium*
CUSPINIANUS, Johannes
(probably De consulibus Romanorum commentarii, Magni
Aurelii chronicon
2°, Basle, Oporinus, 1553; not in Adams)
Historici Romani

absent (probably alienated before 1645; possibly replaced by a
copy of the same work, Frankfurt a. M. 1601, bought with the
Sedley gift, 1618)

OL90    *Bergomensis de Claris mulieribus*
JACOBUS PHILIPPUS, de Bergamo
(probably De claris mulieribus
2°, Ferrara, L. de Rubeis, 1497; Goff J-204)
Historici ecclesiastici

absent (probably alienated before 1645)

OL91    *Aristophanes cum Comentar:*
ARISTOPHANES
(doubtless Comediae novem, *Greek, comm.* S. Gelenius
2°, Basle, Froben, 1547; Adams A1715)
Poetae Graeci

absent (probably sold as a duplicate, 1952)

OL92    *Politiani Epistolæ*
POLITIANUS, Angelus
Omnium operum tom. prior (secundus)
2°, Paris, J. Badius, 1519; Adams P1763
Philologi

G.5.53

OL93    *Legenda aurea*
        VORAGINE, Jacobus de
        (unidentified edition of Legenda aurea; the 1675 catalogue gives
        the date 1516, but no edition of this date found in Adams, STC,
        BM, BN, etc.)

        Historici ecclesiastici

        absent (probably alienated between 1675 and 1700)

OL94    *Bartholomæus Anglicus*
        BARTHOLOMAEUS ANGLICUS
        De proprietatibus rerum
        2°, Nuremberg, A. Koberger, 1492; Goff B–141

        Philosophi recentiores

        VI.15.35; given to Michaelhouse by William Filey

OL95    *Valerius Maximus*
        VALERIUS MAXIMUS
        (doubtless Valerius Maximus cum duplici commentario
        2°, Paris, J. Badius, 1513; Adams V90)

        Historici Romani

        (probably Z.11.73, but early marks lost in eighteenth-century
        rebinding)

OL96    *Plutarchi vol. 2*
        PLUTARCH
        Quae exstant omnia, *Greek and Latin*
        2 vols, 2°, Frankfurt a. M., A. Wechel, 1599; Adams P1608
        Historici Graeci

        II.18.20–21

OL97    *Aristotelis vol. 2*
        ARISTOTLE
        (unidentified 2-vol. edition of Works, *Greek and Latin*)

        Peripatetici

        absent (probably alienated before 1645; possibly replaced by Du
        Val's edition, Paris, 1619)

OL98   *Dionysius Halicarnasseus*
DIONYSIUS, of Halicarnassus
(doubtless Scripta quae extant omnia, *Greek and Latin*
2°, Frankfurt a. M., A. Wechel, 1586; Adams D625)

Historici Graeci

(probably II.3.2, but early marks lost in eighteenth-century
rebinding; possibly acquired after 1607)

OL99   *Simplicius in Aristot. graece*
(doubtless ARISTOTLE, two or more works
Commentaria in tres libros Aristotelis de anima, *etc., Greek,
comment.* Simplicius
2°, Venice, Aldus, 1527; Adams A1752)

Peripatetici

(probably N.5.32², but early marks lost when it was bound up
with a copy of Adams A677 c.1667)

OL100   *Victorius in Aristotelem*
ARISTOTLE, Rhetorica
P. Victorii commentarii in tres libros de arte dicendi, *Greek*
2°, Florence, B. Giunta, 1548; Adams A1941

Peripatetici

T.6.23

OL101   *Ficinj in Platonem vol. 2*
FICINUS, Marsilius
(probably Commentaria V perpetua in Platonem
1 vol in 2, 2°, Florence, de Alpa, 1496; Goff F-152)

Philosophi Platonici

absent (probably alienated before 1667)

OL102   *Gulielmj Altissiodorensis*
GULIELMUS, Altissiodorensis
Aurea in quattuor sententiarum libros explanatio
2°, Paris, F. Regnault, (c.1510); Adams G1594

Scholastici in sententias

E.16.62

OL103   *Philoponus in Aristotelem*
        PHILOPONUS, Johannes

(103¹)   Comentaria in priora analytica, *etc., Greek*
         2°, Venice, B. Zanetti, 1536; Adams P1040

(103²)   In posteriora resolutoria Aristotelis commentarium, *Greek*
         2°, Venice, Aldus, 1534; Adams P1044

         Peripatetici

         N.5.43$^{1-2}$


OL104   *Porphyrius cum Philopono*

(104¹)   PORPHYRIUS, of Tyre
         De non necendis ad epulandum animantibus. Michaelis Ephesii
         scholia in Aristotelis de partibus animantium, *Greek*
         2°, Florence, B. Giunta, 1548; Adams P1910

(104²)   ARISTOTLE, de generatione animalium
         De animalium generatione cum Philoponi commentariis, *Greek*
         2°, Venice, J. Antonius, 1526; Adams A1789

         Peripatetici

         S.4.47 (104¹), S.4.24 (104²); formerly bound together


OL105   *Simplicius in Categorias*
        SIMPLICIUS
        (probably Simplicii commentationes accuratissimae in praedica-
        menta Aristotelis in latinam linguam translatae
        2°, Venice, H. Scotus, 1550; not in Adams)

        Peripatetici

        absent (probably alienated between 1675 and 1700)


OL106   *Themistij opera*

(106¹)   THEMISTIUS
         Opera. Alexandri Aphrodisiensis de anima et de fato unus, *Greek*
         2°, Venice, Aldus, 1534; Adams T447

(106²)  PHILOPONUS, Johannes
Joannes Grammaticus in libros de generatione, *etc.* Alexander
Aphrodisiensis in meteorologica, *etc., Greek*
2°, Venice, Aldus, 1527; Adams P1052

Peripatetici

N.5.37 (106¹), N.5.34 (106²); formerly bound together

OL107  *Didymus in Homerum*
DIDYMUS, Alexandrinus
(probably Didymi interpretatio in Homerum, *Greek*
2°, Rome, A. Collotius, 1517; Adams D440)

Poetae Graeci

absent (probably alienated before 1645)

OL108  *Camerarius in Homerum*
CAMERARIUS, Joachimus, Senior
(probably Commentarius explicationis primi (secundi) libri
Iliados Homeri, *Greek and Latin*
4°, Strassburg, C. Mylius, 1538, 1540; Adams C418)

Poetae Graeci

absent (probably alienated before 1645)

OL109  *Ciceronis Epistolæ*
CICERO, Marcus Tullius
Familiarium epistolarum libri XVI
2°, Paris, A. Parvus, 1549; Adams C1951

Oratores Latini

Z.4.48

OL110  *Hesiodi opuscula cum alijs*
a fragment of
THEOCRITUS, *etc.*
Idyllia, *etc., Greek*
2°, Venice, Aldus, 1495; Goff T–144

Poetae Graeci

N.3.72

OL111   *Alexander Aphrodisiensis*
ALEXANDER, Aphrodisiensis
(unidentified work)

(doubtless Peripatetici)

absent (probably alienated before 1645)

OL112   *Philoponus contra Proclum*
PHILOPONUS, Johannes
(doubtless Contra Proclum de mundi aeternitate, *Greek*
2°, Venice, B. Zanetti, 1535; Adams P1060)

Philosophi Platonici

(doubtless T.17.4²; bound in the late seventeenth century with the
Library's copy of Adams P2139)

OL113   *Gesnerj Bibliotheca*
GESNER, Conrad
Bibliotheca instituta et collecta primum a C. Gesnero. Deinde per
J. Simlerum
2°, Zurich, C. Froschouer, 1574; Adams G514

Lexicographi

IV.13.21

OL114   *Wottonus de different: animal.*
WOTTON, Edward
De differentiis animalium
2°, Paris, M. Vascosan, 1552; Adams W259 (the only edition)

Anatomici

absent (probably alienated before 1645)

OL115   *Titus Liuius Italice*
LIVIUS, Titus
Le deche delle historie Romane, *Italian*
2°, Venice, Giunti, 1547; Adams L1362

Historici Romani

Z.4.56

OL116  *Pausanias de veterj græcia*
PAUSANIAS
(probably Veteris Graeciae descriptio
2°, Florence, L. Torrentinus, 1551; Adams P524)

Historici Graeci

absent (probably alienated between 1640 and 1667; possibly
replaced by a Greek and Latin edition, Hanover, 1613)


OL117  *Thucidides cum Herodoto*

(117¹)  THUCYDIDES
Thucydides cum scholiis, *Greek*
2°, Basle, Hervagius, 1540; Adams T664

(117²)  HERODOTUS
Herodoti libri novem, *Greek*
2°, Basle, Hervagius, 1541; Adams H395

Historici Graeci

II.13.34$^{1-2}$


OL118  *Vitæ Cæsarum per Suetonium*
CAESARES
Vitae Caesarum (by Suetonius *et al.*)
2°, Basle, H. Froben and N. Episcopius, 1546; Adams C91

Historici Romani

Z.16.48


OL119  *Volaterrani Geographia*
MAFFEIUS, Raphael, Volaterranus
(probably Commentariorum urbanorum 38 libri
2°, Basle, H. Froben and N. Episcopius, 1544; Adams M103)

Philologi

absent (probably sold as a duplicate, 1784)

OL120 *Lucianj dialogi græcè*
LUCIAN, of Samosata
Dialogi et alia multa opera, *Greek*
2°, Venice, Aldus, 1522; Adams L1604

Philologi

N.5.16 (possibly alienated temporarily in the late seventeenth century)

OL121 *Munsterj Cosmographia*
MUNSTER, Sebastian
(probably Cosmographiae universalis
2°, Basle, H. Petri, 1554; Adams M1910)

Mathematici

absent (probably alienated after 1800)

OL122 *Nicephori Historia*
NICEPHORUS, Callistus
(unidentified edition of Ecclesiasticae historiae libri 18)

Historici ecclesiastici

absent (probably alienated before 1645)

OL123 *Pauli Jouij Historia*
GIOVIO, Paolo, Bp of Nocera
Historiarum sui temporis tomus primus (secundus)
2°, Paris, R. Fouet, 1598; Adams G658

Historici recentiores

Y.6.22

OL124 *Appianj Historia græce*
APPIANUS, of Alexandria
(doubtless Romanarum historiarum Celtica, *Greek*
2°, Paris, C. Stephanus, 1551; Adams A1340)

Historici Graeci

(doubtless II.17.29, but early marks lost in nineteenth-century rebinding)

OL125  *Nicholaus Gerbellius*
GERBELIUS, Nicolaus
(doubtless Pro declaratione picturae Graeciae sophiani libri septem
2°, Basle, J. Oporinus, 1549; Adams G480)

Geographi

(doubtless U.5.31, but early marks lost in seventeenth-century
rebinding)

OL126  *Stobæus*
STOBAEUS, Johannes
(unidentified edition of Apophthegmata, *Greek and Latin*)

Philosophi Platonica

absent (probably alienated between 1675 and 1700)

OL127  *Fasciculus temporum*

(127¹)  ROLEWINCK, Werner
Fasciculus temporum
2°, (?Cologne, von Renchen, 1483); Goff R–269

(127²)  BREYDENBACH, Bernhard von
Peregrinatio in terram sanctam
2°, Mainz, E. Reuwich, 1486; Goff B–1189

Historici ecclesiastici

NQ.11.32$^{1-2}$; given by William Filey in the period 1546–51; alienated mid-seventeenth century; returned as part of Newton's
library, 1943

OL128  *Æneæ Siluij historia*
PIUS II, Pope (Aeneas Silvius, Piccolomini)
Opera omnia. Gnomologia
2°, Basle, H. Petri, 1551; Adams P1333

Historici ecclesiastici

L.14.7

OL129  *Holinshead Chro: vol: 2*
HOLINSHED, Raphael
The firste (laste) vol. of the chronicles of England, Scotlande, and Irelande, *English*
2 vols, 2°, London, J. Hunne *etc.*, 1577; STC 13568

Historici recentiores

VI.3.36–37; given by Michael Meade c.1595–7

OL130  *Cochlæi historia Huscit:*
COCHLAEUS, Johannes
Historiae Hussitarum libri duodecim
2°, Mainz, F. Behem, 1549; Adams C2272

Historici ecclesiastici

L.14.33

OL131  *Lodouicus contra Alcoranum*
MUHAMMAD, the Prophet
Machumetis eiusque successorum vitae ac doctrina. Confutationes Alcoranum adjecta est Lodovici Vivis Valentini censura
2°, (Basle, J. Oporinus, c. 1543); Adams M1889

Controversiae

Y.19.4, the Confutationes of Vives being bound first

OL132  *Pet: Comestoris historia*

(132[1])  PETRUS, Comestor
Historia scholastica
2°, Strassburg, G. Husner, 1503; Adams P883

(132[2])  EUSEBIUS, Pamphili, Bp of Caesarea, and BEDE, the Venerable
Ecclesiastici historia divi Eusebii, et ecclesiastica historia gentis Anglorum venerabilis Bede
2°, Hagenau, J. Rynman and H. Gran, 1506; Adams E1088

Historici ecclesiastici

C.15.2[1–2]; given to Michaelhouse by William Filey ·

OL133   *Bembi historia venet:*
BEMBO, Pietro, Cardinal
(doubtless Historiae Venetae libri XII
2°, Venice, Aldus, 1551; Adams B597)

Historici recentiores

(doubtless N.5.55, but early marks lost in seventeenth-century rebinding)

OL134   *Nizolius in Ciceronem*
NIZOLIUS, Marius
(probably Observationes omnia M. T. Ciceronis verba complectentes
2°, Basle, J. Hervagius, 1548; Adams N301)

Lexicographi

absent (probably alienated between 1675 and 1700)

OL135   *Pollucis vocabularij index*

(135¹)   POLLUX, Julius, of Naucratis
Vocabularium, *Greek*
2°, Venice, Aldus, 1502; Adams P1787

(135²)   STEPHANUS, Byzantinus
De urbibus, *Greek*
2°, Venice, Aldus, 1502; Adams S1717

Lexicographi

N.4.14 (135¹), N.4.20 (135²); formerly bound together, 135²
being misbound with sections A–D following G–L

OL136   *Licosthenis Apophthegmata*
WOLFFHART, Conrad
(doubtless Apophthegmatum loci communes
2°, Basle, J. Oporinus, 1555; Adams W246)

Historici recentiores

(doubtless III.2.22, but early marks lost in eighteenth-century rebinding)

OL137  *Priscianj Grammatica*

(137¹)  PRISCIANUS, Caesariensis
Institutiones
2°, Paris, J. Badius, 1516; Adams P2108

(137²)  GRAMMATICI
Grammatici illustres XII
2°, Paris, J. Badius, 1516; Adams G939
Lexicographi
III.11.120¹⁻²

OL138  *Victorius in Ciceronem*
VICTORIUS, Petrus, the elder
(unidentified edition of P. Victorii explicationes suarum in Ciceronem castigationum)
Oratores Latini
absent (probably alienated before 1645)

OL139  *Dictionarium latino =gallicum*
STEPHANUS, Robertus, the elder
Dictionarium Latinogallicum, *Latin and French*
2°, Paris, R. Stephanus, 1546; Adams S1804
Lexicographi
IV.4.47

OL140  *Aristotelis pars quædam*
ARISTOTLE
(unidentified work or part of a work in Latin)
Peripatetici
absent (probably alienated before 1645)

OL141  *Alexander ab Alexandro*
ALEXANDRO, Alexander ab
(unidentified edition of Genialium dierum libri sex, *ed.* A. Tiraquellus)
Jus civile
absent (probably alienated between 1640 and 1700)

OL142   *Tiraquelli vol: 4ʳ*
TIRAQUELLUS, Andreas
(unidentified work or works in 4 volumes)

(probably Jus civile)

absent (probably alienated between 1640 and 1700)

OL143   *Sextus liber Decretalium*
BONIFACE VIII, Pope
(probably Liber sextus decretalium
8°, Frankfurt a. M., J. Feyerabend, 1590; Adams B2449)

Jus canonicum

(probably N.12.97, but the early marks are inconclusive, and law
books were not identified in the 1667 and 1675 catalogues)

OL144   *Decretalia Grego: Papæ*
GREGORY IX, Pope
(probably Epistolae decretales
8°, Frankfurt a. M., J. Feyerabend, 1590; Adams G1231)

Jus canonicum

(probably N.12.96, but the early marks are inconclusive, and law
books were not identified in the 1667 and 1675 catalogues)

OL145   *Euripidis Tragœdiæ græcè*
EURIPIDES
(probably Tragoediae octodecim, *Greek*
8°, Basle, J. Hervagius, 1551; Adams E1033)

Poetae Graeci

absent (probably alienated in the mid-eighteenth century)

OL146   *Bembus de virgilij Culice*
BEMBO, Pietro, Cardinal

(146¹)   De Virgilii culice et Terentii fabulis
4°, Venice, de Nicolini, 1530; Adams B586

(146²)   De Guido Ubaldo Feretrio deque Elizabetha Gonzagia
4°, Venice, de Nicolini, 1530; Adams B585

(146³)  De Aetna
        4°, Venice, de Nicolini, 1530; Adams B584

(146⁴)  PICO DELLA MIRANDOLA, Giovanni Francesco
        Ad Petrum Bembum de imitatione libellus
        4°, Venice, de Nicolini, 1530; Adams P1150

        Philologi

        II.3.59$^{1-4}$

OL147   *Pædianus in Ciceronem*
        ASCONIUS PEDIANUS, Quintus
        Commentarii in M. T. Ciceronis orationes
        4°, Paris, M. Vascosan, 1536; Adams A2055

        Oratores Latini

        Z.10.99

OL148   *Libanus Sophista græce*
        LIBANIUS
        (doubtless Μελεται λογοι τε και εκφρασεις, Greek
        4°, Ferrara, J. Macciochius, 1517; Adams L629)

        Oratores Graeci

        (doubtless II.12.2, but early marks lost in eighteenth-century
        rebinding)

OL149   *De verbis latinis epitome*
        ZANCHI, Basilio
        Verborum latinorum ex variis authoribus epitome
        4°, Rome, A. Blado, 1541; Adams Z31

        Lexicographi

        III.10.59

OL150   *Compendium de gestis Francorum*
        (doubtless GAGUIN, Robert
        Compendium super Francorum gestis
        2°, Paris, T. Kerver, 1500–1; Goff G–15, Adams G16)

Historici recentiores

(doubtless VI.14.31, but early marks lost in seventeenth-century rebinding)

OLI51　*Historia Sanctorum patrum*
PALLADIUS, Bp of Aspona
Lausiaca historia
4°, Paris, B. Turrisanus, 1555; Adams P102

Historici ecclesiastici

N.3.67

OLI52　*Missa Sanctorum patrum*
LITURGIES, Greek rite, Leitourgikon
Liturgiae, sive missae sanctorum patrum
8°, Antwerp, C. Plantin, 1560; Adams L843

Liturgiae

C.29.16

OLI53　*Caluinus in Josuam*
CALVIN, Jean
(probably In librum Josue brevis commentarius
8°, Geneva, F. Perrin, 1564; Adams C280)

Commentatores

(possibly D.9.9, but the early marks and catalogue entries are inconclusive)

OLI54　*Redman de iustificatione*

(154¹)　REDMAN, John
De justificatione opus
4°, Antwerp, J. Withaye, 1555; Adams R266

(154²)　GUALTHERUS, Rodolphus, Senior
Servus ecclesiasticus
4°, Zurich, C. Froschouer, (1548); Adams G1412

(154³)  BULLINGER, Heinrich
Series et digestio temporum et rerum descriptarum a Luca in
Actis
4°, Zurich, Froschouer, 1548; Adams B3232

(154⁴)  BULLINGER, Heinrich
De scripturae sanctae authoritate
4°, Zurich, Froschouer, 1538; Adams B3206

(154⁵)  LAVATER, Ludwig
Historia de origine et progressu controversiae sacramentariae de
coena Domini
4°, Zurich, C. Froschouer, 1563; Adams L303

(154⁶)  SIMLER, Josias
Oratio de vita et obitu P. Martyris Vermilii, *etc.*
4°, Zurich, C. Froschouer, 1563; Adams S1177

Tractatus theologicae

K.2.1$^{1-6}$


OL155  *Tuppius in Sinodum Trident.*
COUNCILS, Trent
Adversus Synodi Tridentinae restitutionem a Pio IIII indictam,
*trs.* L. Tuppius
4°, Strassburg, S. Emmel, 1565; Adams C2844

Concilia

M.9.31


OL156  *Bullingerus adversus Cochlæum*
BULLINGER, Heinrich
Ad Joannis Cochlei de canonicae scripturae authoritate libellum
responsio
4°, Zurich, Froschouer, 1544; Adams B3188

Protestantes

K.16.2

OL157  *Latimeri sermones Anglice*
       LATIMER, Hugh
       (unidentifed edition of Sermons, *English*, probably 4° or 8°)

       Concionatores

       absent (probably alienated before 1645)


OL158  *Illyricus de sectis Pontificum*

  (158¹)  FLACIUS, Mathias, Illyricus
          De sectis, dissensionibus, scriptorum et doctorum Pontificionum
          liber
          4°, Basle, P. Quecus, 1565; Adams F560

  (158²)  BRENZ, Johannes
          De personali unione duarum naturarum in Christo
          4°, Tübingen, U. Morhard, 1561; Adams B2755

  (158³)  CHRISTIAN CHURCH, Fathers
          Testimonia S. Patrum an mali et indigni sumant verum corpus et
          sanguinem Christi in eucharistia, collecta per M. Rolandum
          4°, Tübingen, U. Morhard, 1561; Adams C1474

  (158⁴)  BUCER, Martin
          De vera ecclesiarum in doctrina reconciliatione
          4°, (Strassburg, W. Rihelius, 1540); Adams B3029

       Protestantes

       K.14.2$^{1-4}$


OL159  *Caluinus in Ezechielem*
       CALVIN, Jean
       (probably In viginti prima Ezechielis capita praelectiones
       8°, Geneva, F. Perrin, 1565; Adams C300)

       Commentatores

       absent (probably alienated before 1645)

OL160 *Propugnatio Christ: religionis*
(doubtless COLOGNE, Cathedral
Antididagma seu Christianae et catholicae religionis propugnatio)
(probably 8°, Paris, 1549; Adams C2377 or C2378)

Pontificii

absent (possibly replaced c. 1695 by a copy of Adams C2377
given by James Duport)

OL161 *Conciliatio patrum cum Scripturis*
WESTHEMER, Bartholomaeus
En damus lector conciliationem sacrae scripturae et patrum
8°, Basle, B. Westhemer, 1536; Adams W68

Tractatus theologicae

I.13.58

OL162 *Gastius de Anabaptistis*
GAST, Johannes
(doubtless De Anabaptismi exordio, erroribus, libri duo
8°, Basle, R. Winter, 1544; Adams G279)

Controversiae

(doubtless I.5.36, but early marks lost in eighteenth-century
rebinding)

OL163 *Wolfgangus de Missa et Matrimonio*
CAPITO, Wolfgang Fabricius
Responsio de missa
8°, Strassburg, W. Rihelius, 1537; Adams C598

Protestantes

I.13.76

OL164 *Oswaldus in Marcum*
MYCONIUS, Oswaldus
(probably In evangelium Marci expositio
8°, Basle, T. Platter, 1538; Adams M2098)

Commentatores

absent (marked as missing in the 1667 catalogue)

OL165  *Knox de prædestinatione*
KNOX, John
An answer to a great nomber of blasphemous cavillations written
by an Anabaptist and adversarie to predestination, *English*
8°, (Geneva), J. Crespin, 1560; STC 15060

Controversiae

C.7.71


OL166  *Bibliander de Scripturis*

(166¹)  BIBLIANDER, Theodorus
Quomodo legere oporteat sacras scripturas
8°, Basle, J. Oporinus, 1550; Adams B1983

(166²)  CHYTRAEUS, David, the elder
De studio theologiae recto inchoando
8°, Wittenberg, J. Crato, 1562; Adams C1586

(166³)  HYPERIUS, Andreas
De theologo
8°, Basle, J. Oporinus, 1559; Adams H1274

Theologi practici

I.13.77¹⁻³


OL167  *Aurelius Prudentius*
PRUDENTIUS Clemens, Aurelius
Sacra, quae extant, poemata omnia
8°, Basle, H. Petri, 1562; Adams P2185

Poetae Latini

Z.8.139


OL168  *Nowellj Confutatio Dormannj*

(168¹)  NOWELL, Alexander
The reproufe of M. Dorman his proufe of certaine articles continued, *English*
4°, London, H. Wykes, 1566; STC 18742

(168²) BARTHLET, John
The pedegrewe of heretiques, *English*
4°, London, H. Denham, 1566; STC 1534

Protestantes

C.7.74¹⁻²

OL169 *Arnobius in Psalmos*
ARNOBIUS, Afer
Arnobii Afri commentarii in omnes psalmos
4°, Strassburg, J. Knoblouch, 1522; Adams B1405

Patres Latini

D.13.20

OL170 *De residentia Pastorum*

(170¹) DE RESIDENTIA PASTORUM
De residentia pastorum
4°, Florence, (?B. Sermatelli, 1565); Adams D178

(170²) FOX, Edward
Opus eximium de vera differentia regiae potestatis et ecclesiasticae
4°, London, T. Berthelet, 1534; STC 11218

(170³) FLACIUS, Mathias, Illyricus
Refutatio invectivae Bruni contra centurias historiae ecclesiasticae
4°, Basle, J. Oporinus, 1566; Adams F573

Tractatus theologicae

C.7.14¹⁻³

OL171 *Bruno in Epistolas*
BRUNO, Carthusian, St
(probably Brunonis, expositio in omnes divi Pauli epistolas
4°, Paris, B. Rembolt, 1509; Adams B1836)

Commentatores

(possibly E.9.12, but the early evidence is inconclusive)

OL172 *Psalterium hebraicè*
BIBLE, Psalms, Hebrew
Psalterium hebraicum, *Hebrew*
2°, (Isny, 1541–2); Adams B1353

Orientales

A.14.7


OL173 *Compendium talmudicum*
(unidentified; probably 4° or 8°)

Orientales

(probably absent)


OL174 *Christi Victoria et triumphus*
(unidentified; probably 4° or 8°)

(probably Tractatus theologicae

(probably absent)


OL175 *Homerus græco =Latine*
HOMER
(doubtless Omnia quae quidem extant opera Graece, adjecta ver-
sione Latina, *Greek and Latin*
2°, Basle, N. Bryling and B. Calybaeus, 1551; Adams H757)

Poetae Graeci

(doubtless II.6.4, but early marks lost in seventeenth-century
rebinding)


OL176 *Conradus Pellicanus*
PELLICANUS, Conradus
(unidentified commentary, probably 2°)

Commentatores

(absent; possibly replaced by the copies of Adams P596–8 given
by Nevile in 1611–12)

OL177  *Magdeburgensium vol. 8*
MAGDEBURG, Centuriators
Ecclesiastica historia
edition 'A', 13 vols in 8, 2°, Basle, J. Oporinus, 1560–74; Adams
M109

Historici ecclesiastici

L.14.8–15

OL178  *Egesippi Historia*
HEGESIPPUS
De rebus a Judaeorum principibus in obsidione fortiter gestis
2°, Cologne, J. Gennepaeus, 1544; Adams H149

Historici ecclesiastici

L.10.72

OL179  *Abdias Babylonius*
ABDIAS, pseud.
Liber de passione Jesu Christi, *etc., ed.* W. Lazius
2°, Basle, J. Oporinus, 1552; Adams A13

Historici ecclesiastici

L.14.4

OL180  *Abbas Vspergensis*
CONRADUS, Abbot of Auersperg
(unidentified edition of Chronicon, probably 2°)

Historici ecclesiastici

absent (probably replaced by the 2° edition, Strassburg, L. Zetz-
ner, 1609, now W.17.75; but it is possible that W.17.75 is itself
OL180)

OL181  *Vitæ Sanctorum Patrum*
JEROME, St
Vitae sanctorum patrum
2°, Cologne, J. Gennepaeus, 1548; Adams J149, C1473

Historici ecclesiastici

L.14.25

OL182 *Tritehemij Historia*

(182¹) TRITHEMIUS, Johannes
Chronicon monasterii Hirsaugensis, *etc.*
2°, Basle, J. Parcus and J. Oporinus, 1559; Adams T967

(182²) SCOTUS, Marianus
Chronica. Adjecimus M. Poloni historiam
2°, Basle, J. Oporinus, 1559; Adams S759

Historici ecclesiastici

L.10.66¹⁻²


OL183 *Baronij volumen octauum*
BARONIUS, Caesar, Cardinal
(probably Annales ecclesiastici
7 vols in 8, 2°, Antwerp, C. Plantin, 1589–98; Adams B238)

Historici ecclesiastici

absent (alienated by 1667; probably replaced by the Cologne, 1624, edition bought with the Whalley bequest in 1637)


OL184 *Eusebij Historia græcè*
EUSEBIUS, Pamphili, Bp of Caesarea
(doubtless Ecclesiasticae historiae, *Greek*
2°, Paris, R. Stephanus, 1544; Adams E1093)

Historici ecclesiastici

absent (probably sold as a duplicate, 1784)


OL185 *Thesauri Stephani vol: 3*
STEPHANUS, Robertus, the elder
(doubtless Dictionarium, seu Latinae linguae thesaurus, ed. 2a
3 vols, 2°, R. Stephanus, 1543; Adams S1820)

Lexicographi

absent (probably replaced c. 1705)

OL186 *Phauorini Dictionarium*
PHAVORINUS, Varinus, Bp of Nocera
(doubtless Dictionarium, *Greek*
2°, Basle, R. Winter, 1538, 1541; Adams P984)

Lexicographi

absent (probably sold as a duplicate, 1952)


OL187 *Hesychij Dictionarium*
HESYCHIUS, Alexandrinus
(probably Dictionarium, *Greek*
2°, Hagenau, T. Anshelm, 1521; Adams H508/9)

Lexicographi

absent (probably sold as a duplicate, 1784)


OL188 *Eustathij in Homerum vol: 3*
EUSTATHIUS, Bp of Thessalonica
(doubtless In Homeris Iliadis et Odysseae, *Greek and Latin*
3 vols, 2°, Rome, A. Blado, 1542, 1550; Adams E1107)

Poetae Graeci

absent (vols 2 and 3 probably alienated between 1675 and 1700;
vol 1 probably sold as a duplicate, 1784)


OL189 *Suidas græce*
SUIDAS
(doubtless Τὸμὲν παρὸν βιβλίον, Σουίδα, *Greek*
2°, Venice, Aldus, 1514; Adams S2062)

Lexicographi

(doubtless N.5.4, but early marks lost in seventeenth-century
rebinding)


OL190 *Commentarium hebræum in psalm.*
(unidentified; possibly an edition of Kimchi on the Psalms, probably 2°)

Orientales

(probably absent)

OL191* *Francisci Junij vol. 2*
JUNIUS, Franciscus, Senior
Opera theologica
2 vols, 2°, (Heidelberg), Sanctandreana, 1608

Protestantes

I.17.25–26


OL192  *Index Hieronymi*
(probably Jerome, St
index to Omnes quae extant lucubrationes
part of vol. ix, 2°, Basle, H. Froben and N. Episcopius, 1538;
Adams J117)

Patres Latini

absent (probably alienated in the mid-18th century)


OL193  *Athenæus græce*
ATHENAEUS, Naucratita
(unidentified edition of Dipnosophistarum, *Greek*, probably 2°)

Philologi

absent (probably alienated before 1667)


OL194  *Chrisost: in Epistolas vol: 2*
CHRYSOSTOM, John, Abp of Constantinople
(probably Expositio in D. Pauli epistolas, *Greek and Latin*
2 vols, 2°, (Heidelberg), H. Commelinus, 1595; Adams C1541)

Patres Graeci

absent (probably alienated between 1675 and 1700)


OL195  *Titus Liuius Hispanice*
LIVIUS, Titus
Todas las decadas, *Spanish*
2°, Cologne, A. Byrckmann, 1553; Adams L1367

Historici Romani

Z.4.78

OL196   *Josephi Historia Latinè*
        JOSEPHUS, Flavius
        Antiquitatum Judaicarum libri XX, *etc.*
        2°, Basle, H. Froben and N. Episcopius, 1548; Adams J364

        Historici ecclesiastici

        F.5.23

OL197* *Berchorij vol: 2*
        BERTHORUS, Petrus

   (197¹*) Opera omnia
          2°, Mainz, A. Hierat, 1609

   (197²*) Repertorium
          2°, Antwerp, J. Keerbergius, 1609

          Theologi practici

          E.10.33–34

OL198* *Gensneri opera vol 3*
        GESNER, Conrad

   (198¹*) (doubtless Historiae animalium lib. I de quadrupedibus viviparis
          2°, Zurich, C. Froschouer, 1551; Adams G532)

   (198²*) Historiae animalium liber IIII qui est de piscium & aquatilium
          animantium natura
          2°, Zurich, C. Froschouer, 1558; Adams G538

   (198³*) Historiae animalium liber III qui est de avium natura
          2°, Zurich, C. Froschouer, 1555; Adams G535

          Philosophiae naturalis

          198¹: absent (probably sold as a duplicate, 1784)
          198²⁻³: S.6.6., S.6.5
          (OL 198 probably added c. 1616)

OL199* *Thomæ Aquinatis 2ª 2ᵃᵉ*
AQUINAS, Thomas, St
Secunda secundae summae theologiae, cum comment. Caietani
2°, Antwerp, J. Keerbergius, 1612 (coloph. Mainz, B. Lippius,
1611)

Scholastici in Thomam

E.16.11 (probably bought 1616)

OL200* *Minshæi Dictionarium 11ᵐ: linguarum*
MINSHEU, John
Ductor in linguas, the guide into tongues. In undecim linguis,
*Latin and English*
2°, London, J. Browne, 1617; STC 17944

Lexicographi

absent (bought 1617; probably sold as a duplicate, 1784)

OL201* *Registarium Benefactorum*
TRINITY COLLEGE, CAMBRIDGE
Memoriale Collegio Trinitatis
2°, Vellum MS; James 994

Manuscripti

R.17.8

TS1   *Alexandrj Tartagni vol: 2*
      TARTAGNI, Alexander, da Imola
      (unidentified work or works in 2 vols, probably legal commentaries
      in 2°)

      (probably Jus, civile or canonicum)

      absent (probably replaced in 1608 by the Stanhope copies of Adams
      T173, 160, 164, 177, 169, now N.16.20–22)

TS2   *Marantæ praxis Ciuilis*
      MARANTA, Robertus
      (probably Speculum aureum, et lumen advocatorum praxis civilis
      4°, Venice, G. Bonelli, 1568; Adams M513)

      Jus civile

      absent (probably alienated in the mid-eighteenth century)

TS3   *Petrus de Ferrarijs*
      FERRARI, Giampietro, of Pavia
      (unidentified, probably a 4° or 8° edition of Practica)

      (probably Jus civile)

      absent (probably replaced in 1608 by the Stanhope copy of Adams
      F271, now N.7.29)

TS4   *Baptista Porta de Literis*
      PORTA, Giovanni Battista della
      De furtivis literarum notis
      4°, London, J. Wolphius, 1591; STC 20118

      Philologi

      VI.7.37²

TS5   *Gratiani Decretum*
      GRATIANUS, Bononiensis
      (unidentified edition of Decretum, probably 2°)

      Jus canonicum

      absent (possibly alienated after 1800)

TS6   *Consilia Ludouicj*
      PONTANUS, Ludovicus
      (unidentified edition of Consilia, probably 2°)

      Jus canonicum

      absent (probably replaced in 1608 by the Stanhope copy of Adams
      P1874, now N.9.11)

TS7   *Singularia Doctorum*
      SINGULARIA DOCTORUM
      (unidentified edition of Singularia doctorum, probably 2°)

      Jus civile

      absent (probably replaced in 1608 by the Stanhope copy of S1215,
      now N.16.26)

TS8   *Ferdinandi Vasquij vol: 2*
      VASQUEZ Y MENCHACA, Ferdinando
      (unidentified work or works in 2 vols, probably 4° or 8°, possibly
      Controversiarum libri)

      (probably Jus, civile or canonicum)

      absent (possibly replaced in 1608 by Stanhope copies of Adams
      V311, 312, one of which may now be N.12.121)

TS9   *Communes opiniones Gabrielis*
      GABRIEL, Antonio
      (unidentified edition of Communion opinionum syntagma,
      probably 2°, possibly Adams G5)

      Jus civile

      absent (possibly replaced in 1608 by the Stanhope copy of Adams
      G5, now N.15.4)

TS10  *Consilia Criminalia Zilettj*
      ZILETTUS, Johannes Baptista
      (unidentified edition of Criminalium consiliorum, probably 2°)

      Jus civile

      absent (probably replaced in 1608 by the Stanhope copy of Adams
      Z157, now N.8.91)

TS11 *Tractatus Caroli Molinæi*
DU MOULIN, Charles
Tractatus commerciorum
8°, Lyons, A. de Harsy, 1572; Adams D1097

Jus civile

Y.7.129

TS12 *Practica Johannis Berberij*
BARBIER, Jean
Aurea practica
8°, Cologne, J. Gymnicus II, 1576; Adams B189

Jus civile

Y.7.76

TS13 *Hieronymus de Monte Brixiano*
MONTE, Hieronymus de
Tractatus de finibus regendis civitatum, castrorum, ac praediorum
8°, Heidelberg, M. Schirat, 1565; Adams M1697

Jus civile

P.7.35

TS14 *Synopsis totius Juris*
ROSENTHAL, Heinrich von
Synopsis totius juris feudalis
4°, (Geneva), E. Vignon, 1588; Adams R788

Jus civile

N.12.5

TS15 *Mynsingeri obseruationes*
MYNSINGER, Joachim
(unidentified edition of Singularium observationum judicii imperialis camerae centuriae quatuor, probably 4° or 8°)

Jus civile

absent (probably alienated between 1640 and 1700)

TS16 *Lanfrancus de Arbitris*
    ORIANO, Lanfranc ab
    De arbitris et compromissis
    8°, Cologne, J. Gymnicus II, 1590; Adams O264

    Jus civile et canonicum

    Y.7.93


TS17 *Cottæ Memoralia*
    COTTA, Catellianus
    (unidentified edition of Memoralia, probably 4° or 8°)

    Jus civile

    absent (probably alienated between 1640 and 1700)


TS18 *Pruckman de Regalibus*
    PRUECKMANN, Friedrich
    Paragraphi soluta potestas tractatus de regalibus
    8°, Wittenberg, S. Grunenberg, 1592; Adams P2193

    Jus civile

    P.7.62


TS19 *Alciati Compendiarium*
    ALCIATUS, Andreas
    (probably Judiciarii processus compendium
    8°, Cologne, A. Birckmann, 1566; Adams A622)

    Jus civile

    (probably P.7.36, but title-page missing by 1700)


TS20 *Viglij comm. in institutiones*
    AYTTA, Wigle van, of Swichem
    Commentaria in decem titulos institutionum juris civilis
    8°, Lyons, Q. P. Tinghius, 1575; Adams A2354

    Jus civile

    M.7.159$^2$

TS21 *Lanfranci practica iudiciaria*
ORIANO, Lanfranc ab
(unidentified edition of Practica judiciaria, probably 4° or 8°)

Jus civile et canonicum

absent (probably alienated in the mid-eighteenth century)


TS22 *Vigelij Methodus iuris*
VIGELIUS, Nicolaus
Methodus juris controversi
8°, Basle, Oporinus, 1579; Adams V735

Jus civile

P.7.61


TS23 *Tractatus de pensionibus*
GIGAS, Hieronymus
Tractatus de pensionibus ecclesiasticis
8°, Lyons, G. Rouille, 1548; Adams G603

Jus civile

P.7.20


TS24 *Alfonsus a Castro*
CASTRO, Alfonsus de
(unidentified work, probably 4° or 8°)

absent (probably alienated before 1640)


TS25 *Jmberti institutiones*
IMBERT, Jean
Institutionum forensium Galliae pene totius libri quatuor
8°, Lyons, S. Gryphius, 1552; Adams I49

Jus civile

P.7.19

TS26 *Pickius de re nautica*
PECKIUS, Petrus
Commentaria in omnes pene juris civilis titulos ad rem nauticam
pertinentes
8°, Louvain, P. Colinaeus, 1556; Adams P540

Jus civile

Y.7.88

TS27 *Cassadorj Decisiones*
CASSADORIS, Gulielmus
(probably Decisiones aureae
8°, Paris, le Preux, 1545; Adams C837)

Jus canonicum

absent (probably alienated in the mid-eighteenth century)

TS28 *Mantuæ obseruationes*
BENAVIDES, Marco, Mantuano
Observationum legalium libri X
8°, Lyons, G. and M. Beringi, 1546; Adams B621

Jus civile

Y.7.1

TS29 *Panormitani volumu: 4ʳ*
TUDESCHIS, Nicolaus, Panormitanus

(29¹) Prima pars super primo decretalium
2°, Lyons, J. Saccon, 1512; Adams T1037

(29²) Secunda pars super primo
2°, Lyons, J. Saccon, 1512; Adams T1039

(29³) Prima pars super secundo
2°, Lyons, J. Saccon, 1513; Adams T1041

(29⁴) Secunda pars super secundo
2°, Lyons, J. Saccon, 1513; Adams T1043

(29⁵) Tertia pars super secundo
2°, Lyons, J. Saccon, 1513; Adams T1046

($29^6$) Lectura super tertio
2°, Lyons, J. Saccon, 1513; Adams T1050

($29^7$) Ultima pars super quarto et quinto
2°, Lyons, J. Moylin, 1513; Adams T1048

($29^8$) Aurea opuscula
2°, Lyons, J. Saccon, 1512; Adams T1020$^1$

($29^9$) Repertorium
2°, Lyons, N. de Benedictis, 1512; Adams T1049, T1020$^2$

Jus canonicum

N.17.21$^{1-2}$ ($29^{1-2}$), N.17.22$^{1-3}$ ($29^{3-5}$), N.17.23$^{1-2}$ ($29^{6-7}$), N.17.24$^{1-2}$ ($28^{8-9}$). Removed to Caius College Library, probably in the seventeenth century; returned to Trinity October 1874.

TS30 *Durandi speculum iuris*
DURANDUS, Gulielmus I
Speculum juris
2°, Basle, Froben, 1574; Adams D1173

Jus canonicum

M.18.27

TS31 *Sextus liber Decretalium*
BONIFACE VIII, Pope
Sextus liber
2°, Lyons, F. Fradin, 1517; Adams B2435

Jus canonicum

N.17.26

TS32 *Alciati vol: 4$^r$*
ALCIATUS, Andreas
(Unidentified works, probably Opera omnia, 4 vols, 2°)

(probably Jus civile)

absent (probably alienated by 1700; possibly replaced by the Würzburg copy of Adams A582, now N.10.7–10, in the seventeenth century)

TS33 *Rebuffi praxis beneficiorum*
 REBUFFUS, Petrus
 Praxis beneficiorum
 2°, Lyons, C. Senneton, 1564; Adams R248

 Jus canonicum

 M.15.9


TS34 *Regulæ vtriusque Juris*
 REGULAE JURIS
 Regulae juris tam civis quam canonici
 2°, Venice, H. Scotus, 1571; Adams J490

 Jus civile et canonicum

 N.8.81


TS35 *Julij Clari tractatus*
 CLARUS, Julius
 Receptarum sententiarum opera omnia
 2°, Frankfurt a. M., N. Bassaeus, 1590; Adams C2068

 Jus civile

 N.8.82


TS36 *Budæus in Pandectas*

(36$^1$) BUDAEUS, Gulielmus
 Annotationes in Pandectarum libros
 2°, Paris, J. Petit, 1535; Adams B3087

(36$^2$) THEODOSIUS II
 Codicis Theodosiani libri XVI
 2°, Basle, H. Petrus, 1528; Adams T541

 Jus civile

 N.8.68$^{1-2}$

TS37 *Gomesij resolutiones*
GOMEZ, Antonio
Commentariorum variorumque resolutionum juris civilis tomi tres
2°, Frankfurt a. M., G. Corvinus, 1572; Adams G847

Jus civile

N.8.72


TS38 *Domini de Rota decisiones*
ROME, Church of, Rota
(unidentified edition of Decisiones, probably 2°)

Jus canonicum

absent (probably alienated by 1640)


TS39 *Zasius in Pandectas*
FREIGIUS, Johannes Thomas
Zasius in Pandectas commentarii
2°, Basle, S. Henricpetri, 1576; Adams F1026

Jus civile

N.8.98


TS40 *Practica Panormitani*

(40¹) AUERBACH, Johannes (formerly ascribed to TUDESCHIS, Nicolaus, Panormitanus)
Processus judiciarius
2°, Venice, F. Girardengus, 1488; Goff A–1027

Jus canonicum

(40²) ZANETINIS, Hieronymus de
Contrarietates
2°, Bologna, F. de Benedictis, 1490; Hain *16274

Jus civile et canonicum

VI.16.30¹⁻²

TS41 *Lexicon Juridicum*
SCHARDIUS, Simon
Lexicon juridicum juris Rom. simul et Pontificii
2°, Basle, Episcopius, 1582; Adams S625

Jus civile et canonicum

M.15.14


TS42 *Wesenbecius in Codicem*
WESENBECIUS, Matthaeus
(unidentified edition of In codicem Justiniani, probably 2°)

Jus civile

absent (probably alienated by 1700)


TS43 *Petri Rebuffi tractatus*
REBUFFUS, Petrus
Tractatus varii
2°, Lyons, G. Rouille, 1581; Adams R251

Jus civile et canonicum

N.15.13


TS44 *Sigonij historia de regno Jtaliae*
SIGONIUS, Carolus
(probably Historiarum de regno Italiae libri XX
2°, Frankfurt a. M., A. Wechel, 1591; Adams S1124)

Historici recentiores

absent (probably alienated after 1784)


TS45 *Leopaldi Dickij Oeconomia*
DICKIUS, Leopold
*Οἰκονομία*
2°, Basle, B. I. Herold, 1567; Adams D411

Jus civile

N.8.80

TS46 *Bodinus de repub: gallice*
BODIN, Jean
Les six livres de la république, *French*
2°, Paris, J. du Puys, 1577; Adams B2235

Historici recentiores

S.6.25


TS47 *Herodotus græco =Latinè*
HERODOTUS

(47¹) (probably ʽΗροδότου τοῦ ʼΑλικαρνασσέως ʽΙστορία λόγοι θ´,
*Greek* 2°, (Geneva), H. Stephanus, 1570; Adams H397)

(47²) (unidentified Latin version)

Historici antiquiores

absent (probably alienated in the mid-eighteenth century)


TS48 *Cælius Rhodiginus*
RHODIGINUS, Ludovicus Coelius
(probably Lectionum antiquarum libri XXX
2°, Basle, Froben and Episcopius, 1542; Adams R451)

Philologi

absent (probably sold as a duplicate, 1784)


TS49 *Adrianus Turnebus*
TURNEBUS, Adrianus
(probably an unidentified edition of Adversariorum tomi III, probably 2°)

Philologi

absent (probably replaced in the 1590s by the Sledd copy of Adams
T1146, now III.14.5)

TS50 *Cornelius Gemma*
>    GEMMA, Cornelius
>    (probably De arte cyclognomica
>    4°, Antwerp, C. Plantin, 1569; Adams G372)
>
>    Philosophi recentiores
>
>    absent (probably replaced in the 1590s by the Sledd copy of Adams
>    G372, now S.6.39)


TS51 *Petri Rami tabulæ*

($51^1$) RAMUS, Petrus
>    Professio regia
>    2°, Basle, S. Henricpetri, 1576; Adams R115
>
>    Philosophi recentiores

($51^2$) TABULAE
>    Tabulae locorum communium theologicorum
>    2°, Basle, S. Henricpetri, 1575; Adams T19
>
>    Tractatus theologici

($51^3$) FREIGIUS, Johannes Thomas
>    Partitiones juris utriusque; partitiones feudales
>    2°, Basle, S. Henricpetri, 1571; Adams F1015
>
>    Jus civile et canonicum

($51^4$) WECKER, Johannes Jacobus
>    Medicinae utriusque syntaxes
>    2°, Basle, Episcopius, 1576; Adams W34
>
>    Medici

($51^5$) MORUS, Horatius
>    Tabulae universam chirurgicam miro ordine complectentes
>    2°, Venice, G. Zilletti, 1572; Adams M1834
>
>    Medici
>
>    S.5.34$^{1-3,\ 5-6}$

TS52 *Xenophon græco=latinè*
XENOPHON
(probably Ξενοφῶντος ἅπαντα τὰ σωζόμενα βιβλία, *Greek and Latin*
2°, (Geneva), H. Stephanus, 1561; Adams X10

Historici antiquiores

absent (probably sold as a duplicate, 1952)

TS53 *Guido Bonatus*
BONATUS, Guido
De astronomia tractatus X
2°, Basle, (?), 1550; Adams B2382

Mathematici

S.5.17[1]

TS54 *Stanihurst de rebus Hiber:*
STANYHURST, Richard
De rebus in Hibernia gestis, libri IV
4°, Leyden, C. Plantin, 1584; Adams S1634

Historici recentiores

X.10.106

TS55 *Hermogenis vol. 3*
HERMOGENES

(55[1]) De ratione tractandae gravitatis occultae, *Greek and Latin, ed.* J. Sturmius
8°, (Strassburg), J. Rihelius, 1571; Adams H363

(55[2]) De dicendi generibus, *Greek and Latin, ed.* J. Sturmius
8°, (Strassburg), J. Rihelius, 1571; Adams H356

(55[3]) Partitionum rhetoricarum liber, *Greek and Latin, ed.* J. Sturmius
8°, (Strassburg), J. Rihelius, 1570; Adams H364

(55[4]) De ratione inveniendi oratoria, *Greek and Latin, ed.* J. Sturmius
8°, Strassburg, J. Rihelius, 1570; Adams H362

Oratores

II.7.135[1-2] (55[1-2]), II.8.122 (55[3]), II.8.120 (55[4])

TS56 *Dictionarium latino =Hispa:*
NEBRISSENSIS, Aelius Antonius
Dictionarium Latinohispanicum
4°, Antwerp, J. Steelsius, 1553; Adams N122

Lexicographi

III.10.106

TS57 *Plinij naturali historia*
PLINIUS SECUNDUS, Gaius
(probably Historiae mundi libri XXXVII, *ed.* I. N. Victorius
2°, Lyons, A. Vincentius, 1563; Adams P1577)

Philosophi naturales

absent (probably sold as a duplicate, 1784)

TS58 *Selectorum tractatuum vol: 2*
TRACTATUS
Selecti tractatus juris varii, vere aurei, de successione
2°, Cologne, G. Calenius, 1569; Adams T871

Jus civile

N.9.21

TS59 *Tractatus vere aurej vol: 2*
TRACTATUS
Selecti tractatus juris varii, vere aurei, assecurationis
2°, Cologne, G. Calenius, 1569; Adams T870

Jus civile

M.15.12

# INDEX

| | |
|---|---|
| ABDIAS, pseud. | OL179 |
| AENEAS SILVIUS, Piccolomini | OL128 |
| ALBERTUS, Magnus, Bp of Ratisbon | OL40 |
| ALCIATUS, Andreas | TS19, TS32 |
| ALEXANDER, Aphrodisiensis | OL106$^{1-2}$, OL111 |
| ALEXANDRO, Alexander ab | OL141 |
| ANSELM, Abp of Canterbury | OL63 |
| APPIANUS, of Alexandria | OL124 |

AQUINAS, Thomas, St     OL43, OL199*
ARETIUS FELINUS (i.e. BUCER, Martin) OL59
ARISTOPHANES      OL91
ARISTOTLE       OL97, OL99, OL100, OL103$^{1-2}$,
           OL104$^{1-2}$, OL105, OL140
ARNOBIUS, Afer     OL169
ASCONIUS PEDIANUS, Quintus  OL147
ATHANASIUS, Abp of Alexandria, St OL1
ATHENAEUS, Naucratita   OL193
AUERBACH, Johannes    TS40$^1$
AUGUSTINE, Bp of Hippo, St   OL11, OL14
AYTTA, Wigle van, of Swichem  TS20
BARBIER, Jean      TS12
BARONIUS, Caesar, Cardinal   OL183
BARTHLET, John     OL168$^2$
BARTHOLOMAEUS ANGLICUS  OL94
BASIL, Abp of Caesarea, the Great, St OL20
BEDE, the Venerable    OL132$^2$
BEMBO, Pietro, Cardinal   OL133, OL146$^{1-4}$
BENAVIDES, Marco, Mantuano  TS28
BERTHORUS, Petrus    OL197$^{1-2}$*
BIBLE, Latin      OL2, OL5, OL44
  French      OL3
  O.T., polyglot    OL4
  Psalms, Hebrew    OL172, OL190
BIBLIANDER, Theodorus   OL166$^1$
BODIN, Jean      TS46
BONATUS, Guido     TS53
BONIFACE VIII, Pope    OL143, TS31
BRENZ, Johannes     OL29$^{1-5}$, OL29$^{6}$*, OL158$^2$
BREYDENBACH, Bernhard von  OL127$^2$
BRUNO, Carthusian, St    OL171
BRUNUS, Conradus    OL80
BUCER, Martin     OL31$^1$, OL31$^3$, OL59, OL158$^4$
BUDAEUS, Gulielmus    TS36$^1$
BULLINGER, Heinrich    OL154$^{3-4}$, OL156
CAESARES      OL118
CAJETANUS, T. de Vio    OL43, OL199*
CALVIN, Jean      OL153, OL159
CAMERARIUS, Joachimus, Senior  OL108
CAPITO, Wolfgang Fabricius   OL163
CASALIUS, Gaspar, Bp of Coimbra OL70
CASSADORIS, Gulielmus   TS27
CASTRO, Alfonsus de    OL48, TS24
CHRISTIAN CHURCH, Fathers  OL15, OL151, OL158$^3$, OL181
CHRISTI VICTORIA ET TRIUMPHUS OL174
CHRISTOPHORUS, a Castro   OL71*
CHRYSOSTOM, John, Abp of Constantinople OL194
CHYTRAEUS, David, the elder  OL166$^2$
CICERO, Marcus Tullius   OL109, OL134, OL138
CLARUS, Julius     TS35
COCHLAEUS, Johannes    OL52$^2$, OL80, OL130, OL156
COLOGNE, Cathedral    OL160
CONRADUS, Abbot of Auersperg  OL180
COTTA, Catellianus    TS17
COUNCILS      OL6, OL7, OL155

| | |
|---|---|
| CUSPINIANUS, Johannes | OL89 |
| CYRIL, Abp of Alexandria, St | OL10 |
| DEMOSTHENES | OL73 |
| DE RESIDENTIA PASTORUM | OL170[1] |
| DICKIUS, Leopold | TS45 |
| DIDYMUS, Alexandrinus | OL107 |
| DIODORUS, Siculus | OL72 |
| DIONYSIUS, the Areopagite | OL25 |
| DIONYSIUS, Carthusianus, à Rickel | OL49 |
| DIONYSIUS, of Halicarnassus | OL98 |
| DORMAN, Thomas | OL168[1] |
| DRIEDO, Johannes | OL62 |
| DU MOULIN, Charles | TS11 |
| DURANDUS, Gulielmus I | TS30 |
| DURANDUS, Gulielmus, Bp of Meaux | OL45 |
| EPIPHANIUS, Bp of Constantia | OL13 |
| ERASMUS, Desiderius | OL66 |
| EURIPIDES | OL145 |
| EUSEBIUS, Pamphili, Bp of Caesarea | OL132[2], OL184 |
| EUSTATHIUS, Bp of Thessalonica | OL188 |
| FABER, Jacobus, Stapulensis | OL79 |
| FERRARI, Giampietro, of Pavia | TS3 |
| FERUS, Johannes | OL77 |
| FICINUS, Marsilius | OL101 |
| FLACIUS, Mathias, Illyricus | OL28, OL60, OL158[1], OL170[3] |
| FOX, Edward | OL170[2] |
| FREIGIUS, Johannes Thomas | TS39, TS51[3] |
| GABRIEL, Antonio | TS9 |
| GAGUIN, Robert | OL150 |
| GARDINER, Stephen, Bp of Winchester | OL30[1] |
| GAST, Johannes | OL14, OL162 |
| GEMMA, Cornelius | TS50 |
| GENSNER (i.e. GESNER, Conrad) | OL198[1-3]* |
| GERBELIUS, Nicolaus | OL125 |
| GESNER, Conrad | OL113, OL198[1-3]* |
| GIGAS, Hieronymus | TS23 |
| GIOVIO, Paolo, Bp of Nocera | OL123 |
| GOETHALS, Hendrik, of Ghent | OL39 |
| GOMEZ, Antonio | TS37 |
| GORRAN, Nicolaus de | OL65 |
| GRAMMATICI | OL137[2] |
| GRATIANUS, Bononiensis | TS5 |
| GREGORY, Patriarch of Constantinople, Nazianzus, St | OL22 |
| GREGORY I, Pope, the Great | OL12 |
| GREGORY IX, Pope | OL144 |
| GUALTHERUS, Rodolphus, Senior | OL54, OL154[2] |
| GULIELMUS, Altissiodorensis | OL102 |
| HEGESIPPUS | OL178 |
| HENRIQUEZ, Henricus | OL36 |
| HERMAN, of Wied, Abp of Cologne | OL78 |
| HERMOGENES | TS55[1-4] |
| HERODOTUS | OL117[2], TS47[1-2] |
| HESIOD | OL110 |
| HESYCHIUS, Alexandrinus | OL187 |
| HILARY, Bp of Poitiers, St | OL24 |

| | |
|---|---|
| HISTORIA SACRA MULTORUM PATRUM | OL15 |
| HISTORIA SANCTORUM PATRUM | OL151 |
| HOLINSHED, Raphael | OL129 |
| HOMER | OL107, OL108, OL175, OL188 |
| HOSIUS, Stanislaus | OL51 |
| HYPERIUS, Andreas | OL166$^3$ |
| IMBERT, Jean | TS25 |
| IRENAEUS, Bp of Lyons, St | OL19 |
| JACOBUS PHILIPPUS, de Bergamo | OL90 |
| JEROME, St | OL181, OL192 |
| JOHANNES, Grammaticus | OL103$^{1-2}$, OL104$^2$, OL106$^2$, OL112 |
| JOSEPHUS, Flavius | OL196 |
| JOVIUS, Paulus | OL123 |
| JUNIUS, Franciscus, Senior | OL191* |
| JUSTIN, Martyr, St | OL23$^{1-2}$ |
| JUSTINIANUS, Laurentius | OL34 |
| KIMCHI, David | OL190 |
| KNOX, John | OL165 |
| LACTANTIUS FIRMIANUS, Lucius Coelius | OL17 |
| LATIMER, Hugh | OL157 |
| LATOMUS, Jacobus | OL52$^1$ |
| LAVATER, Ludwig | OL154$^5$ |
| LAZIUS, Wolfgang | OL179 |
| LIBANIUS | OL148 |
| LINDANUS, Wilhelmus, Bp of Roermond | OL84 |
| LITURGIES, Greek rite | OL152 |
| Latin rite | OL85 |
| LIVIUS, Titus | OL115, OL195 |
| LUCIAN, of Samosata | OL120 |
| LYCOSTHENES, Conrad | OL136 |
| LYRA, Nicolas de | OL44 |
| MAFFEIUS, Raphael, Volaterranus | OL119 |
| MAGDEBURG, Centuriators | OL177 |
| MARANTA, Robertus | TS2 |
| MARLORAT, Augustin | OL33, OL53 |
| MARSILIUS, of Padua | OL61 |
| MARTINUS, Polonus, Abp of Gniesen | OL182$^2$ |
| MARTYR, Peter, Vermilius | OL30$^{1-4}$, OL154$^6$ |
| MELANCTHON, Philipp | OL58 |
| MICHAEL, Ephesius | OL104$^1$ |
| MIDDLETON, Richard | OL38$^{1-4}$ |
| MINSHEU, John | OL200* |
| MONTE, Hieronymus de | TS13 |
| MORUS, Horatius | TS51$^5$ |
| MUHAMMAD, the Prophet | OL131 |
| MUNSTER, Sebastian | OL4, OL121 |
| MUSCULUS, Wolfgang | OL32$^{1-5}$ |
| MYCONIUS, Oswaldus | OL164 |
| MYNSINGER, Joachim | TS15 |
| NEBRISSENSIS, Aelius Antonius | TS56 |
| NICEPHORUS, Callistus | OL122 |
| NIZOLIUS, Marius | OL134 |
| NOWELL, Alexander | OL168$^1$ |
| OCKAM, Gulielmus | OL41$^{1-4}$* |
| OECOLAMPADIUS, Joannes | OL26, OL31$^2$ |
| OECUMENIUS, Bp of Tricca | OL9, OL27 |

| | |
|---|---|
| ORATORES GRAECI | OL74 |
| ORIANO, Lanfranc ab | TS16, TS21 |
| PALLADIUS, Bp of Aspona | OL151 |
| PANORMITANUS | TS29$^{1-9}$, TS40$^1$ |
| PAUSANIAS | OL116 |
| PECKIUS, Petrus | TS26 |
| PELLICANUS, Conradus | OL56, OL176 |
| PEREZ DE AYALA, Martin, of Valentia | OL83 |
| PETRUS, Comestor | OL132$^1$ |
| PHAVORINUS, Varinus, Bp of Nocera | OL186 |
| PHILO, Judaeus | OL18 |
| PHILOPONUS, Johannes | OL103$^{1-2}$, OL104$^2$, OL106$^2$, OL112 |
| PICO DELLA MIRANDOLA, Giovanni Francesco | OL146$^4$ |
| PIGHIUS, Albertus | OL82$^{1-2}$ |
| PINEDA, Joannes de, of Seville | OL46* |
| PIUS II, Pope | OL128 |
| PLATO | OL86, OL101 |
| PLINIUS SECUNDUS, Gaius | TS57 |
| PLUTARCH | OL96 |
| POETAE GRAECI | OL88 |
| POLITIANUS, Angelus | OL92 |
| POLLUX, Julius, of Naucratis | OL135$^1$ |
| PONTANUS, Ludovicus | TS6 |
| PORPHYRIUS, of Tyre | OL104$^1$ |
| PORTA, Giovanni Battista della | TS4 |
| PRADUS, Hieronymus | OL47* |
| PRISCIANUS, Caesariensis | OL137$^1$ |
| PROCLUS, Diadochus | OL112 |
| PRUDENTIUS Clemens, Aurelius | OL167 |
| PRUECKMANN, Friedrich | TS18 |
| RAMUS, Petrus | TS51$^1$ |
| REBUFFUS, Petrus | TS33, TS43 |
| REDMAN, John | OL154$^1$ |
| REGULAE JURIS | TS34 |
| RHODIGINUS, Ludovicus Coelius | TS48 |
| ROLEWINCK, Werner | OL127$^1$ |
| ROME, Church of, Rota | TS38 |
| ROSENTHAL, Heinrich von | TS14 |
| RULAND, Martin | OL158$^3$ |
| SABELLICUS, Marcus Antonius Coccius | OL87 |
| SAYRUS, Gregorius | OL35$^{1-2}$* |
| SCHARDIUS, Simon | TS41 |
| SCOTUS, Marianus | OL182$^2$ |
| SICHARDUS, Johannes | OL16 |
| SIGONIUS, Carolus | TS44 |
| SIMLER, Josias | OL113, OL154$^6$ |
| SIMPLICIUS | OL99, OL105 |
| SINGULARIA DOCTORUM | TS7 |
| SOTO, Domingo de | OL64 |
| STANYHURST, Richard | TS54 |
| STAPLETON, Thomas | OL50 |
| STEPHANUS, Byzantinus | OL135$^2$ |
| STEPHANUS, Robertus, the elder | OL139, OL185 |
| STOBAEUS, Johannes | OL126 |
| STRABO | OL68 |
| SUETONIUS TRANQUILLUS, Gaius | OL118 |

| | |
|---|---|
| SUIDAS | OL189 |
| TABULAE | TS51[1-5] |
| TALMUD | OL173 |
| TARTAGNI, Alexander, da Imola | TS1 |
| TERTULLIANUS, Quintus Septimius Florens | OL21 |
| THEMISTIUS | OL106[1] |
| THEOCRITUS | OL110 |
| THEODOSIUS II | TS36[2] |
| THEOPHYLACTUS, Abp of Ochrida | OL8 |
| THUCYDIDES | OL69, OL117[1] |
| TIRAQUELLUS, Andreas | OL141, OL142 |
| TITELMANN, Franz | OL76 |
| TOLETUS, Franciscus | OL37* |
| TRACTATUS | TS58, TS59 |
| TRINITY COLLEGE, CAMBRIDGE | OL201* |
| TRITHEMIUS, Johannes | OL182[1] |
| TRUXILLO, Thomas de | OL75 |
| TUDESCHIS, Nicolaus, Panormitanus | TS29[1-9], TS40[1] |
| TUPPIUS, Laurentius | OL155 |
| TURNEBUS, Adrianus | TS49 |
| TUSANUS, Jacobus | OL67 |
| VALERIUS MAXIMUS | OL95 |
| VASQUEZ, Gabriel | OL42* |
| VASQUEZ Y MENCHACA, Ferdinando | TS8 |
| VATABLUS, Franciscus | OL2 |
| VICTORIUS, Petrus, the elder | OL100, OL138 |
| VIGELIUS, Nicolaus | TS22 |
| VIGUERIUS, Joannes | OL81 |
| VILLALPANDUS, Joannes Baptista | OL47* |
| VITAE CAESARUM | OL118 |
| VITAE PATRUM | OL181 |
| VIVES, Johannes Ludovicus | OL131 |
| VORAGINE, Jacobus de | OL93 |
| WECKER, Johannes Jacobus | TS51[4] |
| WESENBECIUS, Matthaeus | TS42 |
| WESTHEMER, Bartholomaeus | OL161 |
| WHITGIFT, John, Abp | OL57 |
| WOLFFHART, Conrad | OL136 |
| WOTTON, Edward | OL114 |
| XENOPHON | TS52 |
| ZANCHI, Basilio | OL149 |
| ZANETINIS, Hieronymus de | TS40[2] |
| ZASIUS, Udalricus | TS39 |
| ZILETTUS, Johannes Baptista | TS10 |
| ZWINGLI, Ulrich | OL31[2], OL55[1-2] |

# THE SEVENTEENTH-CENTURY LIBRARY CATALOGUES

*Memoriale*

*Benefactions and 'register' book, c.1612–c.1675* (TCL MS R.17.8). *Memoriale Collegio Sanctae et Individuae Trinitatis in Academia Cantabrigiensi dicatum,* 1614, pp. 85–133.[1] Entries give authors or short titles; in order of benefactions. Most lists are in shelf order, but without locations. Written c.1612–c.1675 by John Scott and others.[2] Incomplete (See fig. 10.)

*1640*

*Alphabetical Finding list, c.1640* (TCL Add. MS a.103). Eleven broadside sheets, 36cm × 46cm, versos blank, which may have been posted in the Library but which are now bound in folio. Entries give authors or short titles; locations give case, side, and shelf, but not running numbers. Written, probably by William Clutterbooke, Librarian,[3] c.1640; not significantly added to.
*Volume totals*: MS 353; printed 1,819; total 2,172. (See fig. 25.)

*1645*

*Draft class catalogue, c.1645–8* (BL MS Sloane 78, ff. 139ᵃ–154ᵃ). Class catalogue drafted on sixteen folio leaves; lacks classes 22–26; law books not

---

[1] OL201*; see pp. 34–5 above, and Willis and Clark, ii, pp. 671–3.
[2] John Scott is identified in the College accounts as the original scribe (see p. 34 n. 4 above), and he continued to write the majority of the entries until the late 1630s. Other scribes were employed before as well as after the late 1630s, one of them being 'Mʳ Evans writing master' (TC Mun., JB accounts, 1670–1, Extraordinaries).
[3] Clutterbooke signed the admissions book when he was admitted Scholar in 1624; and he signed an admonition in 1638 (TC Mun., *Admissions and admonitions*, p. 257; *Conclusion book A*, p. ²16). These signatures agree with the handwriting of *1640*.

included. Entries give authors or short titles, with class, shelf, and running number. Written c.1645–8, possibly by Thomas Pockley BA;[1] not added to; probably never used.

*Volume totals* (incomplete): MS 198; printed 1,471; total 1,669. (See fig. 26.)

## 1667

*Indexed class catalogue, 1667–c.1675* (TCL Add. MS a.101). Folio class catalogue, drafted by Thomas Griffith, Librarian,[2] in Add. MSS a.101 A, 102; written out by him and dated 1667 in Add. MS a.101; added to until c. 1675; with an index of printed books; bound pamphlets and law books not included. Entries give authors and short titles, and occasionally dates; with class, shelf, and running numbers.

*Volume totals, 1667*: MS 434; printed 2,247; total 2,681.

*Volume totals, c.1675*: MS 453; printed 2,607; total 3,060. (See figs 27, 29.)

## 1675

*Indexed class catalogue, c.1675–95* (TCL Add. MS a.104). Folio class catalogue, written (printed books) by James Manfeild, Librarian,[3] and (manuscripts) by John Laughton, Librarian;[4] begun c.1675–7, added to until 1695; with an index of printed books; bound pamphlets and law books not included. Entries give authors and short titles, with dates, and usually places of printing; with class, shelf, and running numbers.

*Volume totals, c.1675*: MS 501; printed 2,705; total, 3,206.

*Volume totals, 1695*: MS 519; printed 2,937; total 3,456. (See figs 28, 30.)

---

[1] TC Mun., JB accounts, 1645–6, Extraordinaries: 'To the Library Keeper for a booke to take a Catalogue of the bookes – 1ˢ 6ᵈ'. TC Mun., *Conclusion book B*, p. 19: 2 March 1649[50] 'Then concluded that five pounds be given to Sir Pockley as a gratuity, he haveing done something wch is usefull in the Library'. The handwriting of Thomas Pockley's brief entry in the admissions book when he was admitted a minor fellow in 1650 could be, but is not certainly, that of the scribe of *1645* (TC Mun., *Admissions 1645–59*, p. 29).

[2] The distinctive handwriting of Add. MSS a.101, 101A, and 102 is certainly Griffith's; compare his entries in TC Mun., *Admissions and admonitions*, p. 145 (1641); and TC Mun., *Fellows' exit and redit book*, exit 30 July 1673.

[3] See Manfeild's handwriting in TC Mun., *Admissions and admonitions*, p. 159 (1674); and *Fellows' exit and redit book*, exit 6 January 1679.

[4] See Laughton's handwriting in TC Mun., *Admissions and admonitions*, p. 159 (1679); and *Fellows' exit and redit book*, exit 27 July 1685. Laughton's catalogue of the manuscripts, which may have been made in the 1680s, was published in Bernard, E., *Catalogi librorum manuscriptorum*, Oxford 1697, pp. 93–101 (where Laughton's name is wrongly given as Henry).

# ROBERT BEAUMONT'S BOOKS, 1567

See pp. 47–8 above. The following list of books is transcribed from Beaumont's probate inventory of 1567 in CUA, with the addition of serial numbers.

Only a few of the entries in the OL list offer likely identifications with entries in this inventory. The most probable are:

| | |
|---|---|
| OL2 / RB1 | OL29⁵ / RB49 |
| OL4 / RB117 | OL30¹ / RB26 |
| OL6 / RB17 | OL30² / RB15 |
| OL9 / RB30 | OL31¹⁻² / RB22 |
| OL10 / RB2 | OL59 / RB72 |
| OL11 / RB4 | OL156 / RB96 |
| OL12 / RB66 | OL169 / RB51 |
| OL17 / RB54 | OL182 / RB35 |
| OL26 / RB21 | OL184 / RB110 |

[f.3]
Bokys

| | | | |
|---|---|---|---|
| [RB1] | Item biblia Stephani in 2obus volu fo | xxvj s | viiij d |
| [RB2] | opera Cirilli. ba | xiij s | iiij d |
| [RB3] | opera Crisostomi in iiij°ʳ vol: ba | xxx s | |
| [RB4] | opera Augustini in ix vol: ba | lxvj s | viij d |
| [RB5] | opera bede in iiij°ʳ vol: ba | xl s | |
| [RB6] | opera Jeronimi in v voluminibus. frob | xxvj s | viij d |
| [RB7] | opera tertulliani par: | vj s | viij d |
| [RB8] | opera lire in 7 vol: | xxvj s | viij d |
| [RB9] | opera Ambrosij in ij vol: ba | xvj s | viij d |
| [RB10] | opera Athanasij | viij s | |
| [RB11] | opera originis in ij vol: ba | xvj s | viij d |
| [RB12] | opera gregorij nisseni | vj s | |
| [RB13] | opera cipriani et hillarij simul | x s | |
| [RB14] | Gwalterus in Marcum cum busero ad ephes | x s | |
| [RB15] | peter martir in lib Judicum | ·.j s | |
| [RB16] | Annotationes Erasmi in novum testamentum | iiij s | |
| [RB17] | Concilia generalia in 3 vol: | xxvj s | viij d |

| [RB18] | Anselmus in paulum | ij s |
| [RB19] | Gwalterus in prophetas | vj s |
| [RB20] | Musculus in Johannem | viij s |
| [RB21] | Oecolompadius in prophetas | vj s   viij d |
| [RB22] | bucerus ad Romanos \ etc: / | v s iiij d |
| [RB23] | biblia Castalionis | v s |
| [RB24] | Erasmus de ratione concionandi | ij s |
| [RB25] | picus Mirandula | xij d |
| [RB26] | pet Martir adversus gardinerum | v s   iiij d |
| [RB27] | Sermones bullingeri | v s |
| [RB28] | Qwalterus in acta | iij s   iiij d |
| [RB29] | Bucerus in evangel: | vj s   viij d |
| [RB30] | Eucuminius in evangel: | ij s vj d |
| [RB31] | Lutherus in psal: | ij s |
| [RB32] | Distinctiones gratiani | iij s   iiij d |
| [RB33] | Sextus cum Clemen: | ij s |
| [RB34] | Ecclesiastica historia in 4 vol | xxvj s viij d |
| [RB35] | Cronica tritemij | iij s iiij d |
| [RB36] | polidori historia | iij s iiij d |
| [RB37] | Dionisius in epistolas D pauli | ij s |
| [RB38] | Thomas in epistolas | ij s |
| [RB39] | Musculus in Esaiam | ij s vj d |
| [RB40] | Spengilbardi tabule | ij s vj d |
| [RB41] | Musculus in psal | viij s |
| [RB42] | Mantuanus in psal | ij s |
| [RB43] | Dionisius in evang | ij s |
| [RB44] | Augustinus in epistolas | xx d |
| [RB45] | Musculus in Mattheum | v s |
| [RB46] | polianthea | xij d |
| [RB47] | ij paper bokes | iiij s |

[f.4]

| [RB48] | burraus in Judicum | ij s |
| [RB49] | brentius in acta | xx d |
| [RB50] | Destruxtorium | viij d |
| [RB51] | Arnobius in psalm | xij d |
| [RB52] | Lutherus de Judeis | vj d |
| [RB53] | Catena aurea bis | viij d |
| [RB54] | Lactantius | iiij d |
| [RB55] | Cronica Eusebij | xij d |
| [RB56] | Oecolompadius in Danielem | vj d |
| [RB57] | Idem in Jeremiam | viij d |
| [RB58] | Orosius | ij d |
| [RB59] | biblia | ij s |
| [RB60] | bullingerus de verbo dei | viij d |
| [RB61] | beza de hereticis | viij d |
| [RB62] | Emblemata alciati | x d |
| [RB63] | Institutiones Calvini fo. | iij s   iiij d |
| [RB64] | Idem in prophetas | iiij s |
| [RB65] | Idem in genesim fo. | ij s vj d |
| [RB66] | opera gregorij pape in 2 vol: ba | xiij s   iiij d |
| [RB67] | Calvinus in epistolas | vj s |
| [RB68] | Idem in psal | iiij s |
| [RB69] | opera barnardi in 2 vol: | xiij s   iiij d |
| [RB70] | harmonia evang Calvini | v s |
| [RB71] | Idem in Esaiam etc: | v s |

| | | |
|---|---|---|
| [RB72] | Felinus in psal | iij s |
| [RB73] | Pet Martir ad Romanos | iij s   iiij d |
| [RB74] | Loci communes Musculi | iij s   iiij d |
| [RB75] | Idem in genesim | v s   iiij d |
| [RB76] | prodigia Licostonis | ij s   vj d |
| [RB77] | Reformatio hermanni | xx d |
| [RB78] | Draconitus in evang | xij d |
| [RB79] | Calvinus de scandalis | iiij d |
| [RB80] | Idem de vitandis superstition: | vj d |
| [RB81] | pet Martir ad corinthios | ij s   vj d |
| [RB82] | bucerus de reconciliatione Relig | viij d |
| [RB83] | Illiricus contra papam | vj d |
| [RB84] | bullingerus de origine erroris | viij d |
| [RB85] | Decembrius de politia literaria | xij d |
| [RB86] | certayne litle bokes bound in parchement & standyng over the | |
| | cowntynghowse dore | xx s |
| [RB87] | paraphrasis Erasmi in 4 vol: | ij s   vj d |
| [RB88] | Eucomenius in paulum in 2 vol: | ij s |
| [RB89] | Theophilactus in evang | [xx d]   xvj d |
| [RB90] | corpus Doctrine xp'iane | xx d |
| [RB91] | bucerus de vera administr | xij d |
| [RB92] | biblia step in 2 vol: | vj s   viij d |
| [RB93] | postille Corvini | viij d |
| [RB94] | Concordantie | ij s |
| [RB95] | Latomus & bucerus de celibatu | vj d |
| [RB96] | bullingerus contra Cocleum | viij d |
| [RB97] | certayne other litle boke prised at | vj librae |
| | vnbound | |
| [RB98] | Gualterus in epistolas canonicas | xij d |
| [RB99] | bullingerus in epistolas | xij d |
| [RB100] | Idem in Danielem | ij s   vj d |
| [RB101] | opera Damaceni grec et Lat | iij s |
| [RB102] | Defensio pacis | xx d |
| [RB103] | eccliastice historie due partes | iij s   iiij d |
| [RB104] | iiij other bokes in quarto | iij s   iiij d |
| [RB105] | xx other in 8° | vj s   viij d |
| | greke & Ebrew | |
| [RB106] | Opera Aristot grece | x s |
| [RB107] | opera Crisostomi grece in 2 vol: | xiij s iiij d |
| [RB108] | Testamentum novum grecum | vj s |
| [RB109] | F Josephus grece | viij s |
| [RB110] | Eusebius grece | x s |
| [RB111] | Lexicon greco Latine | vj s   viij d |
| [f.5] | | |
| [RB112] | Dictionarium varini grecum | iij s iiij d |
| [RB113] | Tucidides grece | iij s |
| [RB114] | Ilias homeri grece | xx d |
| [RB115] | Onomasticon Julij pollucis grece | xij d |
| [RB116] | certayne litle greke bokes in 8 | x s |
| [RB117] | biblia hebr | vj s   viij d |
| [RB118] | certayne his bokys | x s |

# PASSAGES CONCERNING THE LIBRARY FROM THE WILL OF SIR EDWARD STANHOPE

(Dated 28 February 1603; proved 25 March 1608. From an early transcript in TC Mun., Box 31 no. 2.)

. . .Firste, for that I was from my infancy brought vp in that worthie Colledge, of the blessed, and vndevided Trenitie in Cambridge of the foundation of Kinge Henery the eight and there lived of the Colledge chardge manie yeares, as scholler and fellow there, and therefore nexte vnto God and my good parents, whom hee hath longe since taken to his mercie, doe confesse to haue received of that good Colledge the foundation of all which I haue since bine inhabled vnto I giue vnto the Colledge of the Blessed, and vndevided Trenitie in Cambridge the full some of Seaven Hundred poundes of Currant English monie to bee payde to the saide Colledge by my Executor, or Executors hearafter to bee named vppon the like accquittance as before I haue appoynted for the former paimente vnder the Colledge Seale in such manner and sorte, to such vse, and vppon such conditions as here after doe ensue. That is if the Librarie in the sayde Colledge bee new erected, and finished beefore my Death. And that there shall not bee beefore my Death a sufficiente stipend alloted for a Library Keeper, and hi[s] poore Scholler in the sayde Colledge by any other Benefactor . . .

This Land of two and thirtie poundes by yeare at the least, and soe much more as that seaven hundred poundes will purchase my will is shalby the sayde Colledge yearely be bestowed vppon the maintenance, and findinge of a Librarie Keeper and of his man a poore scholler in the sayde Colledge for ever. The Library Keeper to bee chosen by the M$^r$, and Seniors of Trenity Colledge in Cambridge as all other elections in that Colledge be made with in one fortenight of the receipte of the fore saide seaven hundred poundes, or with in one fortenight after my funeralls yf the

Librarie be finished before my Death and that my Executor bee tied to the paimente of the first yeares Annuitie of Thirtie poundes, he shall alwayes be chosen yf there bee any qualified as heareafter is sett downe that will accepte of it *De gremio Collegii* one that is ore hath bine scholler of the Colledge a single and vnmaried man no dispensation either beefore or after his acceptance of that place to bee allowed him a Bachelor of Artes at the least not deteched of any publike offence or crime, but *Integri famæ,* not havinge when he is chosen, nor acceptinge soe longe as he shall continue in that place any fellowship in that ore any other Colledge, Office, Lecture, preferment, or Prechership, nor servinge any cure, noe Practioner either in Lawe or Physicke, but vppon the verrie first acceptance of any of these functions shall preasantly disable him from continuinge the place of Librarie Keeper, hee shall not accept any Eaclesiasticall livinge whatsoever ore of what value soever either in title by Commendam, or by Sequestrac(-tion) but shall there vppon *Ipso facto*, lose this place, he shall not bee absent from the Colledge at anie time soe longe as hee hold this place vppon anie Licence whatsoever aboue fortie Daies in the yeare in all, and that by leaue of the M^r, or Vise Master and the more parte of the eight Seniors, vnless verie greate extreamitie of dangerous sickness vppon oathe testified doe compell him levinge for his substitute to be allowed by the M^r ore in his absence by the Vise Master of the Colledge one of the same Colledge *De gremio Collegii* and of the same degree in schoole which hee is of at the time of his libertie to goe abroad in Presence of which saide M^r or Vise Master hee shall deliver vnto his Substitue the keys of the Librarie and shall write in the Colledge Booke for those that haue leaue to go forth of the Towne, the day of his departure, and the day of his retorne, and his Substitute shall in the same booke write the day of his receavinge of the Librarie Keyes, and the day of his deliverie of them back. The Librarie Keeper shalbe a Bachelor of Artes at the least, and never aboue the degree of a Master of Artes, his dyet, wages, and Lyverie shall wholie bee borne by the Colledge and his chamber allowed vnto him, and his poore scholler ore vnder keeper in manner followenge. Hee shall take his degree of M^r of Artes soe soone as his time of three yeares Bachelor be expired. Soe longe as he is Bachelor of Artes the Colledge shall beare the whole chardge of his Commons and Decrements in the Bachelors commons. When hee proceedeth M^r of Artes the Colledge shall beare the whole chardge of his Commons and Decrements in the fellowes Commons, which hee shall enter into at the same time when those whoe be chosen *Maiores Socij* doe enter into the fellowes Commons. The Colledge shall at there charge paie him yearelie for his wages Six powndes by the yeare to bee paide quarterlie as the Fellowes are, allowenge him for the first quarter after the rate of the time of his admission yf he be chosen with in eight weekes of the ende of the quarter. But yf he be chosen aboue eight weekes before the end of the quarter then shall the Colledge allowe him 30s for his first whole quarters wages. The Colledge at there chardge shall further paie him yearelie for his Liverie fortie shillinges by yeare paide him in monie at such time yearelie as the Colledge paieth all the fellowes of the howse theire Liverie. He beinge once chosen maie continue his place soe longe as hee attendeth his chardge diligently and liveth honestlie after hee hath bin seaven yeares M$^r$ of Artes with out beinge minister neither shall he at anie time serue anie Cure, or accept anie Preachers place either in the Towne or elce wheare soe longe as hee continueth Librarie Keeper. To the ende that he maie bee more diligent in his place, and the more circumspect in his life, and conversation, hee shall at his admission by the M$^r$ and Seniors subiect him selfe by oath to theise Ordinances, and to the Statutes of the Colledge. And shall receive *Trinam admonitionem*, and expulsion from his place for such offences as the fellowes of the Colledge are subiect vnto. His chardge shalbe to keepe the keyes of the Librarie to see the Bookes, and Mapps in the Librarie and other ornaments of the Library cleanly kepte by his poore Scholler or vnderkeeper, to attend anie of the fellowes of the Colledge when they doe either goe into the Library to Studie; or bringe in any stranger with them and to continue in the Librarie soe longe as anie doe stay in it. Hee shall not suffer anie Booke, Mapp, ore anie other Ornament belongenge to the Librarie to bee caried forth of the Librarie after it is once placed or entered into the same, vnless hee haue the hand writinge of the M$^r$ of the Colledge ore in his absence of the Visemaster of the Colledge for his warrant for deliverie of such particular Booke Mapp, ore other Orna-mente by name. An that not to bee forth of the saide Librarie aboue fowreteene dayes at the most, but hee shall call to the Master, or the Visemaster for it againe. His chardge shall further bee after the first Ledger booke, made, and written at the chardge of the Colledge of all the particu-lar names of everie booke, mapp, or other ornament given to the Colledge to gither with his name, whoe gaue it to continue the writinge in faire Roman or Secretarie hand, at his owne chardges yf hee write not faire him selfe, of all such bookes, mappes, or ornaments as shall come into or bee in the Librarie after his takinge of the Chardge of the Library keeping vppon him and by whome they shall soe bee given. And for writinge of all other thinges for the good preservation of all the Bookes, Mapps, and ornaments

of the saide Librarie hee shall after hee is admitted to bee Librarie Keeper
bee subiect to all such decrees for the good of the Colledge as the M$^r$ and
Seniors shall from time to time at their meetinges appoynte vnto him, for
tyenge of him to keepe such exercises, both in the Colledge and Publique
Schooles as others whoe bee either *Minores* or *Maiores Socij* are tied vnto I
leaue that to the M$^r$ and Seniors of the Colledge to appoynte him accordinge as they shall see his continuall attendance one his chardge shall give
him respect of Studie which I desier hee may soe apply as that when hee
shall leaue that service he may proue a fit member for the Common wealth
in some profession of Learninge. His chamber for him selfe and his man
shall by the saide Colledge bee assignde him neere to the Librarie wheare
hee may bee ready for all attendance, whensoever the saide Lybrarie
Keeper shall loose his place for anie of the causes aboue sett downe, or
shalbe expeld the Colledge for anie publike offence, or cause which by the
Statutes of the Colledge anie *Maior Socius* is to bee expeld for, yf the saide
M$^r$ and eight seniors of the Colledge doe not with in fowerteene dayes
after knowledge of his loss of his place make choise of an other in all sortes
qualified as aboue and admitt him with in seaven dayes after such election
made. Then shall it bee lawfull for the Lord Archbishopp of Canterbury, or
that sea beinge voide, for the Lord Bishopp of London for the time beinge to
nominate a Librarie Keeper of his owne election *De gremio Collegij*, whoe
hath bin Scholler of the Colledge qualified both for degree, and otherwise
as is aboue sett downe, whoe vppon certificate of such nomination vnder
his Archiepiscopall or Episcopall seale made to the Colledge shall stand for
chosen and shall be with oute other election admitted, & sworne by the M$^r$
and Seniors with in three dayes of his exhibiting of the saide nomination as
aforesaide. at everie change of the Librarie Keeper the Officers of the said
Colledge hereafter named shall see him whoe is chosen to receaue all his
chardge in the said Librarie comparinge the Bookes, and other ornaments
with theire Ledger Booke which they are written into. For the Librarie
Keeper his poore scholler or vnder Librarie Keeper hee shalbe chosen and
appoynted by the M$^r$ of the Colledge aboue, vnder his owne hand
writinge, he shalbe such a one as hath bin admitted Pentioner, Siser, or
Subsiser in the Colledge six months at the least before his election to that
place, and after his acceptance of that place he shall not anie more be
pentioner or Siser in the Colledge soe longe as hee holdeth that place, he
shall Lodge in the Librarie Keepers chamber, hee shall twise in the weeke at
least sweepe, and make cleane the Librarie, and the common staires to it,
keepe of the dust from the bookes, the seates, and deskes, the Mapps,

glassed windowes, and other ornaments of the librarie, whensoever hee taketh degree of Bachelor of Artes hee shall loose his place vppon the latter Acte daye followenge and the M$^r$ of the Colledge shall vnder his hand place one other in his place with in six dayes followenge, hee shall never bee chosen vnder fifteene yeares of age nor continue in the place after hee is Twentie fiue years of age. The Colledge shall paie vnto him at their owne chardge fowre poundes by the yeare for his wages to bee paide quarterly as is appoynted for his M$^r$ the Librarie Keeper. And further it shalbe at the election of the M$^r$ and Seniors of the Colledge, whether they will allowe him his diet amonst the Sisers, and at theire bord, ore the Colledge to paye him ten shillinges everie quarter of the yeare, for his commons and diet over and aboue his wages of foure poundes, he shalbe at the commandement, and goverment of the Librarie Keeper and lodge alwaies in his chamber, whoe if hee find him stubborne, disobedient, or negligent of his dewtie hee shalbee complaind of vnto the Senior Deane of the Colledge, whoe vppon his inst[ant] deserte shall giue him open correction, yf he amende not hee shall vppon the second complainte made by his M$^r$ the Librarie Keeper receive correction publike in the hall at dinner time yf he be not Adultus by the Rod, yf he bee Adultus by other publike open shame, vppon the thirde complainte to be caled vp to the Table and admonished by the M$^r$ Visemaster, and the Senior Deane to ammende vppon paine of loss of his place, And vppon the fourth, and last complainte he shall by the M$^r$ and Seniors bee removed from his place fore ever and another chosen in manner as aboue. And for the good and safe preservinge of all the bookes, and other ornaments of the saide Librarie my request to the M$^r$, and Seniors of the said Colledge of the Blessed and vndevided Trenitie in Cambridge, in his absence the Visemaster thene together with the two Deanes, the head Lectorer, and the two Bursers of the same ore yf anie of them bee forth of the towne his ore theire Substitute doe once everie yeare betwixte the ende of theire Audit and St Thomas day thence next following spend one whole day in the Librarie ore at the least two howres of it in the fore noone, and three howers of it in the after noone, in which time they shall pervse over the Cathologe of all there Bookes, Mapps, and other ornaments of there Librarie, and carefullie see that all Bookes, and other ornaments whatsoever brought into the Librarie, ore given to the saide Colledge the yeare before, be entred and faire written by the Librarie Keeper appoynted as aboue or at his chardge into a Ledger parchmente booke for that purpose appoynted. And that all the Bookes, Mapps, globes and the other ornaments laid in the Librarie and commited to the affore sayd Keepers chardge, be safe and well kept w$^{th}$ oute tearinge out of anie leaues blottinge, ore notinge any of them after they shalbe laid vp in the Librarie, wherein if they shall find the Librarie Keeper faultie that anie of those thinges committed to his chardge shall by his negligence haue bine marred, ore defaced and that hee did not presantly vppon such hurte done complaine vnto the M$^r$ or visemaster of yt, whereby the offence of it might have been reformd and the Offender receaue punnishment, then it shalbe Lawfull for the M$^r$, or Vicemaster, and the two Deanes, the Head lecturer, and the two Bursers ore the more part of them to punnish the said faulte in the Librarie Keeper by the purse at the discretion and accordinge to the greeviousnes of the faulte soe yt bee not aboue one quarter of a yeares wages, unless by his over greate dissolutenes the Colledge doe in the thinges committed to his chardge receaue verie greate dammage in which case hee is by the M$^r$ and Seniors to bee removed, and proceded against as anie Officer in the Colledge aught to be, whoe doth *Devastare bona Collegij*. And the affore sayde *Mulct*: emposd as aboue vppon the saide Librarie Keeper shalbe preasantly employde towards the repaire of the booke, Mapp, Globe or other ornament spoild ore wasted as aboue for the paines of the M$^r$ or Visemaster and the other Officers aboue named that day taken, the Colledge shall oute of the Thirtie poundes by yeare by mee given as aboue make allowance of Tenne shillings by yeare to bee bestowed the night one which the M$^r$, or Visemaster, with the other Officers shall meete one as aboue vppon a supper for them over and aboue there Ordinarie Commons to be made in the Chamber of the M$^r$, or Visemaster ore some one of the Officers aboue named, To the ende the Colledge of the blessed, and undevided Trenitie in Cambridge of Kinge Henery the eights foundation may bee perpetually tied to performe all the conditions aboue by mee sett downe . . .

I doe beside giue vnto the saide Colledge of the Blessed and undevided Trenitie in Cambridge to bee kepte in there Publike Librarie to the vse of the saide Colledge, to bee affixed and chained in their new Librarie yf it bee finished and desked with in six months after the receite of them, or elce with in six months after it is finished and desked fitt to receiue Bookes, my Great Ebrew Bible in a lardge folio bound vp in Pastbord in seaven volumes with my Crest and E.S. one the oute side of the covers, commonlie caled Biblia sacra Hebraice, Caldaice, Graece, et Latine, other wise caled Kinge Phillips Bible. I doe further give vnto the saide Colledge all my Bookes of Divinitie, Civill ore Common Lawes, Comon or Statute Lawes, Historie ore other humanitie bookes either in Greeke or Lattin which I shalbe possessed of or haue at the time of my death, and shall by my last will and testament or other Codicill vnder my hand and Seale not haue particularlie and by name given away. And which the Colledge of the Blessed and vndevided Trenitie aboue saide hath not alreadie belonginge to there Publike Librarie of the Colledge ownd at the time of my Death . . .

And yf there bee anie of my Bookes aboue set downe which Trenitie Colledge in Cambridge alreadie hath, yf they desier to change anie of there Bookes with mine as beeinge of a later impression ore more fitlie bounde for them My Will is that the saide Colledge may exchange all such Bookes with anie of mine which I shall die possessed of . . .

I doe further giue vnto the saide Colledge, of the Blessed and vndevided Trenitie in Cambridge the some of twentie poundes of Currant English monie to bee paide vnto them by my Executor, or Executors with in six monthes after my decease where with my will is the Colledge shall provide one verie greate Booke of large velam in severall leaues whereof shall first be faire written, and lyned [=lymed ?] the names, titles, Armes and Dignities of all the Fownders of the saide Colledge sett oute in there propper Cullers. After them the Armes of the Colledge. After that the names of all the Benefactors who haue given anie yearely perpetuitie of maintenance to that Colledge since the first erection there of together with the particuler induments which they haue soe yearelie given to that Col-ledge. After shalbe written the name and estate of everie benefactor, whoe since the erection of that Colldge, anie remembrance of theire loue and kindness to the same where in shalbe expressed the particuler gifte soe by anie of them given bee it more ore less. After that shalbe the names of all the M$^{rs}$ whoe haue governed that Colledge since the first erection thereof together with a particuler of those places whereto anie of them haue bin caled in the Govermente of the Church, or Commonwealth before there death. The Booke must further bee kepte for the publike Register Booke of all the particuler Bookes, Mapps, Globes ore other ornaments what-soever belongenge or hereafter to bee longe to the saide Colledge Librarie. The loue which I am assured the M$^r$ and Seniors of the Colledge doth beare to the kinde remembrance of all the good benefactors to that Blessed Societie I know to bee such as I am assured they will see this small portion of Twentie poundes to bee employed to the full, for keepinge a perpetuall Register and Memoriall garnished in that Booke, to the best and kindest encoragement of all future frends whoe shall hereafter bee encoraged to doe good to that Colledge. This Booke thus written, garnished, and finished with leaues sufficiente to adde what shall hereafter by good men bee suplied, I desier may with such good speede by prepared as that it bee one of the first Bookes which shoul[d]be perfected, bound vp chained, & affixed to there Librarie . . .

# COLLEGE LIBRARIANS AND SUB-LIBRARIANS, 1609–95

The details in the following tables are derived from TC Mun., *Admissions and admonitions*; ibid., *Conclusion books A* and *B*; ibid., Senior Bursars' accounts; Sinker, *Librarians*; *TC Admissions*; Venn; and the references given in Sinker, *Librarians*, and Venn.

The Senior Bursars' accounts which run from Michaelmas to Michaelmas and which record the stipends of the Librarians and Sub-Librarians, are complete for the period 1609–95 except for the years ending Michaelmas 1611, 1613, 1617, 1619–20, 1622–36, 1638–9, 1641, 1649. There were perhaps six Sub-Librarians of whom no record survives in the Senior Bursars' accounts in the period from Michaelmas 1621 to Michaelmas 1636; and possibly others between Barcroft and Ormrod and between Parish and Havercroft; but probably not more than about eight in all.

*Librarians 1609–95*

| Name | Admitted | Scholar/BA | Librarian | Notes |
|---|---|---|---|---|
| HICKES, William | Sizar, 1601 | 1605/1605–6 | 1609–12 (3 yrs) | probably ordained; died 1646 |
| PARKER, Nicolas | (no record) | 1608/1608–9 | 1612–25 (13½ yrs) | Paling Exhibitioner 1614–25; died 1625 |
| HERSENT, Peter | (no record) | 1617 (W)/1620–1 | 1625–31 (5½ yrs) | |
| CLUTTERBOOKE, William | Pensioner, 1623 | 1624 (W)/1627–8 | 1631–41 (10½ yrs) | ordained 1638–9; BD (by Royal dispensation) 1640; died 1665 |
| GRIFFITH (formerly MUTTON), Thomas | Pensioner, 1633 | 1633 (W)/1635–6 | 1641–74 (32 yrs) | suspended for neglect 1645–6; Tutor; Registrar (by Royal dispensation) 1666; died 1674 |
| MANFEILD, James | Sizar, 1664 | 1668/1668–9 | 1674–9 (5 yrs) | ordained 1671; Chaplain 1679–86; University Librarian 1684–6; died 1686 |
| LAUGHTON, John | Pensioner, 1665 | 1668/1668–9 | 1679–83 (4 yrs) | ordained; Chaplain 1678–9, 1683–1712; Tutor; University Librarian 1686–1712; died 1712 |
| ROTHERHAM, Thomas | Pensioner, 1654 | (–)*/1656–7 | 1683–96 (13 yrs) | ordained; Chaplain 1661–83, 1696–1702; died 1702 |

(W): Scholar on the Westminster election

* Rotherham had never been a Scholar of the College, and was therefore ineligible for the post of Librarian under the terms of Sir Edward Stanhope's will.

*Sub-Librarians 1609–95*

| Name | Admitted | Sub-Librarian | Notes |
| --- | --- | --- | --- |
| PARTRIDGE, Alfred | Sizar, 1606 | 1609 (6 months) | BA ?1609–10; ordained; died 1636–7 |
| POLWHEELE, Otho | Sizar, 1610 | 1609–?13 (?4 yrs) | BA (Trin. Hall) 1615–16; ordained; died ?1669 |
| BARCROFT(E), Robert | Sizar, 1614 | ?1613–?18 (?5 yrs) | BA ?1618–19; MA (Emma.) 1622; compounded for Knighthood 1631;* died 1647 |
| ORM(E)ROD, Lawrence | (no record) | by 1620 (? yrs) | BA 1622–3; schoolmaster |
| | – – – (records missing 1621–36) – – – | | |
| PARISH, George | Sizar, 1634 | by 1636 (? yrs) | BA 1637–8; Fellow 1640 (ejected)–63; ordained |
| HAVERCROFT, William | Sizar, 1636 | by 1639–42 (? yrs) | did not graduate |
| NIDD, John | Sizar, 1640 | 1642–5 (3 yrs) | BA 1645–6; Fellow 1647–59; ordained; Tutor, Junior and Senior Dean; died 1659 |
| STEDMAN, Richard | Sub-sizar, 1645 | 1645–7 (2 yrs) | BA 1647–8; Fellow 1649–99; ordained; Tutor, Junior and Senior Dean, Junior and Senior Bursar |
| WHITE, Jeremy† | Sub-sizar, 1646 | 1647–50 (3 yrs) | BA 1649–50; ordained; chaplain to Cromwell, author; died 1707 |
| QUINSEY, Thomas | Sub-sizar, 1650 | 1650–1 (6 months) | Scholar 1651; BA 1653–4; ordained |
| MURIELL, John | Sub-sizar, 1650 | 1651–3 (2½ yrs) | did not graduate |
| RESBURY, Theodore | Sizar, 1652 | 1653–?55 (?1½ yrs) | Scholar 1655; BA 1655–6; Fellow 1658–9 |
| ATKIN(S), Thomas | Sub-sizar, 1654 | ?1655–6 (?1 year) | did not graduate |
| JENNER, David‡ (but possibly his brother Jonathan, Sub-sizar 1655, did not graduate BA) | Sub-sizar, 1653 | 1656–7 (?1 year) | Scholar 1657; BA 1657–8; Fellow of Sidney; ordained; chaplain to Charles II, author; died 1691 |

* Barcroft's composition fine was £13.6s.8d. This would indicate that his Lancashire property was valued at £100+ a year; he did not bear arms, and was probably of the rank of 'parish gentleman' (information from Dr B. G. Blackwood and Dr J. S. Morrill).

† White graduated in the first quarter of 1650, but continued as Sub-Librarian until Michaelmas 1650. See *DNB*.

‡ See *DNB*.

Sub-Librarians 1609–95 (2)

| Name | Admitted | Sub-Librarian | Notes |
|---|---|---|---|
| LAMBERT, Joshua | Sub-sizar, 1654 | 1657 (?6 months) | BA 1657–8; ordained |
| CROSLAND, William | Sub-sizar, 1655 | 1657–9 (?1½ yrs) | Scholar 1659; BA 1659–60 |
| LANE, Henry | Sub-sizar, 1658 | 1659 (?6 months) | Scholar 1661; BA 1661–2; Fellow 1664–92; ordained; Tutor, Junior Bursar, Junior Dean |
| GILLIBRAND, Thomas | Sub-sizar, 1659 | 1659–61 (?1½ yrs) | did not graduate |
| OWEN, Vincent | Sizar, 1660 | 1661–3 (2½ yrs) | did not graduate BA, LLB 1673; probably ordained; died 1703 |
| MAULIVERER, Thomas* | Sizar, 1662 | 1663–7 (3½ yrs) | BA 1665–6; ordained; died 1701 |
| PULLEYN, John | Pensioner, 1666 | 1667–8 (1 year) | BA 1669–70; ordained |
| SAMBEE, John | Sub-sizar, 1667 | 1668–70 (2¾ yrs) | BA 1670–71; ordained; died 1728 |
| SMITHSON, Huntington | Sub-sizar, 1670 | 1671–74 (?3¼ yrs) | Scholar 1674; BA 1674–5 |
| PAGET, Edward | Sub-sizar, 1672 | 1674–6 (2 yrs) | Scholar 1676; BA 1676–7; Fellow 1679–1700; ?FRS 1682 |
| LEAKELAND, Thomas | Sub-sizar, 1675 | 1676–9 (3¼ yrs) | BA 1679–80; ordained |
| ALC(K)HORNE, Charles | Sizar, 1677 | 1679–81 (1¾ yrs) | Scholar 1681; BA 1681–2; Fellow 1684–99; ordained |
| RHODES, Samuel | Sizar, 1680 | 1681–3 (2 yrs) | Scholar 1683; BA 1683–4; ordained; died 1706 |
| FETHERSTON, Leonard† | Sizar, 1681 | 1683–5 (2½ yrs) | BA 1684–5; ordained |
| WATTS, Thomas | Pensioner, 1686 | 1685–8 (2½ yrs) | Scholar 1689; BA 1689–90 |
| MANNING, Lancelot | Sub-sizar, 1686 | 1688 (?6 months) | Scholar 1689; BA 1689–90; ordained |
| PALMER, Joseph | Pensioner, 1688 | 1688–91 (2½ yrs) | Scholar 1691; BA 1691–2; ordained; Chaplain of King's; died 1696 |
| HUMPHREYS, Thomas (but poss. his elder brother John, Sub-sizar, 1690, BA 1693–4) | Sub-sizar, 1689 | 1691–3 (2 yrs) | Scholar 1693; BA 1693–4; ordained |
| VALAVINE, John | Sub-sizar, 1692 | 1693–9 (6 yrs) | did not graduate |

* Mauliverer graduated in the first quarter of 1666, but continued as Sub-Librarian until Lady Day 1667.
† Fetherston graduated in the first quarter of 1685, but continued as Sub-Librarian until Michaelmas 1685.

| | | |
|---|---|---|
| ALC(K)HORNE, Charles | SL | 1679–81 |
| ATKIN(S), Thomas | SL | ?1655–6 |
| BARCROFT(E), Robert | SL | ?1613–?18 |
| CLUTTERBOOKE, William | L | 1631–41 |
| CROSLAND, William | SL | 1657–9 |
| FETHERSTON, Leonard | SL | 1683–5 |
| GILLIBRAND, Thomas | SL | 1659–61 |
| GRIFFITH, Thomas | L | 1641–74 |
| HAVERCROFT, William | SL | by 1639–42 |
| HERSENT, Peter | L | 1625–31 |
| HICKES, William | L | 1609–12 |
| HUMPHREYS, Thomas (or John) | SL | 1691–3 |
| JENNER, David (or Jonathan) | SL | 1656–7 |
| LAMBERT, Joshua | SL | 1657 |
| LANE, Henry | SL | 1659 |
| LAUGHTON, John | L | 1679–83 |
| LEAKELAND, Thomas | SL | 1676–9 |
| MANFEILD, James | L | 1674–9 |
| MANNING, Lancelot | SL | 1688 |
| MAULIVERER, Thomas | SL | 1663–7 |
| MURIELL, John | SL | 1651–3 |
| MUTTON, Thomas = GRIFFITH, Thomas | | |
| NIDD, John | SL | 1642–5 |
| ORM(E)ROD, Lawrence | SL | by 1620 |
| OWEN, Vincent | SL | 1661–3 |
| PAGET, Edward | SL | 1674–6 |
| PALMER, Joseph | SL | 1688–91 |
| PARISH, George | SL | by 1636 |
| PARKER, Nicholas | L | 1612–25 |
| PARTRIDGE, Alfred | SL | 1609 |
| POLWHEELE, Otho | SL | 1609–?13 |
| PULLEYN, John | SL | 1667–8 |
| QUINSEY, Thomas | SL | 1650–1 |
| RESBURY, Theodore | SL | 1653–?5 |
| RHODES, Samuel | SL | 1681–3 |
| ROTHERHAM, Thomas | L | 1683–96 |
| SAMBEE, John | SL | 1668–70 |
| SMITHSON, Huntington | SL | 1671–4 |
| STEDMAN, Richard | SL | 1645–7 |
| VALAVINE, John | SL | 1693–9 |
| WATTS, Thomas | SL | 1685–8 |
| WHITE, Jeremy | SL | 1647–50 |

# DONATIONS OF MANUSCRIPTS, 1604–94

The 532 manuscripts analysed and indexed here are those given to the College from 1604 to 1694 which were recorded in the early lists of donations, or which can be identified by means of inscriptions, arms, etc., in the books themselves. A few other manuscripts may have been given to the College during this period which were not recorded or identified at the time, and which are therefore omitted.

| Date | Name | to 13th cent | 14th and 15th cent | 16th and 17th cent | oriental | unidentified | total |
|---|---|---|---|---|---|---|---|
| 1604 | WHITGIFT, John | 100 | 43 | 7 | | | 150 |
| 1608 | STANHOPE, Edward | 3 | 6 | 3 | | 2 | 14 |
| 1611–12 | NEVILE, Thomas | 55 | 53 | 13 | 1 | 4 | 126 |
| 1608–14 | WILLMER, George | 21 | 15 | 1 | | 2 | 39 |
| 1626–30 | ELWES, Silvius | 1 | | 2 | 1 | | 4 |
| c. 1628 | HARDWICK, William | | | | | 1 | 1 |
| 1628–32 | BOWEN, Adam | | | | 1 | | 1 |
| 1633 | FORTHO, John | | 2 | | | 2 | 4 |
| 1633–7 | HICKS, Thomas | | | 1 | | | 1 |
| 1633–7 | 'Ad Coll. pertinentes'* | 20 | 3 | | 1 | | 24 |
| 1637 | WHALLEY, Thomas | 1 | 5 | 4 | | | 10 |
| 1637 | HICSON, Samuel | | | | | 2 | 2 |
| 1638 | BARRY, George | | 1 | | | | 1 |
| 1641 | CRANE, Richard | 1 | | | | | 1 |
| c. 1641 | KINASTON, Francis | | 2 | | | | 2 |
| by 1645 | PULLEY, William | | | 4 | | | 4 |
| 1657 | PETERS, Hugh | | | 1 | | | 1 |
| 1660–9 | SADLEIR, Anne | 1 | | 3 | | | 4 |
| 1661 | GRESWOLD, Henry | 4 | | | | | 4 |
| 1662 | COPPINGER, Thomas | | 1 | | | | 1 |
| 1662–72 | SCATTERGOOD, Anthony | 1 | 6 | | | | 7 |
| 1663 | DRYDEN, Jonathan | 4 | 5 | | 1 | | 10 |
| 1663–4 | CRANE, Robert | | 1 | 2 | | | 3 |
| 1664 | LYNNET, William | | | 2 | | | 2 |
| 1664–74 | PAWLETT, Thomas | | | 1 | | | 1 |
| 1667 | CORKER, William | | | 1 | | | 1 |
| 1667 | DUPORT, James | | 1 | | | | 1 |
| 1668 | PULLEYN, Benjamin | | 1 | | | | 1 |
| 1669 | HILL, Thomas | | | 12 | | | 12 |
| 1669 | HUGHES, Francis | | | 1 | | | 1 |
| 1669† | STOKES, David | | | 5 | | | 5 |
| 1670 | BATTELY, John | | 1 | | | | 1 |
| 1670 | HACKET, John | 2 | | 1 | | | 3 |
| 1670– | LAUGHTON, John | 3 | 4 | 2 | | ?6 | ?15 |
| 1670–2 | THORNDIKE, Herbert | 1 | | 3 | | | 4 |
| ?1672 | DOCWRA, Thomas | | 1 | | | | 1 |
| 1672 | SPRAGG, John | | | 1 | | | 1 |
| 1673 | GRIFFITH, Thomas | 1 | 2 | | | 2 | 5 |
| 1673 | PETTIT, Valentine | | 1 | | | | 1 |
| 1678 | PERRY, William | | | 1 | | | 1 |
| 1682 | DUKE, Richard | | | | 1 | | 1 |
| 1682 | NORTH, John | | | 1 | | | 1 |
| ?1682 | GRAHAM, Richard | | | | | 1 | 1 |
| 1686– | GREAVES, William | 1 | 1 | | | | 2 |
| 1691– | PUCKERING, Henry | | 5 | 51 | | 5 | 61 |
| 1694 | BLAND, Simon | 1 | | | | | 1 |
| Total | | 221 | 160 | 111 | 18 | 27 | 537 |

* See pp. 83–4.
† Bequeathed in 1669, received in 1677 (*Ben* p. 45).

Most of the manuscripts analysed in this table can be identified by using James's lists of donors of manuscripts (James vol. i, pp. xxii–xxiii; vol. ii, pp. xiii–xxi, xxvi–xxvii). In the following index, 'see James' indicates that the class marks of the manuscripts referred to will be found in these lists.

| | |
|---|---|
| BARRY, George (1638) | see James |
| BATTELY, John (1670) | see James |
| BLAND, Simon (1694) | see James |
| BOWEN, Adam (1632) | see James |
| COPPINGER, Thomas (1662) | see James |
| CORKER, William (1667) | see James |
| CRANE, Richard (1641) | see James |
| CRANE, Robert (1663–4) | see James |
| DOCWRA, Thomas (?1672) | see James |
| DRYDEN, Jonathan (1663) | see James |
| DUKE, Richard (1682) | see James |
| DUPORT, James (1667) | see James |
| ELWES, Silvius (1626–30) | see James |
| FORTHO, John (1633) | see James; *Memoriale*, p. 113 |
| GRAHAM, Richard (?1682) | see *Ben*, p. 44 |
| GREAVES, William (1686–) | James 56, 290 |
| GRESWOLD, Henry (1661) | see James |
| GRIFFITH, Thomas (1673) | see *Ben*, p. 35; James 317, 396, 747 |
| HACKET, John (1670) | see James |
| HARDWICK, William (c.1628) | see TC Mun., *Conclusion book A*, p. 96 |
| HICKS, Thomas (1633–7) | see *Memoriale*, p. 114; James 974 |
| HICSON, Samuel (1637) | see *Memoriale*, p. 120 |
| HILL, Thomas (1669) | see James; *Ben*, pp. 21, 31 |
| HUGHES, Francis (1669) | see James |
| KINASTON, Francis (c. 1641) | see James |
| LAUGHTON, John (1670–) | see James; *Ben*, p. 108 |
| LYNNET, William (1664) | see James |
| NEVILE, Thomas (1611–12) | see James |
| NORTH, John (1682) | see James |
| PAWLETT, Thomas (1664–74) | see James |
| PERRY, William (1678) | see James |
| PETERS, Hugh (1657) | see James |
| PETTIT, Valentine (1673) | see James |
| PUCKERING, Henry (1691–) | see James; the MSS given in 1691 are identified in Bernard, E., *Catalogi librorum manuscriptorum*, Oxford 1697, pp. 101–2 |
| PULLEY, William (by 1645) | see James |
| PULLEYN, Benjamin (1668) | see James |
| SADLEIR, Anne (1660–9) | see James |
| SCATTERGOOD, Anthony (1662–72) | see James |
| SPRAGG, John (1672) | see James |
| STANHOPE, Edward (1608) | see James |
| STOKES, David (1669) | see *Ben*, p. 45; James 779, 786–7, 806–7 |
| THORNDIKE, Herbert (1670–2) | see James |
| WHALLEY, Thomas (1637) | see James |
| WHITGIFT, John (1604) | see James |
| WILLMER, George (1608–14) | see James |
| 'Ad Coll. pertinentes' (1633–7) | see James, and pp. 83–4 above. |

# DONATIONS OF PRINTED BOOKS
## 1601–40

*Donations of printed books 1601–40*

| approx. date of donation* | name | relationship to the college | donation† | | Mem. |
|---|---|---|---|---|---|
| | | | printed vols | £/printed vols | |
| 1601 | SHAW, Peter | past Fellow | 143 | | 99 |
| 1603 | FONT, Henry | past pensioner; tenant | | £10/17 | 97 |
| 1606 | ARNOLD, John | past Chaplain | 7 | | 100 |
| 1607 | JENOUR, Kenelm | Fellow-Commoner | 21 | | 97 |
| ?1607 | LAKES, Sir Thomas | not known | | £20/21 | 96 |
| 1608 | STANHOPE, Sir Edward | past Fellow | 238 | | 94 |
| 1609 | OVERALL, John | past Fellow | 1 | | 98 |
| 1609 | SMYTH, William | past Fellow–Com. | | £20/7 | 96 |
| ?1610 | THELWALL, Eubule | past Scholar | | £5/8 | 97 |
| ?1610 | CHENEY, Francis | tenant | | £3?/7 | 97 |
| ?1610 | SPRINGHAM, Matthew (of London) | not known | 1 | | 97 |
| ?1610 | HAMPTON, Christopher | past Fellow | 1 | | 97 |
| ?1610 | STILL, Nathaniel | past Fellow | 3 | | 98 |
| ?1610 | WAYLAND, Henry | past Fellow | 11 | | 100 |
| 1610 | BIRKHEAD, Daniel | Fellow | 5 | | 101 |
| ?1610 | BATT, Edward | past Fellow | 15 | | 100 |

* Established as far as possible from biographical data and from the dates of the books donated, as well as from the order in which the gifts are recorded in the *Memoriale*, a fair but not infallible guide.

† In the left-hand column are given the numbers of printed volumes apparently donated as books; while in the right-hand column are recorded the sums of money given for the purchase of books and the numbers of printed volumes bought with these sums.

| Year | Name | Status | | Money | Page |
|---|---|---|---|---|---|
| 1611–12 | NEVILE, Thomas | Master | 94 | | 91 |
| ?1612 | HALL, William | past Fellow | 2 | | 100 |
| 1613 | WRIGHT, Richard | past Fellow | | | 100 |
| 1614* | MEDHOP, Thomas | Fellow | | £5/8 | 101 |
| ?1615 | FITZRANDOLFE, Thomas | Fellow | 8 | £?/13 | 101 |
| ?1615 | GOODMAN, Godfrey | past Scholar | 1 | | 101 |
| ?1616 | FORTHO, Thomas | Fellow | 14 | | 100 |
| ?1617 | LAYFIELD, John | past Fellow | 8 | | 101 |
| ?1617 | CROPLEY, John | past Fellow | 8 | | 101 |
| 1618 | SUCKLING, Sir John | co-opted MA | | | 102 |
| 1618 | SEDLEY, Sir William | not known | | £?/50 | 103 |
| 1618 | BENNET, Robert | past Fellow | | £100/120 | 104 |
| ?1619 | FARRINGTON, Lady† | not known | | £20/22 | 104 |
| ?1625 | STANHOPE, Sir Michael | brother of Sir Edward | 2 | | 105 |
| ?1626–30 | ELWES, Silvius | Chaplain | 184 | £100/149 | 107 |
| ?1629 | COLLINS, Samuel | Reg. Prof. Div. | 8 | | 106 |
| 1631 | WHITMORE, William | Fellow-Commoner | 1 | | 111 |
| ?1632 | BOWEN, Adam (of London) | not known | 6 | | 114 |
| 1633 | FORTHO, John‡ | past Fellow | 17 | | 113 |
| 1633–7 | 'Ad Coll. pertinentes'§ | | 11 | | 115 |
| 1637 | WHALLEY, Thomas | Fellow | | £100/205 | 117 |
| 1637 | HICSON, Samuel | Fellow | | £40/23 | 120 |

* The 13 volumes mentioned in the *Memoriale* were probably bought at Medhop's expense when he became a Fellow in 1614; but there are three volumes in the Library with his initials on the binding which were probably bought at the time of his death in 1639 (see Appendix H, S38).

† 'Excellentissima D.na Domina Farrington' (*Mem*, p. 104). There seems to be no trace of her in the peerage, baronetage, or knightage of the period.

‡ Some of the books apparently given by Fortho have strange initials on their bindings. For instance, Appendix H S11 is stamped 'RB' (but has Fortho's signature on the title-page); and S8, S21, and S26 are stamped 'TG'. In spite of the markings, which I cannot explain, these appear to be the books named in the *Memoriale* as having been given by Fortho.

§ See pp. 83–4.

# THE SCIENCE BOOKS IN THE CLASS CATALOGUE OF C.1645

The medical and mathematical books are listed in the order in which they appear in *1645* (see Appendix B). 'Medici' (S1–S34) includes writers on alchemy, botany, chemistry, metallurgy, pharmacology, and surgery. 'Mathematici' (S35–S79) includes writers on architecture, astrology, astronomy, chronology, cosmography, geography, geometry, optics, and perspective.

Each entry consists of a serial number; the original entry from *1645* in italics; an abbreviated description; the present location of each book; and its provenance. The list is followed by indexes of headings and provenances.

## *MEDICI*

S1  *Hippocrates*
HIPPOCRATES
(probably Opera, *Greek and Latin*
Frankfurt 1595; Adams H566)

absent; bought 1618 (Sedley)

S2  *Gallenus Græc: vol. 1(–3)*
GALENUS, Claudius
Opera omnia, *Greek*
5v in 3, Basle 1538; Adams G33

S.5.4–6; bought 1618 (Sedley)

S3  *Idem Lat: vol. 1(–4)*
GALENUS, Claudius
Omnia quae extant, *Latin*
4v, Basle 1562; Adams G39

S.5.27–30; bought 1618 (Sedley)

S4  *Scriptores varij de re medicâ*
SORANUS, *Ephesius, etc.*
De re medica
Basle 1528; Adams S1461

S.5.2; given 1611–12 (Nevile)

S5  *Christophorus a Vega*
VEGA, Christophorus de
Opera
Lyons 1576; Adams V322

S.6.33; given 1633 (J. Fortho)

S6  *Brassavolus in Aphorism: Hyppocratis*
BRASAVOLA, Antonio Musa
In octo libros aphorismorum Hippocratis et Galeni
Basle 1541; Adams B2698

S.5.10; probably given 1633 (J. Fortho)

S7  *Gorræi definitiones Med:*
GORRAEUS, Johannes
Definitionum medicarum libri XXIIII
Paris 1564; Adams G878

S.6.21; given 1611–12 (Nevile)

S8  *Dioscorides de interprt: Saraceni*
DIOSCORIDES
Opera omnia, *ed.* J. A. Saracenus
Frankfurt 1598; Adams D658

S.4.54; given 1633 (J. Fortho)

S9  *Matthiolus in eundum*
DIOSCORIDES
P. A. Matthioli commentarii in libros sex
Dioscoridis de medica materia
Lyons 1563; Adams D670

S.22.37; given 1611–12 (Nevile)

S10 *Camerarius de Plantis*
  MATTHIOLI, Pietro Andrea
  De plantis epitome, novis inconibus et descriptionibus
  a D. Ioachimo Camerario
  Frankfurt 1586; Adams M909

  S.3.56; bought 1637 (Whalley)


S11 *Fuchsij hist: stirpium*
  FUCHS, Leonhart
  De historia stirpium commentarii
  Basle 1542; Adams F1099

  S.5.11; given 1633 (J. Fortho)


S12 *Turners Herbal*
  TURNER, William
  The first and seconde partes of the herbal
  Cologne 1568; STC 24367

  bound with

    BRAUNSCHWEIG, Hieronymus
    A most excellent homish apothecary
    Cologne 1561; STC 13433

  VI.3.32$^{1-2}$; given 1611–12 (Nevile)


S13 *Gerhard$^s$ Herbal 1(–2)*
  GERARD, John
  The herball
  London 1597; STC 11750
  (presumably bound in two volumes)

  absent; given 1633 (J. Fortho)


S14 *Ardoynus de venenis*
  ARDOYNIS, Santes de
  Opus de venenis
  Basle 1562; Adams A1546

  S.5.31; given 1633 (J. Fortho)

S15 *Vessalij Anatomia*
VESALIUS, Andreas
De humani corporis fabrica
Basle 1543; Adams V603

absent; bought 1625 (M. Stanhope)


S16 *Horatij Eugenij Epła & consultationes*
AUGENIUS, Horatius
Epistolarum & consultationum medicinalium
Frankfurt 1597; Adams A2127

S.4.6; bought 1625 (M. Stanhope)


S17 *Idem de Febribus*
AUGENIUS, Horatius
De febribus
Frankfurt 1605

S.17.53; bought 1625 (M. Stanhope)


S18 *Solenandri Concil: Med:*
SOLENANDER, Reiner
Conciliorum medicinalium sectiones quinque
Frankfurt 1596; Adams S1385

S.4.5; bought 1625 (M. Stanhope)


S19 *Scholzij Concil: Med:*
SCHOLZ, Laurent
Consiliorum medicinalium liber
Hanover 1610

bound with

SCHOLZ, Laurent
Epistolarum philosophi earum, medicinalium et chymicarum
Frankfurt 1610

E.15.19$^{1-2}$; bought 1625 (M. Stanhope)

S20 *Foresti observationes 1(–2)*
FORESTUS, Petrus
Observationum et curationum medicinalium ac
chirurgicum opera omnia
2v, Frankfurt 1619

S.11.5–6; bought 1625 (M. Stanhope)

S21 *Herculis Saxonici Praxis*
SAXONIA, Hercules
Pantheum medicinae selectum
Frankfurt 1603

bound with

SAXONIA, Hercules
De pulsibus
Frankfurt 1604

S.17.51$^{1-2}$; given 1633 (J. Fortho)

S22 *Montani opa*
MONTANUS, Johannes Baptista
Medicina universa
Frankfurt 1587; Adams M1685

S.4.3; bought 1625 (M. Stanhope)

S23 *Mercati opa vol. 1(–2)*
MERCADO, Luis de
(probably Opera omnia
5v in 2, Frankfurt 1608–15)

absent; bought 1618 (Sedley)

S24 *Vitalis de furno*
FURNO, Johannes Vitalis de
Pro conseruanda sanitate salutarium remediorum, curationumque
liber
Mainz 1531; Adams F1183

S.4.20; given 1611–12 (Nevile)

S25 *Wickeri tabulæ*
WECKER, Johannes Jacobus
Medicinae utriusque syntaxes
Basle 1576; Adams W34

S.5.39; given 1611–12 (Nevile)


S26 *Paræi chirurg:*
PARÉ, Ambroise
Opera chirurgica
Frankfurt 1594; Adams P314

bound with

    WECKER, Johannes Jacobus
    Antidotarium speciale
    Basle 1588; Adams W33

S.4.4$^{1-2}$; given 1633 (J. Fortho)


S27 *The French Chirurg:*
GUILLEMEAU, Jacques
The French chirurgerye
Dordrecht 1597; STC 12498

VI.5.13; bought 1618 (Sedley)


S28 *Senerti opa vol. 1(–5)*
SENNERT, Daniel
Medicina practica
5v in 3, Paris 1632–5

SENNERT, Daniel
De febribus
Paris 1633

bound with

    SENNERT, Daniel
    De chymicorum
    Paris 1633

SENNERT, Daniel
Epitome naturalis scientiae
Paris 1633

(The missing volume was probably Sennert's Institutionum medicinae libri V, Paris 1631, replaced by Lynnet's copy of the Wittenberg 1628 edition, now S.9.15)

S.9.12–14, S.9.16$^{1-3}$ (1 vol absent); bought 1637 (Whalley)

S29 *Paracelsè vol. 1(–4)*
PARACELSUS, Philippus Aureolus Theophrastus
Operum medico-chimicorum, sive paradoxorum
4v, Frankfurt 1603–5

absent; bought 1637 (Whalley)

S30 *Theatri chymic. vol.(–4)*
THEATRUM
Theatrum chemicum
4v, Oberursel 1602–13

S.25.25–8; bought 1637 (Whalley)

S31 *Avicen: ars chymic:*
AVICENNA
Artis chemicae principes
Basle 1572; Adams A2334

bound with

GUIBERTUS, Nicolaus
De interitu alchymiae metallorum transmutatoriae tractatus
Tulle 1614

S.22.8$^{1-2}$; bought 1637 (Whalley)

S32 *Turba philosophorum*
ARS
Artis auriferae quam chemiam vocant
3v in 1, Basle 1610

S.1.20; bought 1637 (Whalley)

S33 *Tractat: Chymic: Amelungij (-vol.2)*
AMELUNG, Peter
Tractatus primus [de alchemia]
Leipzig 1607

bound with

> AMELUNG, Peter
> Tractatus secundus [de alchemia]
> Leipzig 1608

(The two tracts may at first have been bound separately)

S.1.27$^{1-2}$; bought 1637 (Whalley)

S34 *Agricola de re Metallicâ*
AGRICOLA, Georgius
De re metallica
Basle 1561; Adams A350

S.5.26; bought 1637 (Whalley)

## MATHEMATICI

S35 *Clavius vol. 1(–3)*
CLAVIUS, Christopher
Opera mathematica
5v in 4, Mainz 1611–12

T.64.7–10; bought 1618 (Suckling)

S36 *Vitruvius Pollio de Architecturâ*
VITRUVIUS POLLIO, Marcus
De architectura
Venice 1567; Adams V909

L.10.40; bought 1618 (Suckling)

S37 *Aquilonij Optica*
AIGUILLON, François d'
Opticorum libri sex
Antwerp 1613

Q.17.8; bought 1618 (Sedley)

S38 *Argol: Ephemerides v. 1(–3)*
ARGOLUS, Andreas
Ephemerides iuxta Tychonis hypotheses
3v, Venice, Padua 1638

T.1.47, T.2.52–3; bought 1639 (Medhop)

S39 *Serleius de Architecturâ*
SERLIO, Sebastiano
Architettura
Venice 1551; Adams S974

absent

S40 *Speculum Astrologiæ 1(–2)*
JUNCTINUS, Franciscus
Speculum astrologiae
2v, Lyons 1581; Adams J435

S.6.28–9; bought 1637 (Whalley)

S41 *Euclidis Elementa*
EUCLID
(possibly Elements, *Greek*
Basle 1533; Adams E980)

(bound in the 18th cent. with S54)

S.5.3[1]

S42 *Guido Bonatus*
BONATUS, Guido
De astronomia tractatus X
Basle 1550; Adams B2382

(bound in the 18th cent. with another item)

S.5.17[1] (TS53); given 1592 (Skeffington)

S43 *Bayeri Ouranometria*
BAYER, Johann
Uranomatria
Augsburg 1603

T.6.10; bought 1625 (M. Stanhope)

S44 *Hipparchus*
    HIPPARCHUS, *Bithynus*
    [On the Phaenomena of Aratus]. *Greek*
    Florence 1567; Adams H562

    S.4.48; bought 1618 (Sedley)


S45 *Tychoñ. Astronomia*
    KEPLER, Johann
    Astronomia nova
    [Heidelberg] 1609

    T.18.22; bought 1625 (M. Stanhope)


S46 *Opus Palatinum de triangulis*
    RHETICUS, Georgius Joachim
    Opus palatinum de triangulus
    Neustadt 1596; Adams R443

    (lacks the Magnus canon doctrinae triangulorum, bound separately)

    T.17.23; bought 1625 (M. Stanhope)


S47 *Cluerus de Italiâ antiquâ (-vol.3)*
    CLUVERIUS, Philippus
    Italia antiqua
    2v, Leyden 1624

    CLUVERIUS, Philippus
    Sicilia antiqua
    Leyden 1629

    U.5.16–17, U.5.18; bought 1625 (M. Stanhope)


S48 *Dee in Euclidem*
    (probably EUCLID
    Elements, *English*, preface by J. Dee)
    London 1570; STC 10560

    absent; given 1633 (J. Fortho)

S49 *Strabonis Geographia*
STRABO
(doubtless Rerum geographicarum libri septemdecim
Geneva 1587; Adams S1908)

absent (OL68); 16th cent.

S50 *Ramus*
RAMUS, Petrus
Professio regia, *ed.* J. T. Freigius
Basle 1576; Adams R115

bound with

TABULAE
Tabulae locorum communium theologicorum
Basle 1575; Adams T19

FREIGIUS, Johannes Thomas
Partitiones juris utriusque; partitiones feudalis
Basle 1571; Adams F1015

WECKER, Johannes Jacobus
Medicinae utriusque syntaxes
Basle 1576; Adams W34

MORUS, Horatius
Tabulæ universam chirurgicam miro ordine complectentes
Venice 1572; Adams M1834

S.5.34$^{1-3, 5-6}$ (TS51); given 1592 (Skeffington)

S51 *Topographia Romæ*
(unidentified)

S52 *Pezelij Præcepta Genethliaca*
PEZELIUS, Christophorus
Praecepta genethliaca
Frankfurt 1607

bound with

CAMERARIUS, Johann Rudolph
Horarum natalium centuria una
Frankfurt 1607

L.7.72$^{1-2}$; bought 1637 (Whalley)

S53 *Tycho Brahe Mechan:*
BRAHE, Tycho
Astronomiae instauratae mechanica
Nuremberg 1602

S.13.5; bought 1637 (Whalley)

S54 *Diaphanti Arithmet.*
DIOPHANTUS, *Alexandrinus*
Rerum arithmeticarum libri sex
Basle 1575; Adams D652

(bound in the 18th cent. with S41)

S.5.3$^2$; bought 1637 (Whalley)

S55 *Schoneri Mathemat.*
SCHOENER, Johann
Opera mathematica
Nuremberg 1551; Adams S678

S.4.12; bought 1637 (Whalley)

S56 *Alhazeni thesaurus Opt.*
ALHAZEN
Opticae thesaurus
Basle 1572; Adams A745

absent; bought 1637 (Whalley)

S57 *Coment. in Ptolemæum*
PROCLUS, *Diadochus, etc.*
In C. Ptolemaei quadripartitum enarrator ignoti nominis, *Greek and Latin*
Basle 1559; Adams P2141

S.5.40; bought 1637 (Whalley)

S58 *Cardani Comͫent. in eundem*
   CARDANO, Girolamo
   In Cl. Ptolemaei de astrorum iudiciis
   Basle 1578; Adams C682

   S.5.22; bought 1637 (Whalley)


S59 *Munsteri Cosmographia*
   MUNSTER, Sebastian
   (probably Cosmographiae universalis
   Basle 1554; Adams M1910)

   absent (OL121); 16th cent.


S60 *Bucherus de doctrinâ temporum*
   BUCHERIUS, Aegidius
   De doctrina temporum
   Antwerp 1634

   L.18.7; bought 1637 (Whalley)


S61 *Ouranologion*
   PETAVIUS, Dionysius
   Uranologion
   Paris 1630

   T.18.36; bought 1637 (Whalley)


S62 *Kepleri Mysterium Cosmographicum*
   KEPLER, Johann
   Prodromus diss. cosmographicarum
   Frankfurt 1621

   Q.16.95; bought 1625 (M. Stanhope)


S63 *Johͥis Archͤepi Perspectiva*
   PECKHAM, John
   Perspectiva communis
   Cologne 1580; Adams P536

   bound with

DEE, John
Προπαιδεύματα ἀφοριστικά
London 1558; STC 6463

DIGGES, Thomas
Alae seu scalae mathematicae
London 1573; STC 6871

DEE, John
Parallaticae commentationis
London 1573; STC 6462

FULKE, William
Metromaxia sive ludus geometricis
London [1578]; STC 11444 (?)

VI.1.114$^{1-5}$; bought 1637 (Whalley)

S64 *Gema de arte Cyclonomicâ*
GEMMA, Cornelius
De arte cyclognomica
Antwerp 1569; Adams G372

S.6.39; given c. 1597 (Sledd (v. TS50))

S65 *Johnsons Navigacons*
BLAEU, Willem Janszoon
*The light of navigation*
Amsterdam 1620

VI.4.39; bought 1625 (M. Stanhope)

S66 *Calvisij opus Cronologicum*
CALVISIUS, Sethus
Opus chronologicum
Frankfurt 1620

absent; bought 1625 (M. Stanhope)

S67 *Helvicus*
HELVICUS, Christophorus
Theatrum historicum
Marburg 1639

absent

S68 *Cluerus de antiquâ Germaniâ*
CLUVERIUS, Philippus
Germania antiqua
Leyden 1616

U.5.19; bought 1625 (M. Stanhope)


S69 *Bacons Perspect:*
BACON, Roger
Perspectiva
Frankfurt 1614

L.12.137; bought 1637 (Whalley)


S70 *Albumazar introduct.*
ALBUMAZAR
Introductorium in astronomiam
Venice 1506; Adams A567

bound with

ABDU'L AZIZ ibn Uthman al'Qabisi
Alchabitius cum commento
Venice 1512; Adams A21

T.20.48$^{1-2}$; bought 1637 (Whalley)


S71 *Leovitij tabulæ vol. 1(–2)*
LEOVITIUS, Cyprianus
Tabulae positionum pro variis poli elevationibus
Augsburg 1551; Adams L520

REGIOMONTANUS, Johannes
Tabulae directionum et profectionum . . . Tabulae ascensionum obli-
quarum per C. Leovitium
Augsburg 1551; Adams R289

T.20.20, 19; bought 1637 (Whalley)

S72 *Magini Theor:*
MAGINUS, Johannes Antonius
Nouae coelestium orbium theoricae congruentes cum obseruationibus
N. Copernici
Venice 1589; Adams M119

S.3.96; bought 1637 (Whalley)

S73 *Copnicus*
COPERNICUS, Nicolaus
De revolutionibus orbium coelestium
Basle 1566; Adams C2603

absent;[1] bought 1637 (Whalley)

S74 *Prutenicæ tabulæ*
REINHOLD, Erasmus
Prutenicae tabulae coelestium motuum
Wittenberg 1585; Adams R332

T.20.27; bought 1637 (Whalley)

S75 *Pyrovani defensio Astronomiæ*
PIROVANUS, Gabriel
Defensio astronomiae
Milan 1507; Adams P1275

bound with

   SCEPPER, Cornelius Duplicius
   Assertionis fidei adversus astrologos
   Antwerp 1523; Adams S616

S.6.40$^{1-2}$; bought 1637 (Whalley)

S76 *Petrus de Aliaco in sphæram*
JOHANNES DE SACRO BUSTO
Sphaera mundi (with Petrus de Alliaco, Quaestiones)
Paris 1498; Goff J-418

bound with

Sold as a duplicate, 1859; now in the Brotherton Library, University of Leeds.

JOHANNES DE SACRO BUSTO
Sphaera mundi (with the comm. of Jacobus Faber Stapulensis)
Venice 1499; Goff J–419

BRADWARDINUS, Thomas
Geometria speculativa
Paris 1495; Goff B–1072

VI.15.10$^{1-3}$; bought 1637 (Whalley)

S77 *Machiavells Art of Warre*
MACHIAVELLI, Niccoló
The arte of warre
(probably London 1560, 1574, or 1588)

absent; bought 1637 (Whalley)

S78 *Mucices authores*
(unidentified)

S79 *Genethliacon Edvardi Principis Cambriæ*
LELAND, John
Genethliacon illustrissimi Eäduerdi principis Cambriae
London 1543; STC 15443

absent; probably given 1626–30 (? Elwes)

# INDEXES

*I. Headings, etc.*

ABDU'L AZIZ, S70
AGRICOLA, Georgius, S34
AIGUILLON, François de, S37
ALBUMAZAR, S70
ALHAZEN, S56
ALLIACO, Petrus de, S76
AMELUNG, Peter, S33
ARDOYNIS, Santes de, S14
ARGOLUS, Andreas, S38
ARS, S32
AUGENIUS, Horatius, S16, S17
AVICENNA, S31
BACON, Roger, S69
BAYER, Johann, S43
BLAEU, Willem Janszoon, S65
BONATUS, Guido, S42

BRADWARDINUS, Thomas, S76
BRAHE, Tycho, S53
BRASAVOLA, Antonio Musa, S6
BRAUNSCHWEIG, Hieronymus, S12
BUCHERIUS, Aegidius, S60
CALVISIUS, Sethus, S66
CAMERARIUS, Joachimus, *jun.*, S10
CAMERARIUS, Johann Rudolph, S52
CARDANO, Girolamo, S58
CLAVIUS, Christopher, S35
CLUVERIUS, Philippus, S47, S68
COPERNICUS, Nicolaus, S73
DEE, John, S48, S63
DIGGES, Thomas, S63
DIOPHANTUS, *Alexandrinus*, S54
DIOSCORIDES, S8, S9

EUCLID, S41, S48
FABER, Jacobus, *Stapulensis*, S76
FORESTUS, Petrus, S20
FREIGIUS, Johannes Thomas, S50
FUCHS, Leonhart, S11
FULKE, William, S63
FURNO, Johannes Vitalis de, S24
GALENUS, Claudius, S2, S3, S6
GEMMA, Cornelius, S64
GERARD, John, S13
GORRAEUS, Johannes, S7
GUIBERTUS, Nicolaus, S31
GUILLEMEAU, Jacques, S27
HELVICUS, Christophorus, S67
HIPPARCHUS, *Bithynus*, S44
HIPPOCRATES, S1, S6
JOHANNES DE SACRO BUSTO, S76
JUNCTINUS, Franciscus, S40
KEPLER, Johann, S45, S62
LELAND, John, S79
LEOVITIUS, Cyprianus, S71
MACHIAVELLI, Niccoló, S77
MAGINUS, Johannes Antonius, S72
MATTHIOLI, Pietro Andrea, S9, S10
MERCADO, Luis de, S23
MONTANUS, Johannes Baptista, S22
MORUS, Horatius, S50
'Mucices authores', S78
MUNSTER, Sebastian, S59
PARACELSUS, Philippus Aureolus, S29

PARÉ, Ambroise, S26
PECKHAM, John, S63
PETAVIUS, Dionysius, S61
PEZELIUS, Christophorus, S52
PIROVANUS, Gabriel, S75
PROCLUS, *Diadochus*, S57
PTOLEMAEUS, Claudius, S57
RAMUS, Petrus, S50
REGIOMONTANUS, Johannes, S71
REINHOLD, Erasmus, S74
RHETICUS, Georgius Joachim, S46
SARACENUS, Johannes, S8
SAXONIA, Hercules, S21
SCEPPER, Cornelius Duplicius, S75
SCHOENER, Johann, S55
SCHOLZ, Laurent, S19
SENNERT, Daniel, S28
SERLIO, Sebastiano, S39
SOLENANDER, Reiner, S18
SORANUS, *Ephesius*, S4
STRABO, S49
TABULAE, S50
THEATRUM, S30
'Topographia Romae', S51
TURNER, William, S12
VEGA, Christophorus de, S5
VESALIUS, Andreas, S15
VITRUVIUS POLLIO, Marcus, S36
WECKER, Johannes Jacobus, S25, S26, S50

## II. Provenances

### Gifts of books

| | |
|---|---|
| 1592 (Thomas Skeffington), S42, S50 | (2) |
| c.1597 (John Sledd), S64 | (1) |
| 1611–12 (Thomas Nevile), S4, S7, S9, S12, S24, S25 | (6) |
| 1626–30 (Silvius Elwes), S79 | (1) |
| 1633 (John Fortho), S5, S6, S8, S11, S13, S14, S21, S26, S48 | (9) |
| | (19) |

### Books bought with gifts of money

| | |
|---|---|
| 1618 (Sir William Sedley), S1–3, S23, S27, S37, S44 | (7) |
| 1618 (Sir John Suckling), S35, S36 | (2) |
| 1625 (Sir Michael Stanhope), S15–20, S22, S43, S45–7, S62, S65, S66, S68 | (15) |
| 1637 (Thomas Whalley), S10, S28–34, S40, S52–8, S60, S61, S63, S69–77 | (28) |
| 1639 (Thomas Medhop), S38 | (1) |
| | (53) |

### unknown

| | |
|---|---|
| S39, S41, S49, S51, S59, S67, S78 | (7) |

# LIBRARY REGULATIONS, 1651

(From TC MS O.11a.2[51]; in a scribal hand, not Griffith's)

Ordered by the M$^r$ and Seniors for the better preserving the bookes in the Library this 10th day of February 1650[51] as followeth—

1 That no person whatsoever belonging to this Colledge under ye degree of a M$^r$ of Artes (except hee bee fellow or fellowcommoner) shall bee permitted to study in the Library: neither shall any whither stranger or of the Coll: under y$^e$ degree before mentioned (except y$^e$ before excepted) bee admitted to view y$^e$ Library unlesse by the appointment of the M$^r$, or in his absence of the Vice M$^r$: or yf some one of the Fellowes go alonge with him and there abide with y$^e$ party brought in by him untill his departure thence. Those appertaining to y$^e$ Coll. to bee punished by the M$^r$, or in his absence by the Vice M$^r$, y$^e$ summe of two shillings & six pence for every time they shall herein offend. And if the under library keeper shall bring in any under the degree of M$^r$ of Artes either of this or any other Colledge to bee punished five shillings.

2 That no Fellowcommoner of this Colledg, nor M$^r$ of Artes (not fellow) shall at any time take any booke or bookes out of y$^e$ Library upon any occasion whatsoever under y$^e$ penalty of paying y$^e$ double value of y$^e$ said booke or bookes so taken out. And y$^t$ no fellowcommoner who is now, or shall hereafter bee admitted into this Society, nor any M$^r$ of Artes (not fellow) abiding in the Coll: shall enjoy y$^e$ benefit of y$^e$ library by studying in it, unlesse some one of y$^e$ fellowes engage himselfe to y$^e$ M$^r$ and Seniors in his behalfe y$^t$ the sayd party shall observe y$^e$ orders here made concerning y$^e$ Library and submit to such mulcts as hee shall incurre by violating y$^e$ sayd Orders.

3 That no fellow of this Colledge whatsoever shall take out of the Library any booke or bookes, unlesse hee first note downe with his owne hand in y$^e$ Regester reserved by the under Library keeper for y$^t$ purpose, y$^e$ title, edition, & volumne of y$^e$ booke or bookes w$^{th}$ y$^e$ time when so taken

out, and subscribes his name to y$^e$ same, and shall returne into y$^e$ hands of y$^e$ Library keeper or his deputy y$^e$ said booke or bookes within the space of fortie eight houres.

Whosoever shall transgresse in not subscribinge his name to y$^e$ Regester as above sayd shall pay y$^e$ double value of the sayd booke or bookes: And hee who shall offend in not returning y$^e$ booke or bookes within the time before limited shall bee punished for every one of y$^e$ bookes w$^{ch}$ hee shall retaine. And for every weeke beyond y$^e$ time prescribed 2$^s$–6$^d$.

4 That if any person whatsoever belonging to this Colledge shall privily conveigh away out of y$^e$ Library, or shall imbezell any booke or bookes, or shall conceale any booke or bookes conveighed out or imbezelled hee shall pay y$^e$ price of y$^e$ booke or bookes so conveighed out, imbezelled, or concealed fourefold.

5 That every punishment any where mentioned in these orders upon Complaint made to the M$^r$ (or in his absence y$^e$ Vice M$^r$) and upon either y$^e$ Confession of y$^e$ person or persons offending, or the testimony of one or more witnesses against them, is to bee inflicted by the M$^r$ (or in his absence y$^e$ Vice Master) upon y$^e$ severall offenders, the one third part of y$^e$ summe or summes of money thence arising to bee given to y$^e$ informer, the rest to bee expended for y$^e$ benefit of y$^e$ Library.

6 That every person belonging to this Colledge who hath now in his Custodye any booke or bookes formerly borrowed or taken out of y$^e$ Library shall forth with send in the same, & y$^t$ every person who knowes of any bookes formerly taken out, & not yet brought in give notice to y$^e$ Library keeper or to his deputy Whosoever shall bee negligent herein for y$^e$ space of one weeke after y$^e$ publication of these orders shall pay for every such booke or bookes fourefold and shall moreover bee punished three moneths Commons.

# INDEX

Abdias, *pseud.*, 188
Abdu'l Aziz, 255
Aeneas Silvius, Piccolomini (Pius II, Pope), 175
Aeschylus, 54, 130
Aesop, 57
Agricola, Georgius, 89, 248
Agricola, Rudolphus, 23, 54, 57
Aiguillon, François de, 248
Albertus, Magnus, Bp of Ratisbon, 156
Albumazar, 255
Alciatus, Andreas, 42, 197, 200
Alc(k)horne, Charles, Fellow of Trinity, formerly Sub-Librarian, 230
Aldrovandi, Ulisse, 89 and n.2
Alexander, Aphrodisiensis, 170, 172
Alexandro, Alexander ab, 178
Alhazen, 252
All Souls College, Oxford, library of, 3, 7
Alliaco, Petrus de, 256
Amelung, Peter, 248
Ames, William, 129
Anacreon, 54
Anger, William, Fellow of Trinity, private library of, 53
Anselm, Abp of Canterbury, 161
Apocalypse, the Trinity (MS), 80, 84 and n.3, 121
Appianus, of Alexandria, 174
Aquinas, Thomas, St, 28 and n.2, 157, 193
Archer, Thomas, Acting Librarian of Trinity, 107 and n.4
Ardoynis, Santes de, 243
Aretius Felinus (i.e. Bucer, Martin), 161
Argolus, Andreas, 249
Aristophanes, 45, 167
Aristotle, 8, 23, 40 n.3, 45, 54, 57, 168, 169, 170, 178
Arnobius, Afer, 186
Arnold, John, Chaplain of Trinity, printed books given by, 238
Ars, 247

Asconius Pedianus, Quintus, 180
Athanasius, Abp of Alexandria, St, 40 and n.2, 79, 147
Athenaeus, Naucratita, 191
Atkin(s), Thomas, Sub-Librarian of Trinity, 229
Auerbach, Johannes, 202
Augenius, Horatius, 244
Augustine, Bp of Hippo, St, 8, 11, 52, 54, 149, 150
Avicenna, 247
'Awnswer towchyng mynisters app[arell]', 52
Aytta, Wigle van, of Swichem, 197

Babington, Humfrey, Fellow of Trinity, rents for books given by, 140
Bacon, Francis, of Trinity College, xi n.1, 89 and n.2, 129 and n.2
Bacon, Roger, 255
Bale, John, Bp of Ossory, 79
Ball, William, Fellow of Trinity, 91 n.2
Balliol College, Oxford, library of, 3, 7
Bancroft, Richard, Abp of Canterbury, 80
Banks, James, Chaplain and Librarian of Trinity, 135, 142
Barbier, Jean, 196
Barcroft(e), Robert, Sub-Librarian of Trinity, 78 n.4, 229
Barker, Thomas, of Magdalene College, 55 n.5
Baronius, Caesar, Cardinal, 38, 189
Barrow, Isaac, Fellow and Master of Trinity, xi n.1, 89, 131 n.4, 137, fig. 31
his private library, 131 n.2
books for TCL bought from, 130 and n.6
printed books given by, 91 n.4, 119 n.5, 127, 131 and n.2
Barry, George, Fellow of Trinity, MS given by, 234
Barthlet, John, 38, 186

Bartholomaeus Anglicus, 27, 28 n.1, 168
Basil, Abp of Caesarea, the Great, St, 151
Basle editions, 8, 38, 40–1
Batt, Edward, Fellow of Trinity, printed books given by, 238
Battely, John, Fellow of Trinity, MS given by, 234
Bauhin, Kaspar, 90
Baxter, Johann, 249
Bayer, Johann, 249
Beaumont, John, Fellow of Trinity, private library of, 53
Beaumont, Robert, Master of Trinity inventory of his books, 215–17
    money given by, 47, 63
    printed books given by, 32 n.8, 39–40, 46, 47 and n.5, 48, 49, 51 n.3, 55
    royal portraits given by, 47, 48 and n.3
Bede, the Venerable, 28 and n.1, 176
Bembo, Pietro, Cardinal, 177, 179–80
Benavides, Marco, Mantuano, 199
Benefactions book of TCL, 119 and n.2
Bennet, Robert, Fellow of Trinity, money for books given by, 93, 239
Bentley, Richard, Master of Trinity, challenges library accounts, 140–1
Bernard, Edward, catalogue of MSS, 84 n.7, 115 n.1, 135 and n.1, 214 n.4, 235
Berthorus, Petrus, 192
Bible: polyglot, 8, 38, 224; Greek, 52; Latin, 8, 11 n.5, 147, 148, 157; English (1611), 88 n.4; French, 148
    O.T.: polyglot, 148; Hebrew, 11 n.5, 52; Psalms, Hebrew, 187, 190
    N.T.: Greek, 38, 52, 54, 57; Latin, 52; Epistles, Latin, 28 and n.1
    Concordances, 37 n.6
Bibliander, Theodorus, 185
Bill, William, Master of Trinity, printed books given by, 32 n.8, 45 and n.5, 47 and n.1, 49, 55
binding, 12, 29, 32, 68, 69 and nn.3,4, 81 and n.1, 82, 96–7, 123, 124, 125 and n.6, 132; fig. 7, 20, 21
    arms, 81, 82, 97, 104 and n.1
    boards, 69 and n.4, 96, 97
    edges coloured, 68, 81 and n.6, 82, 97, 104 untrimmed, 81 and n.1, 82
    end-papers, 97; fig. 21
    initials, 97, 104 and n.1; fig. 20
    reinforcing strips, 97; fig. 21
    titling and labelling, 29, 37, 69, 71 n.4, 93, 97, 102, 104; fig. 1, 7, 8, 21, 22, 23
    tabs, fore-edge, 97 and n.2, 102; fig. 21, 23
Birkhead, Daniel, Fellow of Trinity, printed books given by, 238

Bishop's Hostel, 137 and n.1
Blaeu, Willem Janszoom, 254
    globes by, 104 and n.4
Bland, Simon, of Trinity College, MS given by, 234
Bodin, Jean, 42, 129, 204
Boehme, Jakob, 129
Bombelli, Rafael, 90
Bonatus, Guido, 206, 249
Boniface VIII, Pope, 42, 179, 200
book-cases, 10, 93, 96, 113, 125 and n.1, 139; fig. 2, 19
Borelli, Giovanni Alfonso, 131
Boteler, John, Fellow of Trinity, speaking trumpet given by, 122
Bowen, Adam, MS given by, 234
    printed books given by, 239
Boyle, Robert, 131
Bradwardinus, Thomas, 257
Brahe, Tycho, 90, 252
Bramfyld, William, of Trinity College, 56 n.2
Brasavola, Antonio Musa, 242
Brasenose College, Oxford, library of, 8
Braunschweig, Hieronymus, 243
Brenz, Johannes, 38, 153, 183
Breydenbach, Bernhard von, 175
British Library, 12 nn. 8, 10, 20 n.1
Brown, John, of St Nicholas Hostel, 51 n.2
Brownrigg, Ralph, Master of St Catharine's College, Bp of Exter, 84 n.3
Bruno, Carthusian, St, 171
Brunus, Conradus, 165
Bucer, Martin, 8, 38, 52, 154, 161, 183
Bucherius, Aegidius, 253
Budaeus, Gulielmus, 42, 201
Buildwas Abbey, Shropshire, MSS from, 80–1
Bull,—, of Queens' College, 56 n.2
Bullinger, Heinrich, 38, 182
Burgoyne, Robert, of Peterhouse, 51 n.2
Byzantine history, Parisian corpus, 129 and n.3

Caesar, Gaius Julius, 57, 129
Caesares, 173
Cajetanus, Thomas de Vio, 157
Calepinus, Ambrosius, 57
Calvin, Jean, 8, 39 and n.1, 48, 52, 54, 124, 181, 183
Calvisius, Sethus, 254
Cambridge, colleges, libraries of, 3–10; see also under individual colleges
Cambridge University, Statutes, 23 and n.1, 56–7

Vice-Chancellor's Court records, 51–7, 51 nn.1, 3, 215–7

Cambridge University Library, 7 and n.3, 96 n.3, 112 n.2, 113 n.3

Camden, William, 88 and n.4, 129 and n.2

Camerarius, Joachimus, senior, 171

Camerarius, Joachimus, junior, 243

Camerarius, Johann Rudolph, 252

Campanella, Tommaso, 129

Canterbury MSS, 80 and n.6, 81, 82, 83

Canterbury Psalter (MS), 80, 81

Capito, Wolfgang Fabricius, 184

Cardano, Girolamo, 253

Cartwright, Thomas, Fellow of Trinity, xi n.1, 39

Casalius, Gaspar, Bp of Coimbra, 163

Cassadoris, Gulielmus, 199

Cassiodorus, Magnus Aurelius, 20 n.1

Castlemaine, Roger Palmer, Earl of, globe, 121, 122

Castro, Alfonsus de, 158, 198

catalogues and cataloguing, 6, 10, 32–3, 34–7, 44 and n.2, 78, 85, 87; fig. 10, 25, 26, 27, 28, 29, 30

catalogues, case-end, 6, 33, 93, 96, 113, 142 n.2; fig. 1, 2

Catullus, Gaius Valerius, 88 n.5

Ceporinus, Jacobus, 24, 54

chains and chaining, 4, 6, 12, 14, 29 and nn.2,3,4, 68 n.3, 71 n.5, 88 n.1, 97, 123 and n.3, 224, 226; fig. 1, 2, 7, 17

Chamberlain, George, Fellow of Trinity, printed books given by, 119 n.5, 129 n.1

Charron, Pierre, 129

Chaucer, Geoffrey, 81, 82

Cheney, Francis, money for books given by, 238

Chillingworth, William, 128 and n.2

Christ Church, Canterbury, MSS from, 80 and n.6, 81, 82, 83

Christ Church, Oxford, library of, 8

Christian Church, Fathers, 183

'Christi victoria et triumphus', 187

Christ's College (formerly God's House), Cambridge, library of, 4 n.1, 8

Christopherson, John, Master of Trinity, books given by, 40, 46, 47 and nn. 2,3,4, 49, 55, 61, 79, 147

Christophorus, a Castro, 163

Chrysostom, John, Abp of Constantinople, 52 n.3, 191

Chytraeus, David, the elder, 185

Cicero, Marcus Tullius, 23, 25 n.3, 54, 57, 171, 177, 178

Clare College (formerly Clare Hall), Cambridge, library of, 3, 7, 20 and n.2, 93 and n.1

Clarus, Julius, 201

classics, Greek and Latin, in early college libraries, 8

'classes', 69

classification, by donors, 85, 87, 93, 96, 108, 113, 142 and n.3
  by subjects, 39, 89–90, 108–9, 112–13, 113 n.2, 115, 126, 127, 142; plans 5, 6
  private schemes, 112
  traditional schemes, 32–3, 74, 109, 112–13, 112 n.2, 127
  'Ratio Dispositionis', 112

Clavius, Christopher, 90, 248

Clement V, Pope, 42

Clenardus, Nicolaus, 24

Clerke, Henry, Fellow of Trinity, private library of, 53

Clichtoveus, Judocus, 54

Clugh, Alexander, of Emmanuel College, 91 n.3

Clusius, Carolus, 89

Clutterbooke, William, Librarian of Trinity, 77–8, 213 and n.3, 228
  indexes the books, 108, 115; fig. 25

Cluverius, Philippus, 130 and n.3, 250, 255

Clyfton, Robert, of Michaelhouse, 51 n.2

Coaker, Thomas, Fellow of Trinity, 91 n.2

Cochlaeus, Johannes, 159, 165, 176, 182

Cockcroft, Henry, Fellow of Trinity, private library of, 53

coins and medals in TCL, 120–1, 121 n.3, 122

Coke, Sir Edward, of Trinity College, xi n.1, 84 and n.3

Colier, Thomas, Fellow of Michaelhouse, 11 n.5, 51 n.2

college libraries, early, 3–10
  access to, 6
  accessions, 4, 6
  book losses, 7
  catalogues and cataloguing in, 4, 6; fig. 1, 2
  chained books in, 4, 6; fig. 1, 2
  contents, 4, 6–7, 8, 10
  furnishing of, 4–6
  librarians, 6, 10
  loan collections, 4, 6
  objects other than books in, 33
  reference collections, 4
  size and capacity, 4, 6

Collins, Samuel, Reg. Prof. of Divinity, Provost of King's College, 91 n.3
  printed books given to Trinity by, 239

Cologne, Cathedral, 184

Concilia, 52 n.3, 129 and n.1, 148, 182

Conradus, Abbot of Auersperg, 188
Cook, Capt. James, 121 n.3
Copernicus, Nicolaus, 90, 256
Coppinger, Adam, MS given by, 234
Corbie Abbey, library of, 109 and n.1
Corker, William, Fellow of Trinity, MS
    given by, 234
Corpus Christi College, Cambridge, library
    of, 4, 7, 20 n.2
Corpus Christi College, Oxford, library of,
    8
Cotta, Catellianus, 197
Councils of the Church, 52 n.3, 129 and n.1,
    148, 182
Coverdale, Miles, 52 n.4
Cowell, John, Master of Trinity Hall, 45
Cowley, Abraham, Fellow of Trinity,
    printed books given by, 119 n.5, 127
    and n.
Crane, Richard, MS given by, 234
Crane, Robert, Fellow of Trinity, MSS
    given by, 234
Cromwell, Thomas, Chancellor of Cam-
    bridge University, 19
Cropley, John, Fellow of Trinity, printed
    books given by, 239
Crosland, William, Sub-Librarian of Trin-
    ity, 230
Crosse, Henry, of Peterhouse, 11 n.5,
    51 n.2
Crossley, Henry, of Michaelhouse, 11 n.5,
    51 n.2
Cudworth, Ralph, 129
Cumberland, Richard, Bp of Peterborough,
    130
curiosities in TCL, 120–1, 121 n.2, 122
Cuspinianus, Johannes, 167
Cyril, Abp of Alexandria, St, 149

Davies, John, Acting Librarian of Trinity,
    107 and n.4
Dee, John, Fellow of Trinity, books by, 250,
    254
    globes, etc., given by, 33, 104, 122
Demosthenes, 24, 40 n.4, 54, 163
De residentia pastorum, 186
Descartes, René, 130 and n.6
'desks', 10 n.1
Dickenson, Henry, bookbinder, 97 n.1
Dickius, Leopold, 203
Didymus, Alexandrinus, 171
Digges, Thomas, 254
Diodorus, Siculus, 163
Dionysius, the Areopagite, 152
Dionysius, Carthusianus, à Rickell, 52 n.3,
    158

Dionysius, of Halicarnassus, 169
Diophantus, Alexandrinus, 252
Dioscorides, 242
divinity the main study at Michaelhouse and
    Trinity, 11, 22–3, 38, 86–7, 126
divinity books in early college libraries, 8,
    10, 19
Docwra, Thomas, of Trinity College, MS
    given by, 234
Doddridge, Sir John, money for globes
    given by, 104 and n.3, 122
Dodington, Bartholomew, Fellow of Trin-
    ity, money for books given by, 46, 48
    and n.4, 49
Dodonaeus, Rembertus, 89
Dorman, Thomas, 185
Dover Priory, library of, 109 n.2
Driedo, Johannes, 161
Dryden, Jonathan, Fellow of Trinity, MSS
    given by, 84, 234
Duke, Richard, Fellow of Trinity, MS given
    by, 234
Dulwich College, library of, 18
Du Moulin, Charles, 196
duplicates discarded, 120 and nn. 3,4, 141
    and nn.3,5,6, 225
Duport, James, Fellow of Trinity, Master of
    Magdalene, Dean of Peterborough, MS
    given by, 234
    money for Wren Library given by, 139
    printed books given by, 88 n.2, 91 n.4, 141
    and nn.2,3,4, 142 and n.3, 184
    private libraries of, 141 n.2
Durandus, Gulielmus I, Bp of Mende, 28
    and n.2, 200
Durandus, Gulielmus, à Sancto Porciano,
    Bp of Meaux, 158
Durham Cathedral, library of, 80 n.6

Echter von Mespelborn, Julius, Bp of Würz-
    burg, Duke of Franconia, library of, 132
Edward II, king of England, 12
Edward VI, king of England, 22 and n.3,
    48 n.3
electiones, 4, 6 n.3
Elizabeth of York, queen of Henry VII,
    48 n.3
Elizabeth I, queen of England, 22 and n.3,
    48 n.3, 61
Elizabeth I, queen of England, 22 and n.3, 48
    n.3, 61
Elwes, Silvius, Chaplain of Trinity, MSS
    given by, 234
    printed books given by, 88, 91, 129 n.2,
    239, 258
Elzevier classics, 129 n.6

Emmanuel College, Cambridge, library of, 8

Epiphanius, Bp of Constantia, 8, 150

Episcopius, Nicolaus, and Froben, Hieronymus, printers, Basle, 8, 47 and n.4

Erasmus, Desiderius, 38, 48, 52, 54, 57, 162

Essex, Robert Devereux, 2nd Earl of, of Trinity College, xi n.1, 56 n.1

Euclid, 90, 249, 250

Euripides, 45, 54, 57, 179

Eusebius, Pamphili, Bp of Caesarea, 8, 28 and n.1, 176, 189

Eustathius, Bp of Thessalonica, 190

Evans,—, writing master, 213 n.2

Exeter College, Oxford, library of, 3

Fabbe, John, of God's House, 51 n.2

Faber, Jacobus, Stapulensis, 28 and n.1, 165, 257

Fallopius, Gabriel, 90

Farrington, Lady, printed books given by, 239

Ferrari, Giampietro, of Pavia, 194

Ferus, Johannes, 164

Fetherston, Leonard, Sub-Librarian of Trinity, 230

Ficinus, Marsilius, 169

Filey, William, Fellow of Michaelhouse, printed books given by, to Michaelhouse, 11, 19 n.2, 27–8, 28 nn.1,2, 46 and n.1,2,3, 49, 165, 168, 176
to Trinity, 46, 175

Finé, Oronce, 90

Firebrace, Henry, Fellow of Trinity, medals given by, 122

Fitzrandolfe, Thomas, Fellow of Trinity, printed books given by, 239

Flacius, Mathias, Illyricus, 153, 161, 183, 186

Forestus, Petrus, 90, 245

Font, Henry, of Trinity College, money for books given by, 238

formats of library books, 9, 40

Fortho (Furtho), John, Fellow of Trinity, globe given by, 104, 106 and n., 122
MSS given by, 234
printed books given by, 239 258

Fortho (Furtho), Thomas, Fellow of Trinity, printed books given by, 239 and Skeffington's law books, 42 and n.2

Fox, Edward, 186

Fraser, Charles, Fellow of Trinity, printed books given by, 119 n.5

Freigius, Johannes Thomas, 202, 205, 251

Frere, Henry, Fellow of Trinity, bracelets given by, 122

Froben, Hieronymus, and Episcopius, Nicolaus, printers, Basle, 8, 47 and n.4

Frontinus, Sextus Julius, 12 n.10

Frysby, John, of King's Hall, 51 n.2

Fuchs, Leonhart, 89, 243

Fulke, William, 254

Furno, Johannes Vitalis de, 245

Gabriel, Antonio, 195

Gaguin, Robert, 180–1

Gale, Thomas, Fellow of Trinity, printed books given by, 131

Galenus, Claudius, 241, 242

Galilei, Galileo, 90, 131 and n.4

Gardiner, Stephen, Bp of Winchester, 153

Gaskell, Philip, and Robson, Robert, A short history of TCL, amendments to, xiii n. 1

Gast, Johannes, 150, 184

Gellius, Aulus, 57

Gemma, Cornelius, 205, 254

'Gensner' (i.e. Gesner, Conrad), 192

Gerard, John, 89, 243

Gerbelius, Nicolaus, 175

Gesner, Conrad, 89 and n.2, 172, 192

Gigas, Hieronymus, 198

Gilbert, William, 131

Gillibrand, Thomas, Sub-Librarian of Trinity, 230

Giovio, Paolo, Bp of Nocera, 174

globes in TCL, 33, 34, 104 and n.4, 120–1, 122

Goethals, Hendrik, of Ghent, 156

Gomez, Antonio, 202

Gonas, Rudolph, of Clare College, 55 n.5

Gonville and Caius College (formerly Gonville Hall), Cambridge, library of, 4, 7, 20 n.2, 200

Goodman, Godfrey, of Trinity College, printed book given by, 239

Gorraeus, Johannes, 242

Gorran, Nicolaus de, 162

Gospels, Winchester (MS), 81

Gotham, William de, Master of Michaelhouse, 11, 19 n.2

Gower, John, 81

Graham, Richard, of Trinity College, MS given by, 234

Grammatici, 178

Gratianus, Bononiensis, 194

Graves, William, bookseller, 125 n.6

Greaves, William, of Trinity College, MSS given by, 234

Greek, books in, 9, 40, 44, 45, 127–8

Gregory, Patriarch of Constantinople, Nazianzus, St, 151

Gregory I, Pope, the Great, 8, 149
Gregory IX, Pope, 179
Greswold, Henry, Fellow of Trinity, MSS given by 84, 234
Grew, Nehemiah, 131 n.3
Griffith, George, Fellow of Trinity, 108 n.2
Griffith, Thomas, Librarian of Trinity, career, 107 and nn. 1,3, 108, and nn.1,2, 134, 228
    catalogues the books, 115, 126, 214 and n.2; fig. 27, 29
    MSS given by, 84 and n.6, 234
    reclassifies the library, 113 and n.2, 115; plan 6
    Registrary (College scribe), 107 n.3, 108 and n.2
    Tutor, 108 and n.2
Grimalius Goslicius, Laurentius, Bp of Posen, 56 n.2
Gronovius, Johann Friedrich, 130
Grotius, Hugo, 129
Gruterus, James, 130 and n.3
Gualtherus, Rodolphus, senior, 52, 160, 181
Guibertus, Nicolaus, 247
Guillemeau, Jacques, 90, 246
Gulielmus, Altissiodorensis, 169
Gulielmus, Badonensis, 28 and n.3, 79 n.2
Gustavus Adolphus, king of Sweden, 132
Gylpyn, Godfrey, Fellow of Trinity, private library of, 53

Hacket, Sir Andrew, portrait of Bp Hacket given by, 122
Hacket, John, Bp of Coventry and Lichfield, Bishop's Hostel given by, 135, 137
    MSS given by, 234
    portrait of in TCL, 121, 122
    rents for books given by, 135, 137
Hakluyt, Richard, 129
Hall, William, Fellow of Trinity, printed books given by, 239
Hamond, John, map of Cambridge, 21, 63; fig. 3
Hamond, William, bookbinder, 32, 69 and n.3, 96
Hampton, Christopher, Fellow of Trinity, printed book given by, 238
Hardwick, William, Fellow of Trinity, MS given by, 234
Harington, James, 130
Harvey, William, 90, 131 and n.6
Havercroft, William, Sub-Librarian of Trinity, 229
Hawes, Henry, Fellow of Trinity, private library of, 53
Hegesippus, 188

Heinsius, Nicolas, 130
Helinandus, Frigidi Montis Monachus, 12 n.8, 20 n.1
Helperbye, Thomas, Fellow of Trinity, private library of, 53
    and Filey's books, 46
Helvicus, Christophorus, 254
Henriquez, Henricus, 155
Henry VI, king of England, 12
Henry VII, king of England, 48 n.3
Henry VIII, king of England, founder of Trinity College, 22, 47, 48 n.3
Henson,—, book-wheel bought from, 125 n.4
Herbert, Edward, Baron Herbert of Cherbury, 130 and n.5
Herbert, George, Fellow of Trinity, xi n.1
Herman, of Wied, Abp of Cologne, 164
Hermogenes, 44, 54, 206
Herodotus, 54, 173, 204
Hersent, Peter, Librarian of Trinity, 77, 228
Hesiod, 24, 40 n.4, 54, 171
Hesychius, Alexandrinus, 190
Hickes, William, Librarian of Trinity, 77, 228
Hicks, Thomas, MS given by, 234
Hicson, Samuel, Fellow of Trinity, MSS given by, 234
    money for books given by, 239
Hilary, Bp of Poitiers, St, 8, 152
Hill, Thomas, Master of Trinity, 107
Hill, Thomas, Fellow of Trinity, MSS given by, 84, 234
    printed books given by, 128 n.3, 130 n.5
Hipparchus, Bithynus, 250
Hippocrates, 241, 242
'Historia sacra multorum patrum', 150
'Historia sanctorum patrum', 181
Hobbes, Thomas, 130 and n.5
Holden,? John, stationer, 125 n.6
Holdsworth, Richard, Master of Emmanuel, library of, 91 n.5
Holinshed, Raphael, 129 and n.2, 176
Holloway, Thomas, substitute Librarian of Trinity, 107
Holme, Richard, Warden of King's Hall, 12, 19 n.2
Homer, 24, 40 n.4, 45, 54, 57, 171, 187, 190
Hooke, Robert, 131 and n.3
Horatius Flaccus, Quintus, 8, 45, 54, 57, 129
Hosius, Stanislaus, 159
Hugh of St Victor, 11
Hughes, Francis, of Trinity College, MS given by, 234
Humphreys, Thomas (or John), Sub-Librarian of Trinity, 230

Hunkes, John, of Michaelhouse, printed book given to Michaelhouse by, 18
Hutton, Mark, of Trinity College, 56 n.2
Hutton, Timothy, of Trinity College, 56 n.2
Hyperius, Andreas, 185

Imbert, Jean, 198
inspection supper, 124, 125 and n.7
Ireland, Richard, bookseller, 125 n.6
Irenaeus, Bp of Lyons, St, 8, 151
Isabella, queen of Edward II, 12
Isocrates, 24, 54

Jacobus Philippus, de Bergamo, 167
James, Thomas, 40 n.2
Jansen, Cornelius, 128 and n.2
Jardine, Lisa, 56–7
Jenner, David (or Jonathan), Sub-Librarian of Trinity, 78 n.6, 229
Jenour, Kenelm, of Trinity College, printed books given by, 104 n.1, 238; fig. 24; plan 4
Jerome, St, 8, 52 n.3, 188, 191
Jesus College, Cambridge, library of, 4 n.1, 8, 20 n.2
Jesus College, Oxford, library of, 8 n.2
Johannes, Grammaticus (Philoponus), 170, 171, 172
Johannes de Sacro Busto, 256, 257
John, Damascene, St, 18
Jones, Ralph, of Clare College, 55 n.5
Josephus, Flavius, 8, 192
Jovius, Paulus, 174
Junctinus, Franciscus, 249
Junius, Franciscus, senior, 191
Justin, Martyr, St, 152
Justinian I, emperor of the East, 42, 44
Justinianus, Laurentius, 155
Justinus, 57
Juvenalis, Decimus Junius, 45

Kepler, Johann, 90, 131, 250, 253
Ker, Neil R., 3 n.1, 18
Key, James, Fellow of Trinity, private library of, 52, 53, 54–5
Kimchi, David, 190
Kinaston, Francis, MSS given by, 234
King's College, Cambridge, library of, 4, 7, 20, 112
    contents in 1612, 44–5, 44 n.2
King's Hall, Cambridge, buildings of, 14; fig. 4
    dissolved 22
    law the main study at, 12, 23
    library of, 3–4 7, 11–114
        contents, 12, 79

and TCL, 19–21
    converted into rooms, 20–1, 20 nn.4,5
    size of, 14, 19
King's Scholars, Society of the, 12
Kirke, Thomas, of Trinity College, 131 n.7
Knevet, E., of King's Hall, 12
Knolles, Richard, 88 n.4
Knox, John, 38–9, 185
Kyddall, Brian, of Peterhouse, 51 n.2
Kyrke, Richard, of King's College, 55 n.5

Lactantius Firmianus, Lucius Coelius, 150
Lakes, Sir Thomas, money for books given by, 238; plan 4
Lambert, Joshua, Sub-Librarian of Trinity, 230
Lambeth Palace Library, 80, 113 n.3
Lane, Henry, Fellow of Trinity, formerly Sub-Librarian, 230
Langland, William, 81, 82
    Piers Plowman, B-text of, 82
Latimer, Hugh, 38, 183
Latin, books in, 9, 40, 44, 45, 88, 127–8
Latomus, Jacobus, 159
Laud, William, Abp of Canterbury, 77
Laughton, John, Chaplain and Librarian of Trinity, 115 n.1, 134–5, 134 n.1, 228
    catalogues the MSS, 214 and n.4; fig. 30
    curiosities given by, 122, 135 n.2
    MSS given by, 84 and n.5, 135 n.2, 234
    printed books given by, 56 n.2, 135 and n.2, 141 and n.6, 142 and n.3
Lavater, Ludwig, 182
law books, in early college libraries, 8
    in King's College Library, 44–5
    in King's Hall Library, 12
    in TCL, 40, 42, 44–5, 88, 108–9, 124 and n.3, 126 and n.1, 127–8, 131–2, 132 nn.4,5
Layfield, John, Fellow of Trinity, printed books given by, 239
Lazius, Wolfgang, 188
Leakeland, Thomas, Sub-Librarian of Trinity, 230
lectern cases, 4–6, 14–15, 29 and n.5, 45 and n.1, 71, 92–3; fig. 1, 5, 6, 17, 18
Leibniz, Gottfried Wilhelm von, 130
Leland, John, antiquary, 20, 20 nn.1,2, 28 and n.3, 79, 257
Leovitius, Cyprianus, 255
Levins, Christopher, of Corpus Christi College, 55 n.5
Libanius, 180
librarians, college, 6, 10
    of TC, 25 and n.2, 75–8, 123, 227–8
library, see under individual institutions

Liffe, William, Fellow of Trinity, private library of, 52, 53, 54
Lincoln College, Oxford, library of, 3, 7
Lindanus, Wilhelmus, Bp of Roermond, 166
Lipsius, Justus, 130
Liturgies, Greek rite, 181
    Latin rite, 166
Lively, Edward, Fellow of Trinity, 91 n.2
Livius, Titus, 54, 57, 172, 191
L'Obel, Matthias de, 89
Locke, John, 130 n.4
Loggan, David, view of Trinity College, 14 n.3; fig. 4
Lownde, John, of Peterhouse, 51 n.2
Lucas, William, MP, private library of, 91 n.5
Lucian, of Samosata, 57, 174
Luther, Martin, 8, 38, 48, 52; fig. 24
Lycosthenes, Conrad, 177
Lyne, Richard, plan of Cambridge, 21 n.2
Lynnet, William, Fellow of Trinity, buys law books, 124
    MSS given by, 234
    printed books given by, 131 n.1
Lyra, Nicolas de, 8, 157

Machiavelli, Niccoló, 257
Maffeius, Raphael, Volaterranus, 173
Magdalen College, Oxford, library of, 3, 7, 33
Magdalene College, Cambridge, library of, 8, 141 n.2
Magdeburg, Centuriators, 38, 52 n.3, 54, 188
Maginus, Johannes Antonius, 256
Mainardi, A., 52 n.4
Mainstone, William, curiosities given by, 121, 122
Malebranche, Nicolas, 130
Malham, John, Fellow of Trinity, private library of, 53
Manfeild, James, Librarian and Chaplain of Trinity, 134 and n.2, 228
    catalogues the printed books, 126, 134, 214 and n.3
Manley (Manly), R., ? of Trinity College, 84 and n.2
Manning, Lancelot, Sub-Librarian of Trinity, 230
manuscripts, 40 and n.2, 79–85, 233–5
    monastic, justification for removing, 80 and n.6
    preservation of, 79–82
Maranta, Robertus, 42, 194
marginalia, 33
Marlorat, Augustin, 155, 159

Marsilius, of Padua, 161
Martialis, Marcus Valerius, 88 n.5
Martinus, Polonus, Abp of Gniesen, 189
Martyr, Peter, Vermilius, 38, 153–4, 182
Mary I, queen of England, 22 and n.3, 48 n.3, 61
Mason, Charles, Fellow of Trinity, 85 n.1
Matthioli, Pietro Andrea, 242, 243
Mauliverer, Thomas, Sub-Librarian of Trinity, 230
Mayerne Turquet, Louis de, 88 n.4
Meade, Michael, money for books given by, 48 and n.5, 49, 161, 176
Medhop, Thomas, Fellow of Trinity, money for books given by, 239, 258
Melancthon, Philipp, 38, 52, 160
Memoriale, The, of TC, 34–7, 34 nn.3,4, 42, 46–9, 71, 79–83, 87, 97, 113, 119, 147, 193, 213 and n.2, 225–6; fig. 10
Mennall, Robert, of Buckingham College, 51 n.2
Mercado, Luis de, 245
Mercator, Gerardus, globes by, 33, 104
Mersenne, Marin, 129
Merton College, Oxford, library of, 3,7
Metcalfe, Robert, money for books given by, 115 and n.3
Meursius, Johannes, 130
Michael, Ephesius, 170
Michaelhouse, Cambridge, buildings of, 11, 21; fig. 3
    dissolved, 22
    divinity the main study at, 11, 23
    library of, 3, 7, 11–14, 68
        contents, 11, 18, 27–8, 28 nn. 1,2, 79 and TCL, 19–21
        location unknown, 21
        size of, 19
Middleton, Richard, 156
Milton, John, MS of his poems, 85 and n.1
Minsheu, John, 193
Montague, Hon. Robert, medal given by, 122
Montanus, Johannes Baptista, 90, 245
Monte, Hieronymus de, 196
Moody, Henry, bookbinder, 81 and n.6
More, Henry, 128 and n.3
Morland, Sir Samuel, speaking trumpet of, 121, 122
Morus, Horatius, 205, 251
Moxon, Joseph, Castlemaine's globe by, 121, 122
'Mucices authores', 257
Muhammad, the Prophet, 176
Munster, Sebastian, 148, 174, 253
Muriell, John, Sub-Librarian of Trinity, 229

Musculus, Wolfgang, 8, 38, 52 and n.3, 154
Mutton, Thomas (= Griffith, Thomas), 107 and n.1
Myconius, Oswaldus, 184
Mynsinger, Joachim, 196

Nannius, Petrus, 47 n.4
Napier, John, 131
Nebrissensis, Aelius Antonius, 207
Nelson, Peter, of Peterhouse, 55 n.5
Nelson, Richard, Fellow of Michaelhouse, 11 n.5
Nevile, Alexander, brother of Thomas, 82
Nevile, Thomas, Master of Trinity, Dean of Canterbury, 63
  MSS given by, 79–83, 234
  printed books given by, 37 n.6, 81, 88, 91, 96, 239, 258; plans 3, 4
New College, Oxford, library of, 3, 7, 33
Newman (Neuman), Andrew, of Trinity College, 56 n.2
Newton, Sir Isaac, Fellow of Trinity, xi n.1, 90, 175, 131 n.4, 141 n.4
  printed books given by, 131 and n.3
Nicephorus, Callistus, 174
Nidd, John, Fellow of Trinity, formerly Sub-Librarian, 229
  printed books given by, 91 nn.3,4, 120, 127 and n., 131 and n.1
Nizolius, Marius, 177
North, Dudley, brother of John, cup and coin given by, 122
North, John, Master of Trinity, MS given by, 234
  printed book given by, 128 n.3
Nowell, Alexander, 38, 185

objects other than books in libraries, 33, 34, 104 and n.4, 106, 120–1, 122
Ockam, Gulielmus, 157
Oecolampadius, Joannes, 8, 38, 152, 154
Oecumenius, Bp of Tricca, 149, 152
Ogilby, John, 131 n.5
Oratores Graeci, 164
Oriano, Lanfranc ab, 197, 198
Oriel College, Oxford, library of, 3, 7
Orm(e)rod, Lawrence, Sub-Librarian of Trinity, 78 n.6, 229
Ottringham, John, Master of Michaelhouse, 11
Overall, John, Fellow of Trinity, printed book given by, 238
Ovidius Naso, Publius, 54, 57, 129
Owen, Vincent, Sub-Librarian of Trinity, 230

Oxford, colleges, libraries of, 3–10; see also under individual colleges
Oxford University Library, 7 and n.3

Paget, Edward, Fellow of Trinity, formerly Sub-Librarian, 230
Palladius, Bp of Aspona, 181
Palmer, John, Fellow of Trinity, 42 n.2, 49 n.1
Palmer, Joseph, Sub-Librarian of Trinity, 230
Panormitanus (Nicolaus Tudeschis), 199–200, 202
Paracelsus, Philippus Aureolus, 90, 247
Paré, Ambroise, 246
Paris, Sorbonne University, library of, 112
Parish, George, Fellow of Trinity, formerly Sub-Librarian, 229
Parker, John, son of Mathew, MSS of, 80 n.5, 82 and n.1
Parker, Matthew, Abp of Canterbury, MSS of, 79, 82 and n.1
Parker, Nicholas, Librarian of Trinity, 77, 228
Parkinson, John, 89
Parkinson, Martin, Fellow of Trinity, private library of, 52, 53, 54
Partridge, Alfred, Sub-Librarian of Trinity, 229
Pascal, Blaise, 130
Paston, John, Fellow of King's Hall, 12
Pausanias, 173
Pawlett, Thomas, Fellow of Trinity, MS given by, 234
Pearson, John, Master of Trinity, printed books given by, 119 n.5
Peckham, John, 253
Peckius, Petrus, 199
Pellicanus, Conradus, 38, 160, 187
Pember, Robert, Fellow of Trinity, private library of, 53
Pembroke College, Cambridge, library of, 4, 7, 20 n.2
Perez de Ayala, Martin, of Valentia, 166
Perkins, William, 88 n.4, 128 and n.1
Perry, William, Fellow of Trinity, MS given by, 234
  printed book given by, 130 n.5
Petavius, Dionysius, 253
Peterhouse, Cambridge, library of, 3, 7, 20 n.2
Peters, Hugh, of Trinity College, MS given by, 234
Petrus, Comestor, 28 and n.1, 176
Petrus, Lombardus, 57

Pettit, Valentine, Fellow of Trinity, MS given by, 234
Pezelius, Christophorus, 251
Phavorinus, Varinus, Bp of Nocera, 190
Philo, Judaeus, 151
Philoponus, Johannes (Grammaticus), 170, 171, 172
Pico della Mirandola, Giovanni Francesco, 180
Pighius, Albertus, 165
Pineda, Johannes de, of Seville, 158
Pirovanus, Gabriel, 256
Pius II, Pope (Aeneas Silvius, Piccolomini), 175
Plato, 8, 24, 40 n.4, 45, 54, 57, 166, 169
Platter, Felix, 90
Plautus, Titus Maccius, 45, 57
Plinius Secundus, Gaius, 89 and n.2, 207
Plutarch, 57, 168
Pockley, Thomas, of Trinity College, 108, 214 and n.1
Poetae Graeci, 167
Politianus, Angelus, 167
Pollux, Julius, of Naucratis, 177
Polwheele, Otho, Sub-Librarian of Trinity, 229
Pontanus, Ludovicus, 195
Porphyrius, of Tyre, 23, 170
Porta, Giovanni Battista della, 194
portrait of Bp Hacket, 121, 122
portraits, royal, at TC, 47–8, 48 n.3
Pradus, Hieronymus, 158
Preston, ?Richard, Chaplain of Trinity, 20 and nn.4,5
Priscianus, Caesariensis, 178
private libraries, 8, 51–7, 80 and n.2, 91 and nn. 2,3,5, 131 n.2, 132, 141 and n.2, 215–7
probate inventories, 51–7, 51 nn.1,3, 131 n.1, 215–17
Proclus, Diadochus, 172, 252
Proctor, John, of Michaelhouse, 11 n.5, 51 n.2
Propertius, Sextus, 88 n.5
Prudentius Clemens, Aurelius, 45, 185
Prueckmann, Friendrich, 197
Psalter, Canterbury (MS), 80, 81
Ptolemaeus, Claudius, 252
Puckering (alias Newton), Sir Henry, of Trinity College, MSS given by, 84 and n.7, 85 and n.1, 141, 234
    printed books given by, 91 n.4, 141 and n.5, 142 and n.3
Pufendorf, Samuel, 129
Pulley, William, Fellow of Trinity, MSS given by, 234

Pulleyn, Benjamin, Fellow of Trinity, medal given by, 122
Pulleyn, John, Sub-Librarian of Trinity, 230
Purchas, Samuel, 88 n.4

Queens' College, Cambridge, library of, 4, 7, 14–15, 20 n.2, 97 n.2; fig.5
Queen's College, Oxford, library of, 3, 7
Quinsey, Thomas, Sub-Librarian of Trinity, 229
Quintilianus, Marcus Fabius, 57

Raleigh, Sir Walter, 129 n.2
Ramus, Petrus, 54, 205, 251
Ray, John, Fellow of Trinity, xi n.1, 131 and n.5
Rebuffus Petrus, 42, 201, 203
Redman, John, 181
Regiomontanus, Johannes, 255
Regulae Juris, 201
Reinhold, Erasmus, 256
Resbury, Theodore, Fellow of Trinity, formerly Sub-Librarian, 229
Rheticus, Georgius Joachim, 250
Rhodes, Samuel, Sub-Librarian of Trinity, 230
Rhodiginus, Ludovicus Coelius, 204
Rolewinck, Werner, 175
Rome, Church of, Rota, 202
Rosenthal, Heinrich von, 196
Rotheram, Roger, Warden of King's Hall, 12
Rotherham, Thomas, Abp of York, 135 n.3
Rotherham, Thomas, Chaplain and Librarian of Trinity, 134, 135 and n.3, 142 and n.1, 228
Rowe, Cheyney, Fellow of Trinity, 119 n.4
Royal Society of London, The, 131 and n.7
Ruland, Martin, 183

Sabellicus, Marcus Antonius Coccius, 166
Sadleir, Anne, MSS given by, 80, 84, 121, 234
    coins given by, 121 and n.1, 122
St Augustine's Canterbury, MSS from, 80, 81, 82, 83
St Catharine's College, Cambridge, library of, 4, 7, 20
St John's College, Cambridge, library of, 8, 97 n.2
St John's College, Oxford, library of, 8
Sallustius Crispus, Gaius, 54, 57, 129
Sambee, John, Sub-Librarian of Trinity, 230
Sandys, George, 88 n.4
Saracenus, Johannes, 242

Sarpi, P. (Paolo, Servita), 129 and n.4
Saxonia, Hercules, 245
Sayrus, Gregorius, 155
Scattergood, Anthony, Chaplain of Trinity, MSS given by, 234
Scattergood, Thomas, instruments given by, 121 n.3
Scepper, Cornelius Duplicius, 256
Schardius, Simon, 203
Schoener, Johann, 90, 252
Scholz, Laurent, 90, 244
scientific instruments in TCL, 120–1, 121 n.3, 122
Sclater, Thomas, Fellow of Trinity, rents for books given by, 140
Scott, John, scribe, 34 and n.4, 213 and n.2
Scotus, Marianus, 189
'seats', 10 n.1, 69, 125
Sedley (Sidley), Sir William, money for books given by, 88 n.4, 91 93, 167, 239, 258; plan 4
Seignior, George, Fellow of Trinity, printed books given by, 119 n.5, 129 and nn.1.6
Selden, John, 128 and n.3, 130
Sennert, Daniel, 90, 246–7
Sentuary, John, of Corpus Christi College, 51 n.2
Serlio, Sebastiano, 249
Serres, Jean de, 88 n.4
Seton, John, 23 n.5, 54
Sharpe, Nicholas, Fellow of Trinity, private library of, 53
Shaw, Peter, Fellow of Trinity, printed books given by, 37 n.6, 88 and n.1, 91, 96, 164, 238; plans 3, 4
Shaxton, John, Fellow of Trinity, 91 n.2
Sichardus, Johannes, 150
Sidney Sussex College, Cambridge, library of, 8 n.2
Sigonius, Carolus, 203
Simler, Josias, 172, 182
Simplicius, 169, 170
Simpson, Nicholas, Fellow of Trinity, private library of, 55
Singularia Doctorum, 195
Skeffington, Thomas, Fellow of Trinity, printed books given by, 35, 42–4, 42 nn.1,2, 44 n.1, 49 nn.1,4, 50, 55, 127 n., 132, 194–212, 258; fig. 11; plans 3, 4
Greek mottoes inscribed by, 42 n.1; fig. 11
Skinner, Daniel, Fellow of Trinity, medal given by, 122
Skinner, Henry, of Peterhouse, 51 n.2

Sledd, John, Fellow of Trinity, printed books given by, 46, 48 and n.7, 49 and n.1, 204, 205, 258
Smithson, Huntington, Sub-Librarian of Trinity, 230
Smyth, William, of Trinity College, money for books given by, 238
Solenander, Reiner, 90, 244
Somerset, Charles Seymour, 6th Duke of, 142
Sophocles, 54
Soranus, Ephesius, 242
Sorbonne, Paris, library of, 112
Soto, Domingo de, 162
Spanheim, Ezechiel, 130
Speed, John, 88 and n.4, 129 n.2
Spinoza, Benedictus de, 130
Spragg, John, Fellow of Trinity, MS given by, 234
Spring, Henry, of Trinity Hall, 55 n.5
Springham, Matthew, printed book given by, 238
'stalls', 10 n.1
Stanhope, Sir Edward, Fellow of Trinity, career, 75 n.1
Librarianship founded by, 75–8, 219–24
MSS given by, 79, 81 and nn.2,3, 83, 234
Memoriale given by, 34 and n.3, 225–6
money given by, 75, 219
printed books given by, 88, 91, 127 n., 132, 194, 195, 224–5, 238; plans 3, 4
will, 33 and n.4, 34, 68 and n.3, 75–7, 120 n.4, 121, 125 and n.7, 219–26
Stanhope, Sir Michael, brother of Sir Edward, money for books given by, 88 n.5, 91, 128 n.1, 130 n.3, 239, 258; plan 4
Stanley, Thomas, 130
Stanton, Hervey de, founder of Michaelhouse, 11
Stanyhurst, Richard, 206; fig. 11
Stapleton, Thomas, 159
Stapley, Thomas, of Trinity Hall, 55 n.5
Stedman, Richard, Fellow of Trinity, formely Sub-Librarian, 229
Stephanus, Byzantinus, 177
Stephanus, Robertus, the elder, 178, 189
Stevynson, Alan, of Pembroke College, 51 n.2
Still, Nathaniel, Fellow of Trinity, printed books given by, 238
Stillingfleet, Edward, 129
Stobaeus, Johannes, 175
Stokes, David of Trinity College, MSS given by, 234
Strabo, 162, 251

Suarez, Francisco de, 128 and n.1
Suckling, Sir John, money for books given
    by, 91, 93, 239, 258
Suetonius Tranquillus, Gaius, 173
Suidas, 190
Suttell, John, of St Nicholas Hostel, 51 n.2
Switzerland, printing in, 40–1
Sycling, John, of Christ's college, 51 n.2

Tabulae, 205, 251
Tacitus, Cornelius, 130
Talmud, 187
Tartagni, Alexander, da Imola, 194
Terentius Afer, Publius, 54, 57
Tertullianus, Quintus Septimus Florens, 8,
    151
text-books, 40, 44, 54–7
'Theatrum chemicum', 90, 247
Thelwall, Eubule, of Trinity College,
    money for books given by, 238
Themistius, 170
Theocritus, 171
Theodorus, of Gaza, 24
Theodosius II, emperor of the East, 44,
    201
Theophylactus, Abp of Ochrida, 149
Thorndike, Herbert, Fellow of Trinity,
    119 n.4
    MSS given by, 234
Thucydides, 163, 173
Tibullus, Albius, 88 n.5
Tiraquellus, Andreas, 178, 179
Titelmann, Franz, 164
titling and labelling, 29, 37, 69, 71 n.4, 93, 97
    and n.2, 102, 104, 113 and nn. 1,3; fig. 1,
    7, 8, 21, 22, 23
Toletus, Franciscus, 156
'Topographia Romae', 251
Torsellino, Orazio, 130
Tractatus, 207
Trinity Apocalypse (MS), 80, 84 and n.3,
    121
Trinity College, Cambridge, Bishop's Hos-
    tel, 137 and n.1, 140 and n.1
    rents of, 124 and n.2, 137 and n.1
    Bursar, Junior, 123 124, 125, 140, 141
    bursars' accounts, 25 n.3, 123 n.4, 140,
    141, 227
    Chapel, 61 n.2, 63
    constitution of, 22–3, 25 n.2
    curricula at, 22–4
    divinity the main study at, 22–3, 38, 86–7,
    126
    famous men of, xi n.1
    foundation of, 19, 22
    Garret Hostel, 137

Great Court, 63, 66, 68
Hall, 68
King Edward Gate, 61, 63, 68
King's Hostel, 14, 124 n.3; fig. 3
Kitchens, 68
Librarian, 25 and n.2, 75–8, 123, 227–8
    called Library Keeper, 75 n.3, 219–24
    duties of, 76–7, 221–2
    terms of employment of, 75–6, 76 n.1,
    220–2
library of, history summarised, xi–xii,
    86–7
    access to, 121 and n.4, 259
    administration, 28–33, 107–25
    Benefactions book, 119 and n.2
    benefactors, 26–7, 32, 34–5, 45, 46–9,
    79–85, 88, 89, 115, 118–20, 135,
    137, 139–42, 233–5, 237–9
    Fellows reluctant to become, 49, 52,
    54–5, 91
    Fellows encouraged to become, 115,
    118–19
    binding, 29, 32, 68, 69 and nn. 3,4, 81,
    82, 123, 124, 125 and n.6; fig. 7, 20,
    21
    boards, 69 and n.4
    edges coloured, 69, 81 and n.6, 82;
    untrimmed, 81 and n.1, 82
    borrowing system, 26, 104, 121, 123
    and n.2, 221, 259–60
    abuse of, 123, and n.2, 260
    for MSS, 85 and n.2
    catalogues and cataloguing, 32–3, 34–7,
    78, 87, 93, 213–14
    for 1600, 147–212
    1640, 93, 94, 96, 102 n.1, 108, 109,
    115, 132 and n.2, 213 and n.3;
    fig. 25; plans 2, 4
    1645, 102 n.1, 108–9, 108 n.7, 126,
    213–14, 214 n.1, 241–58; fig. 26;
    plan 5
    1667, 102 n.1, 115, 126, 127, 131, 132,
    133, 134, 214 and n.2; fig. 27, 29
    1675, 102 n.1, 115 n.1, 126, 127, 131,
    132, 133, 134, 214 and nn.3,4;
    fig. 28, 30
    of MSS, 85, 134–5, 214 and n.4;
    fig. 29, 30
    of pamphlets, 133 n.1
    Wren catalogue c.1700, 126, 132,
    133 n.1, 142 and n.2
    see TCC, The Memoriale of
    chains and chaining, 29 and nn.2,3,4, 68
    n.3, 71, 88 n.1, 93, 123 n.3, 224,
    226; fig. 1, 7
    classification, by donors, 85, 87, 93, 96,

108, 113, 142 and n.3; plans 3, 4
by subjects, 37 n.2, 39, 89–90, 108–9,
112–13, 113 n.2, 115, 126, 127,
142, plans 5, 6; traditional
schemes, 32–3, 74, 109, 112–13,
127
of MSS, 85, 113
Wren Library, 113 and n.2, 142 and
n.2
contents, 27–8, 34–45, 74, 86–91,
126–33, 139, 141–2, 147–212,
241–258
dates and places of printing, 40–1, 49
English, books in, 40 and n.5, 88 and
n.4
formats, 40
Greek, books in, 40
Hebrew, books in, 40 and n.5, 128
languages represented, 40 and n.5
Latin, books in, 40
MSS, 40 and n.2, 79–85, 96, 233–5;
plans 3, 4, 5, 6; 'ad Coll. pertinentes', 83–4, 234; Canterbury
Psalter, 80, 81; English literature, 81, 82, 85 and n.1; Milton's
poems, 85 and n.1; *Piers Plowman*, B-text of, 82; Psalters given
by Stanhope, 81 and n.3; Trinity
Apocalypse, 80, 84 and n.3;
Winchester Gospels, 81
oriental languages, books in, 128
printed books, 'ad Coll. pertinentes',
83, 239; atlases, 133; Civil War
tracts, 133; divinity, 38–40,
44–5, 46–8, 88, 126–9, 133;
Greek literature, 40, 44, 45,
127–8; history, 88 and n.4,
127–8, 133; humanities, 40, 44,
45, 88, 126–8, 129–30; iatrochemistry, 90, 246–8; Latin literature, 40, 44, 45, 88, 127–8; law,
40, 42, 44–5, 88, 108–9, 124 and
n.3, 126 and n.1, 127–8, 131–
132, 132 nn.4,5; mathematics, 40,
89–90, 127–8, 131 and nn.2,3,4,
241, 248–57; medicine, 89–90,
127–8, 131 and nn. 1,5,6, 241–8;
pamphlets, 133; philosophy,
130; science, 89–90, 126–8, 131
and nn.1,2,3,4,5,6, 241–58; text-
books, 40, 44, 56–7
donations, of books, 26–7, 33, 34–6, 45,
46–9, 54–5, 79–85, 88, 89, 115,
118–20, 135, 141–3, 233–5, 237–9
of money for books, 88, 89, 119,
237–9

of rents for books, 135, 137, 140
donors' marks, 81, 82, 97, 104; fig. 20,
24
arms, 81, 82, 97, 104 and n.1
initials, 97, 104 and n.1; fig. 20
labels, 104; fig. 24
duplicates discarded, 120 and nn.3,4,
141 and nn.3,5,6, 225
establishment of, 19–21
finances, 25–6, 27, 88, 123–5, 139–41
chamber rent, 27, 49, 123–4, 124 n.2,
139–41
furniture and equipment, 29, 69–74,
92–3, 96, 113, 115, 125 and
nn.1,2,3,4,5,6, 143; fig. 18, 19;
plans 1–6
book-cases, 93, 96, 113, 125 and n.1,
139; fig. 19
book-wheel, 125 and n.4
crests, 125 and n.2
lectern cases, 29, 71, 92–3; fig. 18
matting, 125 and n.3
stationery, 123, 124, 125 and n.6
weather glass, 125 and n.5
growth of, 86–7, 92–3, 115, 126–8,
137 n.2, 139 and n.4
inscriptions in books, 29, 32–3,
32 nn.5,6,7,8, 42 and n.1, 104;
fig. 9, 11
inspection supper, 124, 125 and n.7
marginalia, 33
New Library, 61–74; fig. 15, 16, 18
early plans for, 61 and n.3, 63; fig. 12
built 1599–1605, 63, 66, 68
capacity, 63, 74, 92–3, 139
interior, 68 and nn. 7,8, 69, 93,
113, 115 and n.1; fig. 18, 19; plans
1–6
damaged by fire, 135 and n.4
inadequacy of, 135, 137, 139
books moved out of, 142 and n.1
converted into rooms, 142–3
objects other than books in, 33, 34, 104
and n.4, 106, 120–1, 122
coins and medals, 120–1, 121 n.3,
122
curiosities, 120–1, 121 n.2, 122
globes, 33, 34, 104 and n.4, 120–1, 122
scientific instruments, 120–1, 121 n.3,
122
Old Library, 20–1, 26–7, 28–33, 68
lectern cases, 29
OL list and books, 35–41, 44–5, 46, 48,
87, 96, 112–13, 147–93, 207–12,
215; plans 3, 4
purchases of books, 26–7, 49, 76 and

Trinity College, Cambridge, library of, Wren Library – *continued*
  n.4, 88, 120, 123–5, 137 and n.1, 140 and n.2, 258
  purchases of furniture and equipment, 123–5
  regulations, 26, 121, 123 and n.2, 221–2, 259–60
  staff, 26–7; *and see* TCC, Librarian, Sub-Librarian
  statistics, 37–45, 86–7, 89, 92–3, 119–20, 119 n.6, 124, 126–8, 126 n.1, 137 n.2, 139 and n.4
  titling and labelling, 29, 37, 69, 71 n.4, 93, 97, 102, 113 and nn.1,3; fig. 1, 7, 8, 21, 22, 23
  tabs, fore-edge, 97 and n.2, 102; fig. 21, 23
  TS list and books, 35, 37, 42–4, 87, 127, 132, 147, 194–212, 258; fig. 11; plans 3,4
  Wren Library, 113, 126, 134, 135, 137, 139, 140–2
    appeals for funds, 137–9, 137 n.3; fig. 31
    built 1676–95, 139
    building accounts challenged, 140–1
    cost of, 137, 140–1
    books moved into, 142 and n.1
    capacity, 139
    catalogues of, 126
  Library Keeper, 26–7, 75 n.3, 219–24
  Master's Lodge, 66, 68, 142; fig. 15, 16
  *Memoriale, The,* of TC, 34–7, 34 nn.3,4, 42, 46–9, 71, 79–83, 87, 97, 113, 119, 147, 193, 213 and n.2, 225–6; fig. 10
  Michaelhouse buildings used by, 21
  need for books at, 22–4, 86, 115
  Nevile's Court, 137, 140
    rents of, 140
  plan of 1555, 21 n.1, 61 and nn.2,3, 63; fig. 12, 13, 14
  portraits, royal, 47–8, 48 n.3
  Queen's Gate, 124 n.3
  Statutes, 1552 (Edwardian), 22 and n.3, 26–7
    1554 (Marian), 22 n.3, 27
    1560 (Elizabethan), 22 and n.3, 23–4, 27, 56–7
  Sub-Librarian, 75–6, 76 n.2, 78, 123, 222–3, 229–30
    called Under Library Keeper, 75 n.3, 222
Trinity College, Oxford, library of, 8
Trinity Hall, Cambridge, library of, 4, 7, 18, 20, 71 and n.3, 93, 96 n.3; fig. 6, 17
Trithemius, Johannes, 189

Trivet, Nicolas, 40 n.2, 79 and n.1
Truxillo, Thomas de, 164
Tudeschis, Nicolaus, Panormitanus, 199–200, 202
Tuppius, Laurentius, 182
Turbervile, Samuel, of Trinity College, 77
Turnebus, Adrianus, 204
Turner, Thomas, scientific instrument given by, 122
Turner, William, 89, 243
Tusanus, Jacobus, 162

Uffenbach, Zacharias Conrad von, 134 n.3, 142 n.3
University College, Oxford, library of, 3, 7

Valavine, John, Sub-Librarian of Trinity, 230
Valerius Maximus, 57, 168
Valla, Laurentius, 57
Vasquez, Gabriel, 157
Vasquez y Menchaca, Ferdinando, 195
Vatablus, Franciscus 147
Vega, Christophorus de, 242
Velleius Paterculus, Gaius, 130
Vesalius, Andreas, 89, 244
Victorius, Petrus, the elder, 169, 178
Vieta, Franciscus, 90
Vigelius, Nicolaus, 198
Vigerus, Franciscus, 130
Viguerius, Johannes, 165
Villalpandus, Johannes Baptista, 158
Vintner, Edmund, Fellow of King's College, printed books given to Trinity by, 119 n.5
Virgilius Maro, Publius, 8, 45, 54, 57, 88 n.5
Vitae Caesarum, 173
Vitae Patrum, 188
Vitruvius Pollio, Marcus, 248
Vives, Johannes Ludovicus, 57, 176
Voragine, Jacobus de, 168

Warden Abbey, Bedfordshire, MSS from, 84
Watts, Thomas, Sub-Librarian of Trinity, 230
Wayland, Henry, Fellow of Trinity, printed books given by, 238
Webster, Charles, 89 n.3
Wecker, Johannes Jacobus, 205, 246, 251
Wedyr, Roger, of St Catharine's College, 51 n.2
Wesenbecius, Matthaeus, 203
Westhemer, Bartholomaeus, 184
Whalley, Thomas, Fellow of Trinity, MSS given by, 234

money for books given by, 90–1, 91 n.1, 189, 239, 258; plan 4
Whelock, Abraham, 129
Whincop, Thomas, Fellow of Trinity, printed books given by, 119 n.5
White, Jeremy, Sub-Librarian of Trinity, 78 n.6, 229
Whitgift, John, Master of Trinity, Abp of Canterbury, xi n.1, 38, 39, 40, 48, 50
  contra Cartwright, 160
  library catalogue, 80 n.2
  MSS given by, 79–83, 96, 104, 234; plans 3, 4
  tutorial accounts, 56 and n.1
Whitmore, William, of Trinity College, printed books given by, 239
Whynn, Richard, of Trinity College, law books bought from, 124 n.3, 132 n.5
William, of Bath, 28 n.3, 79 n.2
Willis, Nathaniel, Fellow of Trinity, 119 n.4
Willmer, George, of Trinity College, MSS given by, 79, 82–3, 234
Winchester Gospels (MS), 81
Wisdome,—,junior, labels library books, 97 n.1
Wolffhart, Conrad, 177

Wood, John, of Trinity College, private library of, 55
Worcester Cathedral, library of, 80 n.6
Wotton, Edward, 89 and n.2, 172
Wren, Sir Christopher, 139
Wren Library, 113, 126, 134, 135, 137, 139, 140–2
Wright, Richard, Fellow of Trinity, money for books given by, 88 n.4, 128 n.1, 239
Wright, William Aldis, Librarian and Fellow of Trinity, 85 n.1
Wroth, Sir Robert, books given by, 46, 49 and n.2
Würzburg law books, 126 n.1, 132 and n.4, 200

Xenophon, 206

Yotton, John, Master of Michaelhouse, 11, 19 n.2

Zanchi, Basilio, 180
Zanetinis, Hieronymus de, 202
Zasius, Udalricus, 202
Zilettus, Johannes Baptista, 195
Zwingli, Ulrich, 8, 38, 154, 160

For EU product safety concerns, contact us at Calle de José Abascal, 56–1°, 28003 Madrid, Spain or eugpsr@cambridge.org.

www.ingramcontent.com/pod-product-compliance
Ingram Content Group UK Ltd.
Pitfield, Milton Keynes, MK11 3LW, UK
UKHW010033140625
459647UK00012BA/1355